These Are the Days
that Must Happen to You . . .

In 2001 bike journalist Dan Walsh departed London
and headed for Africa to become a biking drifter, pilgrim, and
latter-day heir to Ted Simon. His legendary *Bike* magazine columns
about his travel experiences – lyrical, edgy, fraught with danger,
despair and surreal highs and lows – have earned him a vast cult
following and he has been labelled 'the saviour of motorcycle writing'.
Dan still contributes to *Bike* magazine and is still out on the road.
This is his first book.

DAN WALSH

These Are the Days that Must Happen to You . . .

C

CENTURY

Published by Century 2009

2 4 6 8 10 9 7 5 3

Copyright © Dan Walsh 2008

First published in Great Britain in 2008 by
Century
Random House, 20 Vauxhall Bridge Road,
London SW1V 2SA

www.randomhouse.co.uk

Addresses for companies within The Random House Group Limited can be found at:
www.randomhouse.co.uk

The Random House Group Limited Reg. No. 954009

A CIP catalogue record for this book is available from the British Library

ISBN 9781846053115

The Random House Group Limited supports The Forest Stewardship
Council (FSC), the leading international forest certification organisation. All our
titles that are printed on Greenpeace approved FSC certified paper carry the FSC logo.
Our paper procurement policy can be found at www.rbooks.co.uk/environment

Mixed Sources
Product group from well-managed
forests and other controlled sources
www.fsc.org Cert no. TT-COC-2139
© 1996 Forest Stewardship Council

Printed and bound in Great Britain by
Clays Ltd, St Ives plc

Listen! I will be honest with you;
I do not offer the old smooth prizes, but offer rough new prizes;
These are the days that must happen to you.
WALT WHITMAN, 'Song of the Open Road'

I am not sure that I exist, actually. I am all the writers that I have
read, all the people that I have met, all the women that I have loved;
all the cities that I have visited.
JORGE LUIS BORGES

I'm so drunk I can see my own ears.
BRIAN STOTT

# Warning

This isn't a new book, it's a ragged collection of previously published columns and travel pieces. Most of these words have already appeared in *Bike* magazine. I was given the time, the opportunity, to rework my second-hand views into something fresh, but I failed. Couldn't find new words for these old experiences. And like wood and sleep, freshness can't be faked.

The value of information is measured by its unpredictablity, say the scientists. No novelty in this old news. And I'm sorry if this well-meant attempt at a 'Singles and B-Sides' collection smells stale, sounds cynical like some rushed 'Greatest Hits'.

Contents

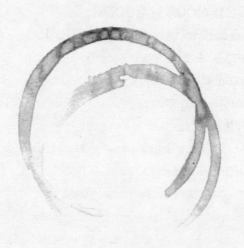

This is a Manifesto, not a Mid Life Crisis.

'What keeps you tied to the corner of the room?' December 2000 I waved goodbye to the best girl and easiest job I'd known, jumped onto a burst-mattress XT600 dirt bike and wobbled through The Looking Glass, headed for southern Spain and the Tangier ferry. A week later I was racing a midget on a monkey bike through Marakesh. A month later I was slurping Christmas Eve mulled wine in the Sahara with French hash smugglers and German car thieves. This Christmas? Probably Venezuela or Brazil. Best thing I ever did for my life, in my life. And, shower me with spittle and pork scratchings, the easiest. Riding away on a bike is easy.

I've never really needed any contrived 'first, fastest, daftest' reason to travel. Oddly, it's what I do for a living – ride bikes, travel, write about it. When I started at Bike magazine back in '97, I'd already spent a couple of psychedelic years puddling around India on clapped-out Enfields, so whenever the editors needed a volunteer to ride some foreign miles, I'd catch the keys. It suited us all – they had wives and lives, I had nothing and no-one better to do.

First trip was to Le Mans on the boss's silver dream machine 900SS. That I dropped on the ferry ramp, then again in a slick petrol station and again in a muddy campsite. Never an expert, always an enthusiast – the boss seethed 'verbal warning' but I was hooked. 'XJR round Normandy battlefields', 'GS1150 to Cannes,' 'K1200LT to Barcelona'

baby-steps grew into 'Electra Glide to Austria', 'Hayabusa to the German autobahns', and 'Falco to a Polish wedding' waddling toddles.

And then the Great Leap Forward. ZX9 to Morocco. And though it was a blast tearing up Marrakech on that inappropriate blue meanie, I could never out-run the feeling that like this, I could never escape. A long weekend here, a fortnight there, wasn't enough anymore. I felt like there was a length of elastic tied round my lad, ready to snap me back to English grey when I strayed too far, when I stayed too long, when I laughed too loud. And that's not half as sexy as it sounds.

Cut the cord. December 2000 I found the finest road sign in Europe, 'Right, town center, left, Africa' and turned left. What started as an over-optimistic round-the-world deteriorated into a too-realistic year-long scramble across Africa that never really found its rhythm. Interrupted by political upheaval ('Now, Donna, with the traffic'. 'Thanks, Mike. Problems in the central region today, bodies on the streets of Bangui after that coup and Congo-Kinshasha has closed its borders after the murder of President Kabila, so expect some delays and if possible, follow the diversion round Chad . . .') and a particularly public sissy fit when I heard that my best girl was taking it up the wrong 'un within two months of me waving bye bye, the trip collapsed when I was kidnapped in Kenya, held hostage in a cage behind a brothel, then slung in jail. When I was released, I found that my best friend Will had been killed in a London cop shop. Back home, his widow cried and smiled and said 'He should have gone with you.'

Maybe he should have. Africa's darkside never obscured the light-highs. Racing across a minefield in Mauritania, wondering how fast you have to move to outrun stupidity. Camping on Christmas night in the Sahara with a convoy of German car-thieves, French smugglers and Portuguese missionaries under a sky so bright with stars that there was no room for black. Living on oranges and kindness in a Guinean mud hut for three days while I begged for passing petrol. And watching a leopard uncoil and leap across a trail like some furious, furry spring while I stopped for a smoke in northern Moçambique after a 2000 mile up-the-coast, off-road epic that everyone said couldn't be done – at least not by a chump like me. Six years on and these memories still shine so bright they light me up like a big, drunk firework.

'One day I'll jack it all in and fuck off on my bike,' slurs everyone at closing time. That ain't me. That ain't this. That's the quiet guy at the bar, the anonymous geezer in the work's canteen, who kisses the missus, pops out for cigarettes and never comes back. Ten years later, an insurance investigator finds him working in a Guernsey chip shop.

No wife, no horse, no moustache. Maybe I found it easier cause I had no 'all' to jack. Not married, no kids. I don't own a house, a car, a tv, a stereo, a phone. You can't drop out if you never signed up.

But you can ride off without dropping out. In Mexico, I ran into an English couple seeing it all on a KTM Adventure. Back home, they run a South London building firm. 'It'll be there when we get back.' Last thing I heard, they were drinking wine on a hotel roof in Bolivia and watching a revolution.

There's a myth, a nonsense surrounding overlanding. Only do-able by Dakar stars like Simon Pavey and John Deacon, bearded men capable of riding with broken ankles, navigating by the moon, lacing DT rims to BMW hubs. Tell that to Trys, my on-and-off riding buddy – he passed

his test in May. In June, he followed me into Mexico. In July, he trotted off on his own to Belize. 'Easy, innit?'

Yes. And has as much in common with the world's toughest desert race as a Sunday bimble has with the TT, as a trackday has with Hour 23 of the Bol d'Or. It's not an endurance test, it's going on holiday on a bike.

Cue the buts. 'But the fear, but the money, but the homesickness.' I've been proper scared twice. In Guinea, crossing a canyon bridged by railway girders. At night. In the rain. Shattered and trembling. Going back would have been ever dafter. So I crossed. [Er, that's not a very good story, is it?] And in Kenya, I was locked in a cage by a taunting, hissing mob of hustlers, jackals, wretches. Which should have been terrifying. And would have been if I hadn't been so damn drunk.

Fear is an instant, a moment, an as yet undecided crossroads of parallel outcomes. Am I gonna hit that? Is he gonna hit me with that? Fear evaporates, leaving a residue of stress. Accident stress, broken-bike stress, skint stress. Stress that exists at home. Stress that fades a lot quicker on a foreign beach than a familiar motorway.

Homesick? Yep, that's why I left. Alarm clocks, Tony Blair, hill town bigots, big city weasels – sick of them all. I'm not overtly aware of their absence – but over the weeks, the miles, I feel my shoulders opening up, feel the curl coming out of my sneer, feel the smiles beaming more often than curses. I miss specifics – roaring Old Trafford Saturdays with my Da, cozy Sunday roasts with my Ma, bed-wetting drunk on a school night with Our Kid. Sometimes it does get lonely. It doesn't last. Just drink a beer, talk to myself, spank that monkey. What?

Miss some people, find more humanity. Same wrong night in Guinea I give up in a village. A filthy, freaked-out foreigner wearing mud skin and weird boots. They feed me, water me, bed me. How would I respond if an unknown West African knocked on my door at midnight needing help?

Could anyone do it? Anyone who's prepared to lose control to gain freedom. Out here, foot-stamping won't shine the sun, won't pay the bribe, won't fill the belly or empty the ferry. Lose control, use patience and groove on the temporary nature of all things. Wet now, dry later. Tired now, sleeping later. Lonely now, laughing later.

If you're reading this, you probably ride a bike in Britain and laugh off all kinds of sarcastic, intrusive, expensive interference just to get your two-wheeled grin on. Which makes you much better suited to life on The Road than your Montego-driving neighbour from Hull.

Anyone can, but not everyone needs to. Maybe the potential is enough. To them, the bike's garage clutter. To us, it's a Beretta, half a mill in cash and a forged passport hidden under the floorboards. It's a great escape route. And whether it's used or not, that choice is always there. These are the days that must happen to you. Que vivan los shambolistas!

Dan Walsh, Salford, 2008
mundogonzo@gmail.com

AFRICA

★ ★ ☆

2000 – 2001

*The only reason monkeys don't speak is so they're not obliged
to pay for all the bananas they eat.*

ETHIOPIAN PROVERB

African Disclaimer

These old words were written on the road, on the run, in Moroccan basement cyber caffs, in Senegalese flophouses, in Ghanaian Irish pubs, in South African beer gardens, by a younger version of me fighting deadline dread, and writing for beer and food. So some of them aren't very good. I never said I was hot stuff. The opening's especially weak — clunky, naïve, and laddy. It picks up in Accra, when I first fuck the pooch — feel free to skip ahead.

'I don't mean to take the piss,' chuckled Chris the Courier, lying through his gold teeth, 'but we've just been overtaken by a funeral procession. Again.'

Monday 4 December, stuck in a drizzly lay-by on the dismal A2, and D-Day is turning into dead-slow day. Or slower-than-dead-slow day, as that late fella in the stretched Austin Princess has just proved. Again.

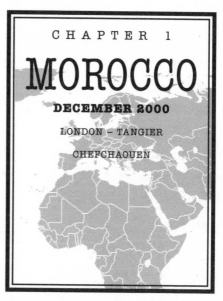

Two forced stops in less than twenty miles. The first time because of a fire – nothing too dramatic, fortunately Chris spotted the smoking strap relatively quickly and we managed to pull over and stamp it out before it had done too much damage to the rest of the luggage.

And then, just as the acrid burning smell had finally cleared, I ran out of petrol. Despite the 25-litre tank and two reserve taps. All this within the familiar confines of the M25. Round the world? At this rate I'll be lucky if I make it to bloody Dover.

Running away's not been as easy as I'd hoped. Having quit the job at *Bike* a month or so before the supposed departure day, I'd envisaged a couple of weeks of laid-back, one-task-per-day loafing, followed by a fortnight as a lout of leisure. Drifting around London town on my XT desert racer, popping into the occasional embassy and the regular pubs, revelling in the conspiratorial cosiness that only weekday-afternoon drinking can provide, overdoing the 'What am I up to? Oh, you know, riding round the world on my motorbike' mystique.

Unfortunately, this balloon of delusion was quickly burst when the bike was impounded. It went back to Yamaha for its crucial yet supposedly uncomplicated pre-trip service, and was instantly declared unroadworthy by a gaggle of crosspatch technicians, shaking their heads and sucking their teeth at the state of my clumsy modifications. Seems that it wasn't such a good idea deciding to fit the Acerbis tank after three hours of liquid lunching. With no tools. In the dark.

So with no bike to distract me, I was freed up to deal with the necessary paperwork, vaccinations, equipment, right? Er, wrong. It freed me up to make lists of all the things I had to sort, diligently updated every morning then urgently ignored. One of the main reasons for getting the funk out of Dodge was the opportunity to escape the claustrophobic clutter and pedantic detail of grown-up life. Instead I found myself staring at more forms than your average tax clerk.

Peter Fonda never made a film about this bit, the sleepless nights worrying whether to take hard or soft luggage, the endless queuing for expensive visas, the fruitless rooting through your mother's drawers (easy, Oedipus) looking for long-lost childhood vaccination records. Frankly, it wasn't very rock 'n' roll.

Eventually, with a lot of cattle-prodding from the girlfriend, I got it sorted and was ready to go. Monday morning showed full of dirty weather that was turning brollies inside out and making the old boys in the bookies wonder why on earth they ever left Jamaica and Galway in the first place. The kit was packed, the documents were photocopied and laminated, I was feeling quietly smug about how compact it all looked.

Until I transferred it to the bike, and the XT was transformed from lightweight trailie to hardcore squat. Park it next to a burst mattress, get a couple of seagulls to circle overhead and you'd swear it was a land-fill site. When Chris turned up on his neatly tail-packed XJR, ready to escort me off the premises, he laughed till he choked.

And it handled even worse than it looked. So, two weeks late, a mess of excess baggage and jangled nerves, I wobbled away from the house like a reluctant drunk at closing time, bouncing off the sides of vans and knocking over traffic signs, before limping down to Dover. We managed, ooh, at least 80 miles in France before retiring, hysterical with cold and ever so slightly demoralised.

But that was then, this is now. The breakdowns (two in two days – I really should learn to use reserve taps) and the fires (yep, plural – eventually I twigged that 'waterproof' and 'fireproof' are not the same thing) and all the other little incompetent defeats have been more than cancelled out by a series of increasingly delightful victories. Soaking up the 'nice one' one nods from the couriers at Vauxhall Bridge lights; the feeling of gay abandon saying 'Just a single for me' at the Dover ticket office; waking up on day two and realising that it really didn't matter that we'd got nowhere; tasting warm wind as I skirted Madrid; waving 'goodbye' to Europe from the deck of the Morocco ferry; and having my mind blown in a Tangier bar as a Berber child acrobat flick-flacked between the tables of dead-eyed hookers and mullet-haired truckers. And the realisation that these are the savagely edited highlights of one short week. Wonder what I did this week last year?

There've been plenty of surprises, some pretty extreme (particularly the Tangier midget on the monkey bike. Laugh? We nearly shat), but no jarring surprises. Travelling slowly by bike blends everything together, puts everywhere in context. Right here, right now, I'm in the Moroccan mountain town of Chefchaouen, plotted up in a five-pound-a-night hotel full of Spanish drug fiends and local commercial travellers. Looking out of the arched window, I can see the whitewashed streets of the kasbah, a cedar valley clouded with clean morning mist, and the green and granite peaks of the Rif mountains. The air's hot, full of fresh mint and ferocious hash and Arabic children's voices. The XT's downstairs, locked to the front desk in reception.

If I'd suddenly jumped here from A1-commuting on the ZX12, it'd be overwhelming. But I've had three days in France to get used to the bike, to practise driving on the right and to sharpen up my dull French, which is the second language round here. I've had two days in Spain feeling winter turn to spring turn to summer. And I've had a long weekend in Tangier, acclimatising to Africa in a Mediterranean environment. So yeah, it's all pleasingly exotic and constantly amazing, but never unnerving or overwhelming. Round the world on a bike? Piece of piss, mate. Bring it on.

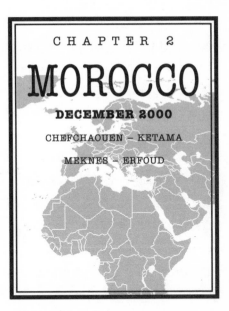

'Don't worry about it, dude,' drawled Kentucky Ken, popping the cap off another cold beer, 'those bad-ass bandidos try to mess with you, just hit the dirt. It'll be like *The Dukes of Hazzard*, man: the car tries to follow you cross-country, winds up in a ditch with the hood and trunk flapping, the fat guys get out, stamp on their hats and curse Dan the Man for getting away. No problem.'

Shooting the shit in the bar of the swanky Hotel Parador, Chefchaouen, Morocco, and the subject for discussion is tomorrow's assault on the notorious Ketama Road, a 100-mile chicken run through the Rif mountains' wild hash-growing region, where tourists are routinely run off the road by overzealous dealers. So come next morning, I'm fairly jittery. But with Ken safely on board the bus back to Tangier, there're no excuses for not hitting the road. Or waiting for it to hit me.

It turns out to be rather lovely, zigging the zag through green and dusty mountains that feel like the Picos de Europa, only busier – rural France and Spain always seem to be empty, closed, but these hills are alive, with old men hissing at plough-burdened donkeys, with boys tending goat herds, and conical-hatted old women struggling under loads so large they'd make an ant sweat.

And, of course, drug dealers. But for the first 60 miles, the most dangerous things I see are the enormous, cloudless views, although the expectation and anticipation of being chased makes it all extra exciting, every car a possible pursuer, every pedestrian a potential hijacker. And I ended up rather disappointed that by the time I reached Ketama town, nothing had happened.

I needn't have worried – the police roadblocks have simply moved the travelling salesmen to the other side of the mountain, and as soon as I left Ketama, it began – a car in the mirrors, lights flashing, horn blaring, closer and closer until it was alongside, swerving violently as its mirror-shaded driver waved a brick of hash, shouting, 'Very best quality, come see my house.'

Apart from the slight embarrassment of being unable to outrun a 25-year-old Renault 9, it was quite a laugh – a proper car chase. After a mile or so he gave up and passed the spliff baton to a 4x4, parked across the road ahead. As Ken said, hit the dirt, so I foot-down-wobbled past, onto the next. And the next. And the next. To be honest, it all got a bit much. After an hour of this nonsense, I'd gone from excitement to anger to jaded weariness – there's only so many car chases a man can take – even the Dukes of Hazzard had the occasional break from the action to splash around in the creek with Daisy.

As suddenly as it began, it ceased, and the road took me past Fes and on to a quiet night in old Meknes town. Meknes was mainly remarkable as a contrast – in the morning I used a cashpoint, and bought a copy of the *Guardian Weekly*, by lunchtime I was in the desert, freaking out over the impossible landscape, or the rapidly changing series of landscapes. In less than a day the green Rif had given way to the dark ochres of the

Atlas and the burnt reds of the desert. But in the distance I could clearly see snow-capped peaks.

Sand and snow at the same time? That's not right, like seeing a cat's head on a dog's body, or some mystic poet's drug-induced ramblings about Kubla Khan's sunny domes with caves of ice. But there's no opium-pipe magic carpet or Frankenstein scientists here, just plain old me on a plain old XT, less than two weeks' ride away from familiar Britain. As a wise Englishwoman said, 'Morocco is the closest faraway place I know.'

I was heading for Erfoud and the ironically named Hotel Majestic, a grubby little gaff notable only for the nosiness of its patron. He started slowly, leafing through my passport, graduated to watching me unpack and for the finale picked up a postcard I was in the middle of writing, examined the front and then started reading on the back in a Stavros accent, 'Hello Mum and Dad, how are you ?'

But people don't come to Erfoud for the hospitality, they come for the Erg Chebbi, Morocco's only section of rolling dunes. So the next morning I dumped the luggage, kinda guessing that within ten minutes of my departure the patron would be running round the lobby with my pants on his head, shouting, 'Look! Now I am the Eengleesh man!', and took the surprisingly perky XT on the 36 km trek to the sand, dreaming crusty-demons-of-dirt fantasies in my motocross helmet.

The dunes just sort of appeared – one minute I'm bouncing along a dusty track, dodging potholes, experimenting with standing up but feeling self-conscious so sitting down again, the next I'm staring up at three enormous, looming, very yellow sandcastles.

Like getting your first erection, or your first proper chance to touch a breast (same for girls if you just swap the nouns around), when they're right in front of me, I don't know what to do with them. How exactly do you ride up a dune?

So I stop, have a cigarette, have a good look and, like all virgins, approach things too tentatively, panic when it all goes soft and engage in a flurry of right-hand activity – which just leaves me axle-deep in sand, sweaty and rather foolish-looking, having travelled, ooh, all of five yards. The Bedouin lounging in the nearby pickup laughed so hard at the 'all the gear, no idea' European, I thought he was going to choke.

Discretion being the better part of valour and all that, I shat out and turned around. There'll be plenty of opportunities to arse around in the sand when I cross the desert. That's the Sahara Desert. Ah, how hard can it be? Bring it on.

'You! With the bike! To the front! Now!'. Bugger. Crunch time at the Moroccan frontier, and the soldier's not taking no for an answer. It's all eyes on me as I reluctantly paddle to the head of the convoy. In front of me, beyond the rusty

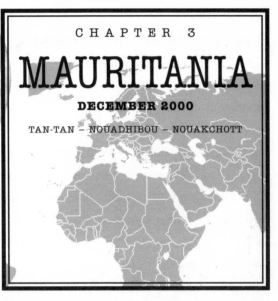

nail stingers and the bored border guards, lies the literal end of the road and 60 km of sandy piste through the mined no-man's-land that separates Morocco and Mauritania.

Behind me, there're sixty-three vehicles, a French, German and Mauritanian mixture of butch 4x4s, family-size camper vans and second-hand or freshly stolen saloons. And up front, the XT and me, the only bike and the only Brit, not so much flying the flag as mincing around in Geri Halliwell's Union Jack frock, smoking nervously and wondering how on earth I'd ended up leading the proceedings.

Heading south overland from Morocco involves joining the convoy from Dakhla, a dusty administrative town three days' ride south of the beach resorts of Agadir. The convoy leaves every Tuesday and Friday, and you have to register a day in advance. This registration is a potential nightmare, involving extended exposure to the worst of all possible human combinations, the uniformed bureaucrat. Fortunately, I had Chris

Scott's indispensable *Adventure Motorcycling Handbook* up my sleeve, which clearly outlines the unwritten rules.

Once officially official, the next thing to do was to change the tyres, or more accurately, find someone else to change them for me. The XT's OE Dunlop Trailmaxes had squared off, and I was desperate to change into the Pirelli MT21s, mainly so I wouldn't have to carry the bloody things any further. Fortunately, I bumped into a Moroccan kid on a battered Cagiva motocrosser. Yes, he knew a local shop, yes, he'd take me there, but he's just on his way home for dinner, and would I like to join him?

So we had a pleasant hour in his apartment with his wife and extended family, and filled up with food and hospitality. We found the mechanic, who fitted and balanced the tyres, hosed clean the air filter and adjusted the chain (yes, all right, I know), all for a fiver. And when we were finished, the three of us went off together for coffee. Motorcycle City? Bite me.

We'd been instructed by the cops to meet at ten the next morning, which gave me my first chance to check out my fellow travellers. There were sixty-plus vehicles divided into three categories – the 4x4s, Mitsubishi Pajeros, Nissan Hiluxes and assorted Land Rovers, plastered with rally stickers and sand ladders and grey beards. Next the happy campers, in converted Transits or purpose-built Fiats, filled with married couples and excited kids and garden furniture. And finally, the cars, a couple of 524 turbo diesel Beemers and various French and Japanese saloons. There's a healthy living to be made buying or stealing motors in Europe and driving them down to West Africa to sell.

What they all had in common was an air of confident capability, expertly tinkering with fan belts, topping up radiators or rustling up three-course lunches. I tried to join in, absent-mindedly fiddling with my luggage, but fumbled a tight bungee and twanged myself in the face so hard it cut my lip. Nothing more to do but sit and wait. And wait.

At eleven o'clock, a man from the Department of Health checked our yellow fever vaccination cards. At midday, a soldier wandered over and amused himself by telling a little French girl that her mummy was going to leave without her. At one o'clock, a cop ordered us to line up on the other side of the road. At two o'clock, absolutely nothing happened. And then at three o'clock, all of a sudden 'Dépêchez ! Allez!' and we're off, 360 km of potholes and the Tropic of Cancer crossed in one hit, arriving at the fort at La Garia well after dark.

Whereupon everyone set about transforming the car park into a holiday village, bustling about with Gaz stoves and head torches and portable barbecues. Everyone, that is, apart from me. For some reason, I'd chosen to interpret the guidebook's advice to 'bring enough food and water for two days' as 'bring a bottle of coke, a packet of biscuits and an orange'. And despite the mountain of baggage, I didn't have a tent. Which is why I ended up sleeping in a blockhouse, engaged in a fiercely contested snoring competition with a dozen Moroccan squaddies.

When reveille sounded at dawn, we saw the real reason we'd arrived at the barracks after dark — the starry Saharan campsite was in fact a rubbish tip. After another session of lining up and faffing about, I was summoned to the front by a well-meaning soldier with the mistaken belief that bikes are faster than cars, and shooed into no-man's-land and my first proper off-road experience.

That was the point when the road trip became an adventure – me and the XT, bouncing along a sandy track through a north African minefield, swerving round potholes, juddering over corrugations and, damn it, trailing dust. I'm aware that for regular trail riders, getting overexcited by the fact that I was producing dust is on a par with getting overexcited about broom-broom noises, but as far as I was concerned, I was riding across the land, kicking up sand, sheriff's posse on my tail 'cause I'm in demand. Remember when you first got a black visor and spent a week with a wing mirror angled upwards, so could check how good you looked ? I was doing exactly the same thing.

Which may explain how I managed to get lost. My *Vanishing Point* fantasies were brought to a clanging end by the realisation that although the next checkpoint was only 20 km away, I'd covered 30 miles. Arse. Maybe I should have gone right rather than left at that fork? Fortunately, it was that simple, and the first to leave was the last to arrive, to a mixed response of ironic applause and genuine concern.

The Mauritanian border post was something else – passport control was a dry stone shack, behind which were two tatty pickups – also known as the visa office and customs. It was all manned by the shadiest-looking soldiers imaginable, masters of African military chic, effortlessly blending combat fatigues and assault rifles with mirrored shades and Tuareg headscarves. (A quick word about these headscarves – wearing them correctly isn't as easy as you might think. The idea is that they transform you from everyday Joe into piratical Omar Sharif-lookalike. Unfortunately, they just make me look like my gran, or a low-rent drag act called Florence of Arabia or Dune Whitfield.)

Despite their formidable appearance, the soldiers were friendly and immigration hassle-free and I was waved towards the town of Nouadhibou, over another 30 km of unescorted piste through another minefield. And into another opportunity to get lost. Properly lost. Not lost as in 'confused by London's one-way system' but lost like a child at a fairground – confused, scared and absolutely helpless. I don't know how, but I followed the wrong set of tyre tracks and wound up at an unambiguous dead end, a couple of tons of sand and razor wire blocking the way.

I tried to retrace my steps, but there were no familiar landmarks to head for, no clear junctions to return to, just a messy scribble of paths leading left, right and sideways, and somewhere, a hidden muddle of mines. A mental stocktake revealed eight cigarettes, a couple of swallows of Coke and half a biscuit. I noted a cave that looked dry, and a tyre that looked like it'd smoke, and waited for divine intervention.

It came in the unlikely form of the two BMWs, moving fast about half a mile away on a parallel piste. I never thought I'd be so pleased to see a German. I blame the following piece of exceptional stupidity on this elation. Deciding it would be impossible to accurately track back and find the origin of their path, I thought light thoughts, held my breath and headed straight for them, cursing and praying across the minefield, wondering how fast I'd have to go to outrun an explosion, for some reason singing 'Bigmouth Strikes Again' at the top of my quivering voice.

In the universe next door, I didn't make it, and spent the rest of my life being humiliated by the question 'How exactly did you lose your leg, Dan?' In this one, I got away with it. 'The desert is not a playground,'

said Peter the German, sternly, before leading me to Nouadhibou and safety.

In Nouadhibou the convoy splintered into smaller groups. The next section was a 530-km trip across Mauritania, a notoriously difficult stretch that demanded the services of a local guide. Despite (or maybe because of) my obvious incompetence, Peter the German asked if I'd like to join his group.

We'd arranged to meet the guide at 8 a.m. At 8.20 I struggled out of bed to find a curt note pinned to the door: 'Gone – meet at petrol pump.' But when you're late once, you're late for the rest of the day. By the time I arrived at the pump, they'd already filled up and were impatiently revving their engines or lashing boxes of water to roof racks. Which is why I found myself stocking up for three days in Africa's harshest wasteland at a newspaper kiosk. And ended up with five packets of Marlboro, three litres of Coke (already warm), three baguettes (already stale) and a tub of Nutella chocolate spread.

I didn't remain the bad guy for long. As we approached the city limits we were pulled up by the police. Without explanation they arrested the guide – 'I'll see you at the customs post,' he shouted optimistically as he was cuffed and dragged away.

The guide never showed, but the world's longest train did – this record breaker's 2.3 km long and carries iron ore from the mines at Zouérat to the port at Nouadhibou. And as it clattered by, we got to know each other. The self-appointed leader was Peter, a capable, arrogant German, travelling to the Gambia with his girlfriend in the two BMs. Next were two Mitsubishi Pajeros – one driven by a hippy German couple, who kindly helped me with my luggage (and lent me a tent, and made me coffee), the other crewed by a permanently angry Portuguese and his permanently angry dog. The rank and file consisted of two quiet Belgian classic-bike buffs in a Mazda 626, two villainous-looking but chirpy French drug dealers in a Peugeot estate van, and the Fall Guy, me.

Word must have got round that this motley crew was stranded at the drive-in, 'cause within half an hour another guide arrived in a taxi, and after an energetic bout of negotiating, we were off to play in the world's biggest sandpit.

There are no gentle introductions to the desert – all of a sudden, it's just there, you're in it, and you'd better deal with it. The first day was hard and fast, as long as it was wide, mile after mile of crusty dust punctuated by splashes of soft sand. The hard dust was fine, it was the soft stuff that terrified me. Every time I saw it I'd panic and slow right down, and consequently the front would slap, the back would sink and I'd shit my pants, convinced I was off.

Eventually, more out of frustration than courage, I found the bottle to do the right thing and attack it with the power on. And what do you know, the bike was transformed, the front skipping, the rear gently weaving, not exactly under control, but certainly less out of it, and I actually started to enjoy myself.

Every hour or so we'd hit a patch too wide to blast across – three, four, five hundred yards of churned-up powder. One by one, the cars would line up, take off and get stuck. And one by one, we'd attack them with shovels and sand ladders, and push and pull them to the far side. As the day went on, these patches grew bigger and more regular, until we were reduced to hopping between small islands of rock in an ever-expanding sea of sand.

At 10 p.m., we called it a day – it'd taken eleven hours to cross 100 km, and the last three klicks took two hours. The cars were parked in a wagon circle, and we got on with an exhausted but cheery Christmas Eve. Peter brewed up some mulled wine, the hippies cooked a stew, the Portugeezer made a fire, the Frenchies built spliffs and I dug out a couple of beers before happily collapsing into a borrowed tent and sandy dreams.

The only thing better than falling asleep in a desert is waking up in one. While the rest of the world was opening presents and watching *The Great Escape*, we were gasping at where we'd come from and groaning at where we were going. The first couple of hours were fantastic – tearing across a vast open plain, 60 mph, seven abreast, beeping and waving at each other as we chased the horizon and tried to outrun the sun. Then the piste narrowed, snaking round sandbanks and clumps of thorny trees and I discovered a new challenge – corners.

I just couldn't get the bike to turn. Every time I tried, it'd just go mental, slewing and wriggling and trying to throw me off. Realising this wasn't the time to learn foot-down berm riding, I gave up, and whenever the cars hit a bend, I'd just go straight on, careering up and down dunes, crashing through bushes, tacking like a supertanker and laughing like a drain.

I wasn't the only one with problems – the hammering route was destroying the cars. First, a BM shredded a tyre, then the Peugeot sheared its exhaust, the Mazda's fan packed up and a Pajero radiator burst. We limped along like this for the rest of the day, stopping to bodge repairs, finally arriving at the coast bedraggled, sunburnt, but happy to be out of the worst of it.

We were woken at 8 by the angry dog barking angrily at the sea. Over coffee, cigarettes and by now extremely crunchy bread, we chatted to the local fishermen – the last section was a run down the beach to the capital Nouakchott, passable only at low tide. That would come around at 2.30. Nothing to do but wait.

There's something pleasingly humbling about being delayed by a phenomenon as enormous as the ocean, knowing that no amount of tutting or swearing or watch-checking will make the blindest bit of difference. This liberating relinquishing of control seemed to chill everybody right out – the Germans took to canoodling and beach-combing, the Portugeezer shared out the last of his biscuits, I spent a couple of hours listening to the waves then idly chatting with the Belgians about Joey Dunlop and Manx Nortons. At 2.30 we packed up and lined up. And this time I was happy to be at the front.

Once again it was me, the XT and Africa. On my right, the sparkling Atlantic, roaring to and fro; to the left, the desert, textbook Technicolor cathedral dunes crashing down into the water. And beneath me, the engine thumping and the knobblies strumming over fresh, wet, hard-packed beach. Forget everything else I've ever done, from riding a

Harley through Vegas to blasting a Busa down the autobahns, this was the reason I learned to ride a bike. A real right-here-right-now moment.

And this shit goes on for 100 miles, which at 45 mph is more than two hours of slithering over slippery rocks, inadvertently jumping dunes, scattering angry gangs of seagulls, alternately axle-deep in sand or knee-high in the surf, past more shipwrecks and ramshackle fishing villages, until finally arriving at Nouakchott and tarmac and a hotel. And over a table of cold Chinese beers and fresh African fish we toasted the desert for letting us pass and tried to work out exactly how we'd just crossed the Sahara.

The point is that we weren't steely-eyed professional adventurers, just ordinary men and women taking a chance to do something extra-ordinary. 'What a man can do, a man can do,' a wise Gambian kid said to me a couple of weeks after, and he was damn right. If a useless chump like me can do it, anyone can. Forget Skeggy bike week and think big.

No more excuses. Keep drifting.

'Cool, fine, nice,' croons Maurice the wrestling fisherman, making it up as he goes along, 'that's how we speak the English.' Lounging in the Campement Palmarin, sipping seaside sundowners, watching girlfriend Lou scoot up the beach on the XT, chuckling along to Maurice's pidgin nursery rhymes and fluent djembe drumming, and the living is easy – Senegaleasy.

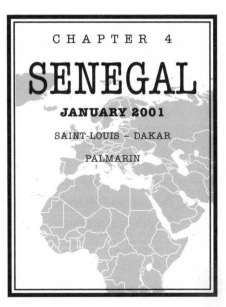

CHAPTER 4

SENEGAL

JANUARY 2001

SAINT-LOUIS – DAKAR

PALMARIN

Heading south from Saharan Mauritania into laid-back Senegal, and the contrast is stark. Mauritania is hot, harsh and hard-faced. This is a country where slavery lasted till 1980, where they've sold their limited natural resources for short-term dollars, and where cash-crop deforestation means that the deserts are eating the cities. So it's every man for himself, and the 100-mile stretch from Nouakchott to the frontier is an increasingly difficult rat run of bribe-chasing cops and robbers. Then you hit the Senegal River and breathe a sigh of relief – the water has held the sand and its attitudes at bay, the yellows become greens, the sulks become smiles, the veiled women become half-naked beauty queens and I think I'm gonna like this place.

Even getting around is easy. Unlike Mauritania, with its pistes and guides, Senegal has roads. Proper tarmac roads. Which could almost be boring if it wasn't for the scenery, a blend of mangrove swamps buzzing with butterflies, salty lagoons humming with wading birds and forests of upside-down baobab trees. And an awful lot of awfully big roadkill. In England we get squashed squirrels and pancaked hedgepigs. Here it's donkeys, camels and long-horns, flyblown and bloated, strewn around like rotting potatoes with stick legs akimbo. And where there's roadkill, there's vultures, mooching around in menacing gangs, giving everyone 'one day' stares, baldy heads and hunched shoulders making them look like skinheads in Crombies. The vultures are everywhere, and even make it into Dakar, the only part of Senegal that isn't laid-back. 'This is the second most beautiful city in West Africa,' said my hitch-hiker proudly as the skyscrapers appeared over the gridlocked shanty suburbs. And it is a beautiful city, if you can see beyond the hustlers, touts, pickpockets and con men, lowlifes with tall tales who haunt its busy squares and narrow streets.

As usual, the most effective crooks are wearing uniforms, and within five minutes of hitting town I've been stung by a yellow-eyed, beery-breathed cop for failing to comply with some invisible sign. I could almost have lost my temper until I remembered that the CFA3000 fine was really only three quid.

I'd come to Dakar to watch the last stage of the famous race – but I was rather surprised when I ended up competing in it. Cruising down the highway from Saint-Louis, minding my own business, I spot a too-bright light in my mirror (that's mirror, singular, after the other was smashed in Dakhla by feral street kids – cue 'I got stoned in Morocco' gag), and next thing I've been chewed up and spat out by two cigarette-liveried V8 howling Pajeros, a thundering six-wheel-drive Merc truck and a team of open-piped XR650s. God damn! They're racing along open roads, three times the speed of everyone else, swerving round buses, beeping at bicycles, tearing up the inside of ox carts, hundreds and thousands of pounds' worth of too fast reckless arrogance forcing their way through the rush-hour slow-down. Try to imagine an African outfit getting away with this kind of behaviour on the Périphérique. It can't be done.

The condemnation came later – at the time, it was a blast. Underpowered and out of my depth but ever the courier, I couldn't help thinking, 'Just wait until they hit some traffic – then I'll have them.' And sure enough, as the roads narrowed and the gaps tightened, I caught up and joined in, acknowledging the cheers of the crowds, ignoring the stares of the factory drivers, saluting cops as they waved us through red lights, generally feeling like a streaker at Wembley, finally creating confusion by going straight on rather than right at the last checkpoint. And there's now a northern quartier of Dakar where the rally will never be taken seriously again, after locals witnessed a scruffy English rider abandon the race fifteen minutes from the end and dive into a notoriously sleazy bar where he spent the night drinking heavily with a crew of Liberian refugees, mooning at the Naomi Campbell-lookalike waitress and trying to teach the bemused band to play 'Baker Street'.

That was enough big-city nonsense, so I headed down the coast to Palmarin and Maurice. And the best thing about this place isn't that it only costs seven pounds a night for full board in a thatched-roof beach hut, nor that you wake up and fall asleep to the sound of the ocean, nor even that the only other guests are foot-long lizards and month-old puppies. It's the fact that the campement is government-built and locally run, with a share of the profits funding the village school and clinic. Which means that mid-afternoon drinking isn't a selfish indulgence, it's an act of selfless philanthropy. So, Ahmed, another round of beers, s'il vous plaît, and Maurice, why don't you grab the guitar and sing us the song about the chauffeur and the boss's wife? Those kids deserve it.

Keep singing.

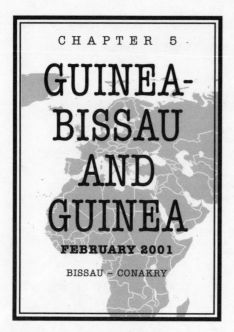

CHAPTER 5

GUINEA-BISSAU AND GUINEA

FEBRUARY 2001

BISSAU – CONAKRY

The map is not the territory. And that is not a bridge. It's an iron-clad kick in the crotch. Six slippery steel railway lines over a steep river canyon glint yellow in my headlight. No guard rails, no chance of surviving the fifty-foot drop-off, and no way round. I nearly fell off just walking the son-of-a-bitch, and returned to the bike on all fours, whimpering like a puppy. 'But it looked so much easier on the map . . .'

It looked so much easier in the pub. Sat sipping in the Palestinian's breeze-block bar, across from the bullet-scarred French Embassy and the ETA-owned casino in the Praça Che Guevara, relaxing with a cold beer, a spicy shwarma and a Michelin map, that backdoor route from backwater Bissau to neighbouring Guinea somehow seemed very doable. Just follow the dotted red line. Bissau, border hop, Boké. Looks to be less than a hundred miles. If I leave in the morning, I'll be plotted up in the Hotel Benda before dark . . .

Fool. A couple of weeks off the bike, in the bars, on the islands, had left me soft in the head. A couple of weeks playing war correspondents with the spooks and mercenaries, aid workers and arms dealers, angels and demons who circle Africa's unfashionable civil conflicts, had left me feeling dagger-proof, dangerously deluded that I was as capable as the whisky-drinking, cigar-smoking, front-line doctors and priests who'd been showing me round this abandoned, shattered capital.

But I'm not a good man on a mercy mission. I'm just some twat on a bike. Out in the dirt and sand, nothing ever goes as planned. Especially when you break the Three Rules of Overland Travel – never assume there's another petrol station; never assume the border crossing will be easy; and never, ever ride off-road at night.

Rule one was broken for the daftest of reasons – I coulda shoulda woulda filled my tank, but the pumpster offered me a couple of cartons of smokes for my last francs. Real Marlboro, not the Chinese counterfeit coughing fits I'd been forcing down for a fortnight. There'll be another garage later, right?

Wrong. The tarmac became gravel became dirty red dust, but I was too tickled by trees full of monkeys and a town called 'Shithole' to notice, and too full of better men's confidence to care that after a three-hour frontier hold-up the quiet afternoon had become a noisy jungle dusk. I knew I was in trouble when the dotted red line became a track became a gap between the trees and my butterfly flit became a caterpillar track along a dried-up riverbed, now knotted rocky and knuckled, now axle-deep in powder-puff sand, so narrow that the soldier on the bicycle had to squash himself into the bushes to let me squeeze past. 'You'll never cross that bridge,' he called as he disappeared into the screeching gloom.

No choice. Ride it. I'll either make or it I won't. I made it. Just before the bike ran out of petrol. Cock. Take stock. I'd rather not. No petrol, no food, no water. No tent, no sign of life. What the hell am I going to do? Somewhere close by, a donkey coughs. Here, Donkey. Donkeys mean people. Maybe I can ride him to the next village? The donkey doesn't look convinced. Maybe I can rein him to the bike with a bungee, make him pull it like a cart? The donkey looks less convinced. Leave the bike here, lock it to the donkey? Thrice neigh. There's nothing to do but push. The donkey laughs and follows behind. I suspect he's as lost as I am.

One, two, three hours later, deranged and deliriously dehydrated, I slouched into a sleeping village. Only the nightwatchman was still awake. He said there was no petrol here, and none for another fifty miles. Said he was glad I'd found their donkey. Said he'd have to speak to the Chief.

'I have always depended on the kindness of strangers' sounds more convincing coming from a flirty Southern belle than a barely intelligible, oddly dressed and filthy foreigner on a broken bike, with eyes full of muddy tears and a pocketful of another country's useless currency. So it's especially special when the Chief turns up with a flask of sweet tea, a bag of oranges and the offer of a bed – his brother's bed. Tonight, because of me, his brother will sleep on the floor.

The only thing weirder than falling asleep in a one-roomed, mud-walled, straw-roofed hut is waking up in one. My internal clock shocks me awake at dawn with an alarming volley of clangs. I wander outside and have a smoke. Children's singing voices float from the open-air, chalk-circle classroom on the early morning mist, mixing with the pecking chickens' cluck, and curling round the fresh tea that's been left on the doorstep. I shit in a bush and wash in a well. This is gonna be a long day.

Make that two long days. I sat by that track, and waved down the one, two, three tractors that crawled past, but the farmers kept shrugging: 'Diesel'. Eventually, the border guards changed shifts, and the driver of their Russian truck sold me a bottle of worryingly red petrol for the price of a four-star weekend in Moscow.

The Chief waved goodbye. 'Tell them that we just want to be left alone. Tell them that we just want to farm.' I'd like to say it was a beautiful human moment. But it wasn't. Too exhausted to translate a fitting response, I just smiled and gave him another packet of cigarettes. As I rode away, the bed-swapping brother ran alongside. 'Take me with you. Please.' I shrugged, pointed at the bags full of junk on the pillion seat and rode away.

I rode away. They're still there. And I still wonder how I'll respond the first time a lost African traveller stumbles out of the darkness, bangs on my locked door and asks for my help.

But it wasn't that black and white. Africa never is. Guinea was especially confusing – I could never tell whether it was gonna buy me a beer or banjo me with the bottle. A klick outside the village I was stopped by angry men demanding money for the bed. When I shrugged and smiled 'Je n'ai pas d'argent', they clattered me with sticks. Five klicks outside the village I was stopped by smiling soldiers offering petrol. When I shrugged and smiled 'No money', they filled me up for free.

Friend and foe. Saint and sinner. Dead and alive. This schizophrenic double-bind has me knotted nuts, confused as Schroedinger's Cat. Morning mist has gifted the jungle a dewy green sheen, and damped down the dust on this giggling, wriggling red trail that splashes across chuckling streams, through dense bush jumping with cheeky monkeys and gossiping birds, but I'm too tense to take it in. Hobbled by my own sloppy lack of planning. One day I'll come back and do it properly.

I burst out of the bush near Boke's new road works. A Chinese engineer rubs his eyes in cartoon disbelief at where I've sprung from and directs me to the only hotel in town. Desperate, starving, and still broke, I explain to the manager that I need a room, a meal and a beer, but I'm only carrying sterling. The hotel's full, but he'll find a staff room. The restaurant's shut, but he'll cook me a chop. The bar's dry, but he'll send a boy and a bike. The bank's gone, but his brother has a bureau de change. All he needs now is my passport as a deposit. I know what's coming, but I need to eat, drink, sleep. And when he announces next morning with a crocodile smile that the room rate's doubled and the exchange rates halved, I surprise him with a grin.

Four days late, I hit capital Conakry and an ATM. Funny how a little money makes everything alright. A bike cop stops and I'm ready for his 'donnez moi un cadeau' tale of woe. Then thrown when he leads me to a hotel, negotiates a better room rate, lets me park up in the police compound. 'And in the morning, we will meet and I will buy you breakfast'. Yeah, we'll see.

Next morning he buys me breakfast, leads me to my cleaned bike, and palms me a handwritten letter of safe passage. When he asks me why I'm look like I'm gonna cry, I tell him I've been having a few problems with corruption. He looks genuinely sad. Apologises. And reminds me that people are especially tense because the country is at war.

War. Twat. I'd forgotten about that. While I'm fannying around in the bush, Guinea's fighting Liberia in the jungle. I should leave. Grab a visa from the Malian embassy and head north through the Fouta Djalon highlands. After months in dry deserts and damp tropics, I'm happy high off this green mountain air. Plenty of cadeau checkpoints, but the laisez passez gets me waved through. Dump the bags in a Kourossa flophouse, grab a beer in a truckstop. A citizen sits down next to me and buys me a drink. Half an hour later he banjoes me the bottle. I gotta get out of this place.

By the time I get to Bamako I'm bollocksed, busted, bushed. What I need is a couple of days off in some bourgoise oasis, some air-conditioned r&r with cable tee vee and a wet bar. But I'm not just broken, I'm also broke. And that means no break. So what I get is beer that stinks of mutton and a chipped ceiling fan and a Hotel Delwende cry and a wank. Wa-Wa – West Africa Wins Again.

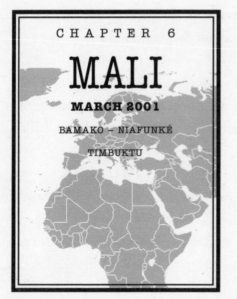

CHAPTER 6

MALI

MARCH 2001

BAMAKO – NIAFUNKÉ

TIMBUKTU

Never get off the bike. Absolutely goddamned right. Another stagnant day in Bamako, Mali's dusty, chock-a-block capital, and this road trip has seriously stalled. So it's another idle morning sitting with the goats on the hotel's rubble-strewn patio, watching the wheels go round on the midget Mobylettes, municipal minibuses and ministerial Mitsubishis. Another impotent afternoon in the generator-powered cybercafé, waiting for visas to be approved and invoices to clear and money to appear. And another drunken night listening to a local John Lee Hooker soundalike sing the Malian Blues while the Congolese government-in-exile murders the schmaltz-French karaoke machine.

Every hour that the XT spends locked to the hotel freezer makes the trip lose more momentum and purpose, degenerating from soul-stirring adventure into just another cheap holiday in other people's misery. Africa is no place to get the blues – attack it with energy and enthusiasm and all you see is life and vitality. Stumble around feeling sorry for yourself and all you see is poverty and disease. I needed a mission and, for my sins, they gave me one, sent it right up just like room service. There on a mineral water bottle label – 'Bottled at source in Tombouctou'. Just the tonic.

Tombouctou – that's the French name for Timbuktu, famous for being famous, a cipher for the middle of nowhere, a word my gran used instead of swearing. Timbuktu – half-remembered from playground rhymes about Constantinople, from Beau Geste comic-book romances, from the final frame in Donald Duck cartoons. According to the guide-book, it's 'a thousand-odd kilometres from Bamako'. A thousand odd kilometres sounds ideal.

As soon as I get the show on the road and take my thumb out of my arse, the fugue lifts, the kids start waving and the coincidences begin again. Sometimes when you have a good idea it feels like the universe conspires to help you realise it. Two hundred and thirty klicks outside Bamako, I hit the town of Ségou, a fork in the road and a big decision. Right, with the tarmac, the hotels and the traditional tourist route, or left, into the Niger's inland delta, dunes and off-road adventure?

I want to fork left, figuring that if Timbuktu's gonna make any sense, then it must be difficult to reach. But 400 km alone in the Malian desert strays beyond 'difficult' into 'reckless'. Right on cue, I run into two Land Rovers, one Dutch, one Swiss. Mike and Angela, the enthusiastic Dutch couple, are obviously in charge, and apparently struggling with the same decision. I needed assistance, they needed encouragement, and after half an hour's getting-to-know-you banter about bikes, beers and a particularly filth Dutch joke (punchline – 'because the first kut is the deepest'), we decide to team up. I sling a 25-litre jerrycan on their roof, we stock up on groceries at a market and that's us – into a week of deep wilderness.

A week of deep wilderness means a week turning the lines and names on a map into remembered jolts, faces and landscapes. And ruts. Just as eskimos have a thousand words for snow and couriers a thousand moans for rain, overlanders have a thousand curses for ruts. Those bastard, bleeding, Jesus-weeping ruts . . .

The first batch we come across are corrugations, cross ruts, bloody furious ruts. Wherever there are man-made tracks that have been used regularly by heavy vehicles, these little fuckers appear. It's like riding across a washboard, it's like racing a skateboard down a cobbled hill, it's like commuting on a tumble dryer. Nothing to do but grimace and bear it, while roaring a stammered, juddering 'B-b-b-b-bastards!'

Cross ruts are uncomfortable and punishing for the bike, but at least they're not scary. That's for the sandy ruts. (Sandy Ruts? Great porn-star name – Sandy Ruts is Rut Buster in *Going Down With the Wind*. Maybe.) Easy to spot – the bike suddenly starts wriggling like a lizard in a tin and shouting, 'Buck off!' Funny how close you can come to binning it out here without actually falling off.

Two types of sandy ruts, the most common caused by trucks. Deep and wide, they're surprisingly comfortable to ride. The problem is that once you're in, there's no way out, slotted-stuck in a giant sandy Scalextric track. Navigation becomes irrelevant. Once you're in, you're in, and you're following that truck till it stops. Not a problem if the driver took a direct route, but kinda tiresome if you have to follow him to his mum's for tea, then to the next village to visit his mistress.

The real bastards are the little skinny fellas left by 4x4s, at their absolute wriggling worst when they're climbing steep dunes. Back off?

Fall off. Simple as that. Nothing to do but get on the pegs, get on the gas and go for it, bucking and weaving and slewing and sweating, and if luck holds and gravity fails, somehow make it to the top. And get ready to do it all over again.

It isn't all hard work and sweary spills. Between the bumps and the grinds are miles, hours, days of big, mad, natural beauty. Allah was having one of his better days when he wrote this part of the world. We're following the River Niger, running on a sharp, red piste chasing a deep, wide blue across irrigated splashes of soft, wet green. I never had a favourite river before.

When the river kinks south, we keep north-east across a dandruff-dry lake bed, a vast disappearing flatness of white dust and skeletal thorn trees. It's just me, the XT and Africa, naked. Life sans intermediaries. 50 mph, sand spiralling off the back wheel, chasing a horizon that looks like a flag – white, green and blue in three stripes of pure broad colour – into one of those moments when I could just let go, hop off and let the ghost-riding guardian Hell's Angel ride while I float alongside. And that's real road tripping, baby.

A week in deep wilderness means a week of wild camping. I'm more red-nosed indoors than ruddy-cheeked outdoors. Why bother when you can get a cheap hotel room instead? But with no hotels out here, there's no option, no choice but to be positive. By the time we pull over for our first night, I'm even looking forward to it – back to basics, just me, my new friends, under the stars. So it's a bit of a shock when the two gas barbecues are unloaded. Followed by the garden furniture. And the lap-top with CD-rom atlas to chart today's progress and load tomorrow's GPS waypoints. While sipping ice-cold drinks. And taking a shower.

And enjoying a three-course meal. Under the savage glare of halogen spotlights. All set to a six-speaker Chili Peppers soundtrack. Everything but the, er, no, that's there too. I spent a month in Bissau without seeing running water and you've got it in the back of a car? Never seen a jeep with better facilities than a capital city before.

Just don't write Mike and Angela off as weekend Winnebago warriors. They caught the overlanding bug in Australia, touring the Outback in a knackered Land Cruiser for six months. And when they returned to Holland, they bought an ex-army ambulance and spent eighteen months' worth of after-work nights and long weekends designing and building this travelling home. 'The idea is to be completely self-sufficient,' says Mike. 'Avoid expensive cities, live out in the country with real people, make this trip last as long as we possibly can. The cold Cokes are just a bonus.'

Despite all the home comforts, four days of shitting in the bushes, sleeping in a bag and drinking from a tube is more than enough for me. So when the others plot up 50 km outside of Timbuktu, I decide to plough on, the desire for a city stronger than the fear of a piste that was difficult at dusk and downright dangerous in the dark.

The final half-hour ran as if it was scripted – the city lights twinkle in the distance, the piste gets nastier, stickier, slippier, before catapulting me onto the short stretch of tarmac that links the airport to the town, past a petrol station and a bank and a roundabout with street lights. A small boy enters stage left, pedalling furiously in the soft sand, and leads me to a hotel, ushering me up the steep front steps, across the lobby, past a gaggle of French tourist extras who all gasp and coo appropriately, into the courtyard beyond and right to a room. Run through the shower, dive into the bar and the coldest, wettest, beeriest beer I've ever tasted, slurped, savoured. *Ice Cold in Alex* with added shish kebab spice. Then the telly comes on and guess what? Manchester United v Arsenal, extended highlights from Old Trafford. And while I'm sinking my third and United are sinking their sixth and the Tuareg barman's got the hang of 'We often score six but we seldom score ten', an older American couple waddle in . . .

'Good evening, bonsoir,' sings the barman. 'How are you? Ça va?'

'Exhausted. Dreadful,' whines the Rupert-trousered old trout. 'We just arrived on the flight from Bamako and the air-con in our room is so noisy we can't sleep.'

And they really couldn't understand why I was laughing so hard that suds frothed out of my sun-scabbed nose.

In the hot light of day, the first thing that strikes you about Timbuktu is the sand – the dunes start just as the last house stops, and the streets are so full of it that you have to step down through front doors. And if you're not careful, the second thing that strikes you is a pickup truck. Because the streets are so soft, everybody has to drive like the clappers just to avoid getting stuck.

Timbuktu – 'Well of the woman with the large navel'. According to local legend (and that fat fella in the bar), the town was founded in the late 11th century by Tuareg nomads. Crazy name, perfect location, an oasis on the most northern stretch of the Niger, a port where all trans-African trade had to make the switch from camel to boat and vice versa. Gold and slaves from the south, salt from the east, textiles and spices from the north all passed through here, and the locals got their cut of every shipment. Easy to see how the place became a legend – after three months in the desert on the camel train from Morocco, three months of sun, sand and sweat, the thought of any city, any bed, any peaceful mosque and lively market, would inevitably become exaggerated in your hot head, in the tales you told other tired travellers. The oasis became a port became a holy university city as the world's most famous belly button became the world's first service station and the world's longest umbilical cord, Old Ma Bouctou's juices feeding her children for generations to come.

All that's left now is the name – over the centuries the river has moved, the old harbour is now a sandy amphitheatre, the old trade routes have become highways and flight paths. Only the Tuareg remain, the blue men of the desert, wafting about in their skin-staining indigo robes, showing out for the tourists. Their name has become an international brand for deep wilderness mystery and, boy, are they aware of it. I have never come across such effective salesmen. The service-station philosophy of delaying visitors for as long as possible while taking as much money off them as possible was invented here, and this blue man group are past masters. First morning, I pop out for two minutes to get a pack of smokes. I return two hours later with two cartons of fake Marlboro, two unusable Tuareg pipes, a bale of unsmokeable Bedouin tobacco and a haircut. Damn, they're good.

Some visitors hate the persistent hard sell, but as always in Africa, there're at least two sides to this story. Truth is, the Tuareg hate their new role as dramatic photo fodder, but times have changed, borders have closed, minefields have been planted and the old roaming ways have been closed down. 'We used to say we were as free as the birds in the sky,' says new friend and camel driver Abdul. 'If we needed wood, we took it from the forest. If we needed water, we took it from a well. But in the city, everything costs money.' And if that money's skilfully extracted from passing tourists, all the better.

Three days, like one egg, is enough, and we head south. A good Tuareg driver in a fast 4x4 can reach Douentza and the tarmac in eight hours. We gave ourselves two days. Which turned into three when the road from Timbuktu bit back.

First, we all suffered punctures. After a week of slapping at my handlebars with thick, muscular arms and trying to scratch my eyes out with nasty, thin fingers, the thorn trees settled for my front wheel and popped the tyre once, twice, three times. And then I had my first serious tumble. I'm not too sure exactly how it happened, and Rossi aside, I'm always deeply suspicious of anyone who can talk you through an off, second by second. Christ knows – one minute I was slewing my way up a dune, the next I was under the bike with a properly banjoed knee. What started as a dull ache quickly became a stabbing yelp and I found out that the dabbing leg wasn't just for psychological-crutch effect – twice I felt the bike sinking to the left, twice I tried to save it on an injured leg and twice it mutinied, buckled and threw me off again.

And then the bike started misbehaving, running out of breath at 4000 revs. After the usual fuel-line checks, I started to panic. Last time I felt a bike struggle like this was in India when I destroyed a two-stroke

Yamaha by putting the oil into the gearbox rather than the two-stroke tank . . . When did I last check the oil? Christmas? Dover? But it wasn't the oil, and that was me stumped.

Out of the blue, Mike announces he's actually a motorcycle mechanic, and after ten minutes of grunting, knuckle skinning and double-Dutch cursing, he emerges from under the tank.

'I think maybe the problem is here.'

Christ, an octopus – how the hell did that get in there?

'No, Dan, it's not an octopus, it's a carburettor. This is where the petrol goes.'

Stupid Dutchman. Petrol goes in the tank – everyone knows that. But just to humour him, I stripped the so-called 'carburettor', cleaned out the sand that was snagging the vacuum and, guess what?, good as new. And what do you think caused the problem, Mike?

'Because your air filter is so dirty you could clean it with dog shit, maybe?'

Upside of this mechanical mucking about was another night in the wilderness. And it turned out just perfect – a last evening under the stars, listening to the crickets chirp and the fire pop and the Chili Peppers croon 'Road Trippin'', and if this isn't nice, what is? 'Isn't that Venus?' coos Angela. All together now – it looks more like Uranus to me . . .

Last day, 60 km to the tarmac and I take off on my own for one last wild waltz, skidding around in the thick white dust, scaring the goats from the trees, stopping at a village under an escarpment that's just too beautiful to photograph, until suddenly I'm back on the tarmac and a thousand kilometres of off-road adventure is over. And as I nursed my popped knee and a bottle of iced water in the last-slash-first petrol station for three days, it all, briefly, made sense. I'd ridden to Timbuktu and back. And for ten long, quiet, relieved, exhausted, triumphant, silent minutes, sat sitting on a chest freezer in a breeze-block gas stop in the literary middle of nowhere, that somehow meant something. Even if the whole escapade had been a self-conscious device to drive the blues away.

So the last words go to Malian bluesman Ali Farka Touré: 'You people think that Timbuktu is at the end of the world. But I am from Timbuktu. And I know that we are at the very heart of the world.'

Timbuktu – so far, so good. Keep drifting.

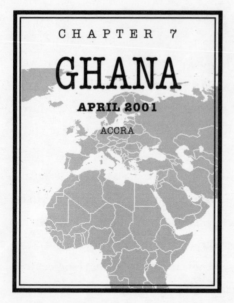

CHAPTER 7

GHANA

APRIL 2001

ACCRA

I love my bike. 'I love your bike too much,' snorted Buffalo the soldier, giving me a punch that might have been considered matey if it hadn't been for the AK swinging from his bowling ball-muscled arms. 'In Accra, it is under my protection. If I see anyone else riding it, I will shoot them dead.' Which was reassuring only as long as he remembered my face. And transformed my XT into the vehicle for the perfect crime. Enter stage left the mockney shyster who's been trying to sleep with my girl while I've been away. 'Hi. Dan. Nice bike.' 'Hi, Mac. Sure is. Tell you what, why not take it for a spin – I know a great route across the cliffs past the barracks.' Praise the Lord and pass the ammunition.

I hated my bike. 'You're going round the world on that?' sniggered girl-friend Lou. 'But it's a kid's bike!' And my wagging tail drooped dish-rag limp. Forget power-to-weight ratios, to hell with race-track geometry, I want a bike that makes me sexy. The only time it ever looked sexy was with Lou on board, all tippy-toes cowboy boots and too-tight Levi's, zipping up and down the beach in Senegal. 'Gosh, you must be a real woman to handle a beast like that. Fancy some taboo sex?'

Not sexy, just slow. Changing down to maintain an asthmatic uphill 60 mph was something I hoped I'd left behind years ago when I jumped off the CG125 into the brave new world of a CX. But the further south I got, the more versatility overtook top speed. And by the time I'd reached Tangier and effortlessly bounded up a set of steps into the hotel courtyard, I knew I was riding a winner. Last time I tried the same manoeuvre was on a ZX9 – it took three men, an hour and some particularly filthy cursing. Can't be that slow if it gained me an extra hour in Africa's sleaziest bar.

I crash my bike. 'I can't believe I've made it all the way across the Sahara without throwing it away' was all the subvocal encouragement that the God of Counted Chickens (the most malicious of deities) needed to kick away my front wheel and scud me into a sandbank. Crashing on tarmac is shocking – skid, gasp, slam, followed by nervous body and bike damage report. But crashing off-road is just silly clowning – yelp, tumble, dead-cat bounce, pick yourself up and do it all over again.

More than crashing, I like dropping my bike. Side stand on wet sand is a recent favourite. Always seem to look up just in time to see it swaying like a waddling toddler before, whoops-a-daisy!, it flops onto its cushioning saddlebag nappies. Last year a couple of clumsy scallies knocked over a Busa I'd borrowed. The invoice touched two grand. Eight comedy drops later, and the only damage to the XT is a banana'd clutch. Perfect for overlanding monkeys.

I fix my bike. 'Punctures will be your most common problem,' warned wise overlander Chris Scott. Most common and least dignified. Last time was in Burkina Faso – strutting into a dusty village, imperiously waving a cheery 'Bonjour!' when the front went bang!, and I veered into a ditch. Big crowd, but no mechanics – so it was up to me to get the spoons out and dive in. And, dayum, after thirty years of paying a buck to pass the buck, it felt good. Me, the bike and no intermediary, a proper bloke doing proper blokes' work. The fact that I had to take the tyre off three bastard times 'cause I couldn't get the patch to stick and then holed the tube with the levers barely ruffled my new-found Zen-like serenity.

I trust my bike. 'Start, you vicious, vicious bastard' is a quote from Rupert Paul that pops up every time I unfaithfully think maybe the trip would have been groovier on a Husquvarna or WR400, and I picture that hard man of publishing sweating like a sieve on a chilly day in Cheshire, pumping away at the recalcitrant Husky. What with border guards, dunes, bandits and my own riding handicaps, the last thing I need is to worry whether the bike will start. Glad as I am that Yamaha went to such trouble to fix the kicker, I've only ever used it in London as a pose. I'll save my kicking for something that deserves it.

I even talk to my bike. 'Come on, little hmar, don't fail me now!' was the superstitious battle cry that led Germans and Tuaregs alike to turn away, slightly embarrassed, tapping the sides of their heads. Divvy as it sounds, it's even got a name – the Yamahmar, 'hmar' being the Arabic word for donkey. The parallels are obvious – both much-maligned beasts of burden, overloaded and abused by cruel owners. And I like donkeys 'cause they invariably wink when I say hello.

Yep, I love my bike. Which is good, because it's all I've got left. 'Dear John,' said Lou as she made a laughing-stock April Fool of me. Home no longer exists. So I'm packing my bags again, and hitting the road again, whistling 'Hey Joe' while pushing hard for motorcycle emptiness.

Keep drifting? I've got no fucking choice.

Rainy night in Ghana. 'Are you all right, Mr Dan?' It was a rhetorical question. Four thirty in the morning and I'm lying underneath my motorcycle, half-way up lobby steps that now crunch with mirror shards and bits of broken indicator, petrol sloshing down my vest, staring up at the embarrassed hotel manager with crying eyes.

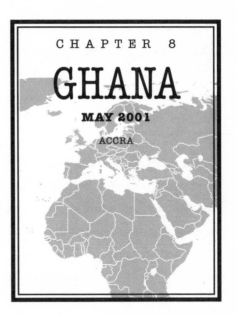

CHAPTER 8

GHANA

MAY 2001

ACCRA

It was a rhetorical question. I answered it anyway. 'No, Kwesi my friend, I'm not all right. Far fucking from it.'

Rewind. 'Welcome to Ghana. Er, are you all right?' It was a rhetorical question. Midday at the Ghanaian frontier and I'm lying underneath my motorcycle, halfway between Burkina Faso and Ghana, petrol dribbling onto my chest, staring up at the customs officer with laughing eyes.

It was a rhetorical question. I answered it anyway. 'Yes, my friend, I'm all right. Any chance of helping me up?'

Couple of hours earlier I'd goophered my left leg footing down at fifty when the front blew out. Miles away on a Burkinan highway, thinking about nothing but TL1000 flat-trackers, Scott Walker and 'Am I in top?'

when, whoopapa!, the front sinks, folding like dough and I'm slaloming left to right, riding the rim into a busy, jumbled too-long half-minute – 'Please bike, don't fall over.' 'Damn that tarmac looks sore.' 'Why am I wearing slacks rather than armour?' 'Has the bus behind me realised what's going on?'

By the time I'd patched the hole, my foot had swelled too big for my boot. Which is why I ended up hitting the border wearing one Tech 6 and one flip-flop, squealing like a pig with Tourette's at each and every jarring movement. No wonder the Burkinan officials shooed me through so quickly. I made it as far as the barrier, lost my balance, the leg buckled and I entered Ghana horizontal and dusted.

The tumble I was expecting – it was the reception that surprised me. I've come to hate borders. 'No harm done, sir. My name is Charles,' said a round-faced soldier, all chins and grins. No beer-breathed, yellow-eyed, crocodile-smiling demands for money with menaces? 'Why don't you sit down? I'll deal with the paperwork.' The worst was in Guinea, a lecherous lieutenant decided he wanted CFA10,000 to stamp my passport. 'Manchester? Ah, Manchester United. I'm a Leeds fan myself. Tony Yeboah is Ghanaian, you know?' We sat in that breeze-block office for two hours, Big Brother President staring down from the wall, watching me smoke and the lieutenant play with a dead fly. 'Have you ever been to London? I have cousins in Chiswick.' Eventually he dismissed me without a stamp – which at best made me an illegal immigrant, and at very worst, in a paranoid country engaged in a couple of undeclared, hazy wars, it made me a spy. 'All done. Would you like a drink? I'm afraid we don't have beer, but there's ice-cold water.'

New country, new people, new environment. The last 500 miles had been all sahel — sub-Saharan savannah, dry, dusty and featureless. Savannah, savannah, savannah — like riding across a piece of toast with a mouthful of crackers. But Ghana is as exotic as monkey curry. It's Tarzan country, a European archetype of Africa, raised road sitting on a red dirt dyke stealing through the shadows of vine-covered dorsal-fin escarpments, wandering down evergreen ravines bubbling with weed-choked rivers, politely slowing for Bible-belt towns full of old-fashioned-looking kids in long shorts and knee-high socks, arms full of textbooks and wooden pencil cases, skipping obediently from American-funded Sunday schools to whitewashed Presbyterian churches.

I picked a town at random and settled into the Toronto Guest House. Five pounds bought me a clean bed, a dirty shower and a bag full of food — sticky rice, spicy eggs and gristly meat. I didn't ask what the meat used to be — I might not have liked the answer. In hard times, euphemistic menus disguise dog as 'red goat', cat as 'Joseph meat', field rat as 'grass cutter' and monkey as everything. I couldn't eat a monkey — I could never eat anything that makes me laugh, and besides, monkeys have Christian hands. I turn on the TV and go to bed with a government information programme about palm oil production.

The Upper Volta, the Mole National Game Park (cue image of pith-helmeted hunter, action-posed foot on pile of furry little blind fellas) and Kumasi, the ancient seat of the Gold Coast's Ashanti empire — I skip past them all heading for a city. I need passive entertainment, busy anonymity and big-smoke sleaze. 'You need Oxford Street,' says a white-gloved cop, directing the traffic jams in Accra's low-rise suburbs. Oxford Street?

Oxford Street, Accra. A mile-long capitalist African dream in flickering neon and coloured glass, Shell station at either end, American banks, Japanese electronics, French supermarket, Italian restaurant, Lebanese hotel and an Irish pub. Fly direct from Gatwick and 'What's all the fuss about, Amish boy? Never seen a city before?' But in context, in West Africa, this sho nuff is one bizarre sight.

In Timbuktu, miners are still paid in slabs of salt; here the money comes fluttering out of Barclays banks, air-con cold. In Ouagadougou, the traffic's bicycles and hand carts, hard-bodied kids in Tupac T-shirts muscling and hustling everything from rice to light bulbs on wooden trolleys; here the jams are caused by uniformed flag-waving and baton-wielding parking attendants obsequiously ushering new Beetles and Merc ML320s out of drive-thru ice-cream parlours and on to the taxi-packed carriageways. In Bamako, the cops had one flat-batteried flat-twin Beemer, fat rider getting a sweaty running bump start at every call-out; here the cops ride Pan-Europeans, standing on the pegs as they get airborne escorting officials across bumpy intersections, overexcited ministers whacking off into tennis shoes behind limousines' tinted windows. It's all a sham, Vegas-fake, counterfeit prosperity. The cars are all stolen, the restaurants can't afford to pay their bills, so the utility companies can't afford to be useful and the blackouts get longer and more frequent. The national average wage is less than a dollar a day, inflation's running at 60 per cent, the newly elected government's just discovered that their predecessors plundered everything, leaving the Treasury coffers bell-empty, and have reluctantly joined the world's least desirable club, Heavily Indebted Poor Countries.

Broke but not broken, Accra bounces. Every day's like Notting Hill Carnival. As the graffiti reads on a downtown shopfront ('Alcoholic

Drinks, Wall Clocks, Plates' – an often overlooked retail combination in England), 'Thank you Lord for another day, my belly's full and my pocket's OK.'

And Accra speaks English – after five months struggling with clumsy French, I feel like the star pupil in an adult literacy programme, roaming streets that suddenly make sense, reading everything aloud: 'Blood of Christ Electrical Gadgets', 'No Food For The Lazy Man Hairdressers', 'Adult Entertainment Movies – the Icing on Wedding's Cake', 'Stick Naked Fools! Don't Urinate Here!'

I come for a week and stay for a month. I pretend I'm resting my leg – I am, but it's only a sprain and I play up the b-boy limp. I pretend I'm sorting a new passport – I am, but that only takes a week. I pretend I'm servicing the bike – I am, but an oil change, filter scrub and pad reconditioning only takes a morning.

I pretend to do some work and check out the local bike scene. Pot-puttering along the beach road I'm buzzed by an R6 and a Blade, plastics ripped off, guts hanging out, helmetless riders' shirts riding up their backs as they large it up and down. We arrange to meet that week-end at Calypso Circle. Turns out they're a right little Ruff Ryders crew – as well as the Blade and R6, there's a ZX12, a GSXR11, a VFR800, a couple of CBR600s and a ZXR400. Like the cars, they're all stolen. In a part of the world where smugglers deal in Liberian diamonds and child slaves, vehicle crime is small potatoes.

Ride it like you stole it – these boys certainly do. Watching them beating up the traffic makes me wince. Don't you get problems with the cops? 'Sometimes – but not if Rawlings is riding with us.' Flight

Lieutenant Jerry Rawlings, charismatic and corrupt former president, and stunt-riding speed freak. When democracy got tiresome, he'd jump on his Blackbird, bodyguard in two-wheeled tow, and let it all hang out. Imagine Tony Blair in fur-collared flight jacket and aviator Ray-Bans, tearing across Westminster Bridge on the back wheel – it can't be done.

I pretend I'm waiting for the weather to clear – April is the beginning of the monsoon season and that means storms – serious tropical storms that roll in from the sea, bad-mood black clouds smelling of wet rain and ozone, thunder that sounds like buildings fighting, dazzling lightning strobing left, right and sideways. I think it's the end of the world, Kwesi thinks it's just a shower. 'This is nothing – people here only pay attention when the lightning starts demolishing apartment blocks.'

What am I waiting for? The fall. My girl don't love me no more. It comes in a two-fingered, two-word text message.

'It's over.' Is there someone else? 'No.' Is there someone else? 'Why do men always think it's about someone else?' Is there someone else? 'Yes.'

Like fingers being slammed in a car door. Like a wire brush scrubbing a burn. I felt like Hillary Clinton. I felt like the Ethiopian navy – when Eritrea won independence in a vicious civil war, Ethiopia lost its coastline. The navy were left stranded in the Indian Ocean, home port occupied by hostile forces, condemned to drift for ever in a life of rum, sodomy and the lash. As easily as a fist becomes a hand, Lou broke my heart and I fell into a very dark place.

Happy hour at Ryan's Irish Pub. 'Good evening, Mr Dan. The usual?' It was a rhetorical question. Mr Thomas was already pouring a pint of porter. Ryan's is the perfect fake Irish pub, draught stout, beef and Guinness pie, 'Cead Mille Failte' over the door, Beckett and Joyce on the walls, Sky Sports on the TV.

Casting Central had been busy – the barfly extras tonight included Kiwi Chris, a man-mountain gold miner, Ecko the lawyer arguing the politics of violence with Callum the Irish aid worker, a couple of Peace Corps types called Abigail (motto – 'digging latrines for Jesus') and Mike, an American Special Forces Technical Sergeant out of Fort Bragg, sniffing round Sally the Pornstar, hoping to get a taste of her superstar techniques. Oh, and two more girls, but I can't work out whether they're supposed to be KLM stewardesses or Russian hookers.

I pick on Josh (Boston, exchange student, gawky, dry, dreams of being Kurt Cobain). My girl's left me for someone else. I'm gonna get shit-faced drunk. And if that doesn't level things out, I think I'm gonna kill myself.

'Right on. Can I watch?'

Seven hours later we were thrown out after I'd stood on the bar, declared 'I'd rather be known as murderer than a chump', broken a glass over my head and striped my arm with the stem.

'Before you get on the back, know this – it's all gone darkside and I'm as drunk as the devil. I accept no responsibility for your safety.'

'Right on. Can we score some drugs?'

The boys were hanging outside Macumba, stained with pink neon, rocking fluently to a muffled highlife bass. Macumba's a typical posh-end-of-common clip joint, full of men called Terry (Croydon, engineer, pot belly, Bic biro in pocket of sweat-stained short-sleeved shirt, erectile dysfunctions) clumsily dance-groping girls called Comfort (Lagos, wants to be a model, cheap and cheerful peekaboob whoredrobe, HIV positive).

A kid who calls himself Sisqo stops kicking a dead cat and saunters over. We swap money for spliffs, a Marlboro box stiffed with fat pre-rolleds.

'I also got some top quality pussy.'

I hate pimps – they bring out the Travis Bickle in me. 'Yeah, your sister's. I hear she slings it for chump change.'

'Fuck you, white man.'

And I'm off the bike, throwing shapes I thought I'd forgotten, chasing him down an alleyway between run-down timbered warehouses. Same old vain old ding-dong, big-prick, who's-the-biggest nonsense. It should have got me killed. Round a corner and he's there, six or seven on either shoulder. 'Get back on your bike before you get chopped.' I pick up a rock – they laugh. I smash it on the ground – they laugh. I swear and retreat, tail between my legs.

Back on the bike, back into the night, charging round the deserted ring road, past Janet Jackson Pepsi billboards, under the flyover with its 'Tiny Drops of Taxes Make Mighty Nation' slogan, searching for that feeling, eyes streaming from 60 mph winds, breathing through my mouth, faking it. I feel like an old lame hound making that last trip to the vet's, hanging his head out of the window, letting his tongue loll and his ears flap one last time.

I drop Josh at a taxi rank.

'Thanks for a wild ride. Are you gonna be OK?'

'I have called for executioners – I want to perish chewing on their gun butts.'

'Right on. So, same time tomorrow?'

It was a rhetorical question. I didn't answer it.

One last wild waltz. For the first time in my life, I rode without fear. For the first time in my life, I was happy to take reckless risks. I've always been scared of bikes, wary of opening the throttle, afraid to lean them over. Round Nkrumah Circle, heading for Independence Avenue, and I'm getting on the gas hard and early, smiling as the back drifts, squidges and bites. Oh, that's what they were on about.

Down Independence Avenue, past the Standard Chartered Bank and Ghana Cocoa, pick the front up over a bump and don't back off and, oh, that's what it feels like. Past Jamestown Prison, past the barracks, on to the cliffs. Watching someone else stop, struggle to light a cigarette with wet matches in the rain, and go, head full of static, eyes fixed on the starboard lights of a Korean trawler way out in the bay. Hearing someone else ask, 'If you're really planning to kill yourself, why are you wearing a crash helmet?' It broke the spell. I locked the brakes, skidded in the mud, bounced off a cable drum and fell off. Got back on, into the hotel, fell off, dozed off.

Rainy night in Ghana. 'Are you all right, Mr Dan?' It was a rhetorical question. Four thirty in the morning and I'm lying underneath my motorcycle, halfway up lobby steps that now crunch with mirror shards and bits of broken indicator, petrol sloshing down my vest, staring up at the embarrassed hotel manager with crying eyes.

It was a rhetorical question. I answered it anyway.

'No, Kwesi my friend, I'm not all right. Far fucking from it.'

To prove it, I struggled up, fell over the other side of the bike and ran away. Into my damp hut, knocked over a bottle of piss, threw a boot at the rats, snapped open a razor and tried to cut my wrists. It was just too sore and teenage – I made a half-hearted slash which barely drew blood and still managed to sting like a bastard. Fell asleep with tissue paper stuck to my pathetic wounds, BBC in the background. 'This is London bahbbbahbbahbbbah . . .'

It's alright, Ma. It only took two weeks for the sulking to ease off a bit. Time, strong drink, wise parents, big singles, baby elephants and fat white lines off slim tawny bellies are all great healers.

'What else did you expect?' said everyone. They were right. Last December I stepped through the looking glass and into a road movie. 'I will come back with limbs of iron, with dark skin and angry eyes. In this mask they will think I belong to a strong race. I will have gold. Women nurse these ferocious invalids come back from the tropics.' I reduced Lou to a non-speaking extra riding pillion on my star vehicle, the astronaut's wife, the prison widow, the cantina señorita. Reduced to a walk-on role, it was no surprise she chose to walk off. And I learned something vital – that the truly wild at heart know that sunrises over the Sahara, sunsets over Timbuktu and absinthe-stained adventures on intriguing foreign shores are all shoddy, second-hand substitutes for love. Man.

Fast forward. 'What did you do that for?' It was a rhetorical question. Late afternoon in a sunny Ghanaian rainforest and Lou's lying underneath my motorcycle, half drowned in a muddy puddle that could swallow a horse, petrol splashing onto her breasts, giggling up at me with big, brown eyes. It was a rhetorical question. She answered it anyway.

'Because I felt like it. Now are you going to help me up or what?'

Happily ever after? We'll see. For now, we're gonna keep drifting.

I ride west down Liberia Street but I don't really know where I'm going. Even after 10,000 miles, six months and a dozen countries it still feels good to go, just go. Nothing to do with blustering across deserts, trippin with the Tuareg or childishy forging visas, just getting on the bike and riding.

There's usually a trigger. This time it was hard news – 'Man Savaged By Cock'. I'd already started sniggering out-loud when I clocked the real headlines next to the tabloid trash. '123 Die in Football Stadium Tragedy'. The news vendor stared at me like he was looking down a well and I knew that I had to get out of town.

'We interrupt this programme for a newsflash,' monotoned the hotel tee vee. 'Nema police station under siege . . . relatives of stadium dead demand inquiry . . . area boys setting fire to cars . . . traffic inconvenience expected'.

Nema's north so I'd better head west. And better head out the back way. I owe a week's rent and a fortnight's beer and right now my money doesn't fold, it jingles. I'll deal with that when I get back.

I ride west down the old port road but I don't really know where I'm going. My head's so full of nonsense I could get lost in a vest. Opt instead for a dead-end full of lively kids playing Frisbee with a Mercedes hub-cap.

'No mister – you must go back – then left – then straight – then straight, straight – then maybe ask again'.

The traffic's racked tighter than spoons in a drawer, 'I worship at the Police church' bumper-sticker to bumper. No room between lanes for claustrophobic bikers – that's cheap retail territory, every over-heating tailback a polluted, open-air market. I get impatient with the clogging kids selling everything and nothing for as long as it takes to imagine my own sister selling J-cloths and razors through finger-trapping electric windows to air-con-cold-eyed commuters.

I ride west round the ring road but I still don't know where I'm going. Or what I'm doing. It's been a week since I've ridden anything but barstools and toilets, a month since I've ventured further than the beach. Pushing the bike out of the watchman's hut was like meeting a mate at the prison gates – anticipation, nostalgia, and do we still have anything in common. The old security guard really couldn't understand why I suddenly yelped 'Can't get the sex you want and don't want the sex get', as I bump-start lurched into the crosstown traffic.

The ring road's fast and dirty, but I'm slow and grubby. Some days you get on the bike and just know it's gonna flow, other days it's instantly apparent you'll be doin nuthin but stutterin. Today I'm Elmer Fudd, mistiming gaps like old white claps, believing deceptive indicators, sticking too close to diesel-coughing wagons, hitting every pothole with rim-bending clumsiness.

Take a time out in Edward Joy's Rest Spot, an almost-converted shipping container caff. I ask Eddie for a menu.
'Sorry, no chop today'.
No problem, I'll just get a Coke.
'No drinks till tomorrow. But you are very welcome'.
I was and it was. I smoke and leave.
'Hey man, you forgot your hand-shoes.'
Eddie follows me out, waving my gloves, giving me a wink that says poet not pidgin.

I ride west along the coast road although I don't really know where I'm going. Or how I got there. Or where all the traffic went. Can't remember overtaking anyone, can't remember anyone overtaking me, but suddenly I'm on my own and I've found a little of what I fancy.

Tension and release. No adrenalin-stained flurry of bends, just two-wheels and some rolling peace and quiet. Hunch over a downshift, lean back, wind it on and breathe. Tension and release. Past a rubbish-strewn lagoon sparkling in the afternoon sunlight, round a roundabout squatted by marooned goats, and dust down a dirt road to the sea. Tension and release.

The Sir Charles Tourist Centre – a peculiar and peculiarly empty art deco holiday camp, crumbling patiently on a rocky ledge, waiting for a tourist boom that will never explode, abandoned by a planned airport that never flew off the drawing board. 'There's the pool,' straight faces receptionist/cook/cleaner/barmaid Hannah, cocking an eyebrow at the Gulf of Guinea's wild waves. 'You can have any room you want,' dropping a wink that suggests that room could be hers. 'Dinner's at 7'. There's a hole in the roof that lets in the rain and the birds.

I don't unpack cause I've brought nothing but a toothbrush and a paperback, and besides, tomorrow I'll be moving on, meeting Lou. But next monsoon morning, put the key in the ignition and cock a doodle don't. It won't turn. Engine oil, brake fluid, Hannah's hand cream, blistered fingers and a crowd of fishermen who aren't at sea cause it's taboo to sail on Tuesdays all fail flat. It won't turn.

I call for a locksmith and get a mason with a lump hammer and a carpenter with a cutlass. If anymore cowboys get their hands on my bike I'll have to rename her Calamity Jane. And the key still won't turn. So I'm stuck, wondering if it's possible to ride round the world with the steering lock on. Keep drifting? I'll do my best, but it may be in ever decreasing circles . . .

Trust me, I'm a doctor. 'You can trust him, he's the doctor,' chirped Alfred, wiping a bogey on his 'Pray for Me, I Married an Italian' T-shirt. 'He's the second best moto fitter in Winneba. Shall I pass you your trousers?'

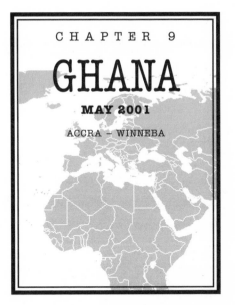

Eight something in the morning by the Ghanaian seaside and I'm crusty-eyed, crosspatch and confused. Confused because there's a 14-year-old boy picking his nose in my front room. Confused because I'm naked. Confused because, shit, I've got an erection.

'Alfred, will you please get out? I'll be with you in a minute.'

'Yes, Mr Dan. I'll be outside with the doctor.'

Through the fly-screen window I can see Doctor Godfrey, looking capable despite his '24 Hour Bitch' T-shirt, attacking the headstock collar with a breeze block and a bayonet. Shit, I'd forgotten about that – the bike's ignition barrel's seized.

'Which doctor?' called Lou from the bedroom.

I think so. Have you seen my trousers?

By the time I've got my bottoms on, he's tugged the head off and is setting about the steering lock with a file. And once that's done, we just hotwire the fucker?

'Yes. It shouldn't take longer than a day.'

Shouldn't, but does. And I should have paid more attention, should have taken more responsibility, should have helped him push the bike up the mile-long hill to his shop. Should've, but don't. I'm too busy shredding Lou.

Lou, the is-she-or-isn't-she dark angel at the centre of my public private life, has flown in out of the blue. We plot up in a trailer park and play at being white trash, Rothman's for breakfast, lager for lunch, spending angry afternoons kissing and crying, fucking and fighting, emotional evenings drinking and dancing in the monsoon waterfalling rain. Fuck, I hate her. But, dayum, she moves me in designer-dirty boot-cut hipsters and oversized shades.

Every day we take time out to check on the bike. Every day the bike changes shape as Godfrey strips the carbs, decokes the exhaust, changes the plugs. The moto that won't became the talk of the town. Every day, strangers stop me to pass on lack-of-progress reports. Every day the crowd outside the workshop gets bigger and more partisan, old men and small boys gathering to mock and encourage, cheer and sneer, smoke and spit, as the bike turns over, backfires and dies.

'Maybe it's the CDI?' I bluff.

'What's a CDI?'

Arse. 'I don't know.'

We came for a day, we stayed for a week. 'The moto is ready, Mrs Lou,' called Alfred through the bathroom window. 'Are you looking for your dress?'

The good witch doctor's looking well pleased in his 'Roger Moore Visits Ghana' T-shirt. The problem?

'A condom.'

I beg your pardon?

'Bits of condom in the barrel.'

Ah, right – old thieves' trick. Wrap a key in a johnny, squeeze it into the barrel and twist. Sometimes the rubber will open the chambers – sometimes it won't.

I ask Godfrey if he'd like to take the XT for a celebratory spin. He says he already has. Glancing at the speedo I see he's not kidding. 123 miles? 'You might need petrol,' he mumbles as we chug off, Lou to the airport and me back to Accra and Ryan's Bar.

Trust me, we're a nurse. 'We're shipping the Land Cruiser to South Africa,' chirped Miriam and Olivier, the adventurous Swiss nurses. 'There's room in the container. Why not come with us?'

Round the world – shit, I'd forgotten about that. Shipping south is the sensible-if-shithouse option now the route east is such a mess. In Africa the map is not the territory. The Michelin 953 doesn't show para-military paranoia, bombed-out bridges or regional desperation in the face of impending famine. Overlanders use the World Service like break-fast TV traffic reports.

'Thanks, Alan. Today's attempted coup in the Central African Republic spells bad news for travellers heading east – from our eye in the sky we can see looting soldiers and bodies on the capital's streets. And avoid the likely looking diversion through Congo – since President Kabila's assassination in January the borders have been slammed shut. Last week's murder of six Red Cross workers not helping the situation there. To the north, the rainy season is causing commuters washed-out problems. And there's still no services on the N'Djamena–Khartoum road – which means 1500 miles of mud with no petrol or water. I'll be back on the hour. Alan.'

I have me a big decision. Ship out and shit out or keep on keeping on? Shipping makes sense, but I'm loath to break the road that has run uninterrupted from my front door to Timbuktu, from west London to West Africa.

At 3 a.m. I email everyone with the news that I'm going for forty days and forty nights in the Sudanese wilderness. By 8 a.m. I'm flapping up Ghana's only motorway, reluctantly heading for the docks and the end of the road.

Trust me I'm a docker. 'Of course it will be safe,' schmoozed Nicholas the shipping agent, flashing a mirror-practised smile that was all light and no heat. The end of the road turns out to be a muddy parking lot in a dockside industrial estate. A container is forklifted down, first the Land Cruiser then the bike are slotted in, strapped up, nailed down by Swiss Olivier, who was a chippie before he was a nurse (cue images of blood-spattered white-coated psycho wheeling vasectomy patient towards a band saw).

And that's that. For the next two weeks I'm a backpacker. Keep drifting? Not quite the same on a bus.

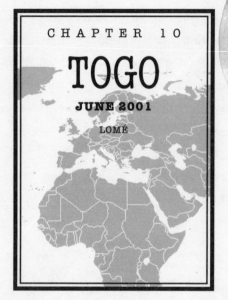

CHAPTER 10

TOGO

JUNE 2001

LOMÉ

So I rock up to the Togolese border with Ben the Cab and wait for the shit to hit the fan. With the bike on a boat en route to South Africa, it should be the easiest crossing so far. Should be fun standing in that jolly, shuffling queue with a gaggle of Ghanaian market women in wraparounds as loud as their laughter and as colourful as their language, as they mock my white legs, wide-eyed babies papoose-strapped to their backs, bags of rice and bundles of fabric nesting comfortably on their heads. Should be, but isn't. Why? Because I'm an illegal.

My sixty-day entry visa expired three weeks ago. Extending it would have been as simple as buying smokes. I was obviously busy – must have had some important swimming or coffee drinking to do that day – and came up with the bright idea of extending it myself. Just change the six into a nine and, voilà, ninety days. I probably shouldn't have tried it drunk. It looked about as convincing as the Turin Shroud.

Here we go. Behind the desk is a big woman in a tight, grey uniform, slurping away at a bowl of lunchtime fufu. I'm rumbled instantly.

'You have overstayed,' she says with her mouth full. 'You are under arrest.' Words expressed through the medium of food.

Arse. A cross-looking cop with a stern moustache takes me and the passport to one side.

'This visa has been forged. You did this.'

'I most certainly did not.' Bluff outrage. 'The immigration officer did it when I entered from Burkina Faso.'

'No he didn't. The maximum allowance for any nationality at any port of entry is sixty days.'

Keep digging. 'But see how the sweep of the "9" matches the sweep of the "y"?'

'No. This is very serious. Come with me.'

I go with him. I wait outside a bungalow that suddenly looks sinister. I try to act innocently nonchalant but it's not easy when you're chain-smoking. I finger my gris-gris, a leather, tooth and bone juju charm gifted to me by Senegalese wrestling fisherman Maurice. 'Now you will always travel invisible,' he explained. 'My cousin used one to fly to France without a passport or a ticket.'

I consider making a run for it – the ocean's just yards away. I try to forget the section in the Lonely Planet guide that reads 'penalties for overstaying are severe'.

'I have a brother who works in Jamestown Prison,' says Ben. I think he's trying to be reassuring.

I'm summoned inside. Stern moustache is standing next to sterner-looking Chief in gold braid cap sat behind a headmaster's table. They both look extremely unbribeable.

'You have overstayed. You have forged your visa. This is very serious.'

Enough already. 'Yes, OK, you're right. I'm sorry. I feel very foolish now. Can we settle this?'

'You must pay a fine.' The headmaster consults a dusty ledger that looks like *The Book of the Dead.* 'You must pay . . .' dramatic pause while he stabs two-handed at the calculator like a maniac Mozart, 'forty thousand cedis.'

I try not to look too smug. Forty thousand cedis is four quid. Get in. And get out.

At the risk of stating the bleeding obvious, borders are odd, the way that an arbitrary line in the sand denotes a change in culture, language, lifestyle and life expectancy. Five yards of littered no-man's-land separates familiar from foreign, democracy from dictatorship, English from French. Togo is Francophone – French speaking, French architecture, French-backed despot. In the kilometre from the frontier to the city centre, we're stopped three times by plain-clothes military. Togo's the first African country I've visited where no one wants to talk politics.

I plot up in the French-run Hotel Galion. I'm woken at 4 a.m. by shouting, banging, screaming, an American bellowing, 'Open the goddamn door.' The visa police? Nah, it's downstairs. An angry man barking, a terrified woman shrieking. I wander down – there's a Yank in his late forties, holding his gut in and his dick down (damn that Viagra's strong), very naked and very drunk, hammering on a bedroom door. The female voice is coming from the other side.

The manager turns up with security. I leave them to it.

I get the story over sausage-and-eggs breakfast. He works at the US Embassy, she works the bars. Seems he had his native-girl fantasy then baulked at the bill. Got a little rough-house, tried to throw her out but she sidestepped and closed the door behind him. The manager calmly demanded he pay the girl, pay for the room and leave. 'Or I call the embassy and the press.' Diplomatic relations, baby.

I've come to Togo 'cause it's a chance to see another city and the flights to South Africa are cheaper. Waiting for the airport bus I get picked up by a Yamaha Townmate. I can't work out whether he's an official moto-taxi or a chancer.

'You're sure about this? Me and my bag?'

'Pas problème.'

It's good to be back on two wheels, pillion-perched on the back of a step-thru, fifteen stone of laughing nonsense, kitbag on my lap like a corpse in a carpet. It's 10 km to the airport. It takes us an hour. Later that evening I'm doing 600 mph 30,000 feet over the Congo Basin. It's nowhere near as exciting as the scoot. Two wheels better.

Next stop Johannesburg.

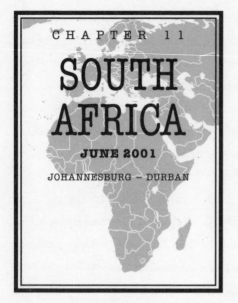

CHAPTER 11

SOUTH AFRICA

JUNE 2001

JOHANNESBURG – DURBAN

'Excuse me,' squawked the fat girl with the clipboard. 'Are you looking for bickpickers' accommodation?' Christ. Sunny 7 a.m. at Johannesburg International Airport and I'm jaded, jet-lagged and jangled. Last time I got off the plane was in Congo-Brazzaville – good thing about flying with agreeably laid-back Air Afrique is that when they stop to refuel, the driver asks if anyone needs to smoke. I spent a humid half-hour on the runway with a posse of sleepy, jungle-striped soldiers, lanky geezers with inappropriate pot bellies, half scared and half excited by the idea of the plane leaving without me. It didn't. And now I'm in South Africa, feeling as disorientated as Terry Waite. First time in seven months I've seen sliding doors, the *Sunday Times* or so many white folk. Damn, they look miserable.

'It'll be a lot of fun,' says the girl, and she screws up her eyes and nose – I think this is supposed to make her look fun. 'We've got a trampoline.' Oh, really? Do I look like the kind of man who's impressed by trampolines? Obviously. How did I get from motorcycle adventurer to this? By shitting out and shipping out, putting the Yam on a boat out of Ghana. And now I'm just another tourist squid. Never get off the bike? Absolutely goddamn right. The alternatives are grotesque.

The Bickpickers Mafia bundle me into a people carrier and whisk me away in a blur of false smiles and Tears for Fears to a white-flight suburb. It looks like a sinister version of *Neighbours*, sprawling bungalows and swimming pools cowering behind electric fences, fish-hook railings and 24-hour surveillance cameras. I am being surveilled. Cages with golden bars, pictures of attack dogs instead of Dunroamin, armed-response private-security wagons instead of ice-cream vans. I never knew there was so much razor wire. Cue – 'That's Pieter, he's a razor-wire millionaire.' Insecurity is job security.

Joburg, baby – the number plates read GP, Gauteng Province, but locals call it the Gangsters' Paradise. This place and Rio fight with knives over the 'Highest Crime Rate in the World' crown. Lots of money, lots of poverty, lots of guns – the shooting ranges are full of blue eyeshadow, business suits and designer-label Glocks; the townships are full of post-Struggle smuggled AKs slung under trenchcoats; the newspapers are full of the consequent gunfight catastrophes. No wonder everybody seems so paranoid.

The Lodge is littered with Gap-wearing, gap-year kids, self-consciously enjoying themselves (Whoo! Frisbee!) while lying to each other (Where are you from? 'London, innit.' Whereabouts? 'Er, Winchester.'). English, Italian, Australian, Israeli, all in transit to the Solar Eclipse Party in Zambia. With the high walls and noticeboard covered in 'don'ts', it feels like an open prison. In a country where they jail you for being a twat.

I try to escape downtown. Barman Paul, a Londoner with the rattled look of a man who's just been caught abusing a German shepherd, tries to warn me off. It's no go, he says. *Escape from New York* come to life, he says. Capital has pulled out in the face of a 1000-dead-cops-per-year criminal tidal wave, banks and business abandoned, skyscrapers smashed up and squatted, laundry fluttering from 55th-floor windows, he says. A communist plot, he says. 'You'll come back at best in an ambulance, at worst in a hearse,' he says, coughing on a roll-up and humming along to Nik Kershaw's 'The Riddle'.

The Lodge radio, like every radio in South Africa, is tuned to the eighties. 'Walking On Sunshine' follows 'Take My Breath Away' follows 'The Heat is On' and on and on in a kitsch nostalgic loop. For the first hour it's kinda funny. After a week it's enough to make you chew your own foot off.

I'm intrigued by Downtown but no one will take me there. The only way is with an official Soweto Township Tour, but that stinks of human zoos. Eventually I find a local (read 'black') bus. *Escape from New York*? It's as threatening as Stockport. No squatted skyscrapers, no bodies in the streets, just a lot of Victorian architecture, a lot of cheap supermarkets and a lot of workaday black folk getting on with it. Plus the only street ever to have produced not one but two Nobel Peace Prize laureates, Archbishop Desmond Tutu (respect) and Nelson Mandela (amandla!). Best of all there's a coach station. Only losers take the bus, but I've got no choice. I've gotta get the bike from Durban docks.

'Open up, it's the police.' What? It wasn't me. Killing time in Durban turned out to be just that. Last night a woman was murdered in front of the hotel, cold-cocked with a beer bottle then stabbed in the neck. She collapses on the pavement, crying and sticky and fading fast. The whole street's hanging out of windows, throwing bottles, whistling, clapping. The drunks outside the liquor store keep drinking Christ-knows-what out of paint tins. A radio's blaring Huey Lewis and the News. A fight kicks off. He's disappeared. She's bleeding to death but no one wants to touch her. Endemic Aids doesn't make for Good Samaritans. The ambulance stops at the top of the street, waiting for a police escort. They're too late and she's too still.

'Dan, it's Steve. We've gotta get to the docks.' Oh yeah, I'd kinda forgotten about that. The bike arrives today, inshallah. Steve's a mate of the Swiss overlanders I shipped with, and just happens to be a police captain. No sense of humour, but very handy at getting containers fast-tracked through customs. I open the door. He looks at me like I'm a piece of shit on his shoe. I just wink. He's whistling Spandau Ballet's 'Gold'.

The Grand Opening – me, the Swiss kids, Steve and a customs officer with a set of bolt croppers. It's a tense moment. Steve's been regaling us with horror stories – skippers jettisoning containers in high seas, containers arriving upside down, empty or full of illegals. The fear is that the Land Cruiser will have slipped the leash and slid about. We're expecting to see the XT embossed in a crushed Nissan beer can.

Lucky again. The bike's exactly as I left it, nailed down and strapped up. It starts first time. Damn, I've missed this. It's only been two weeks, but that's long enough to start jonesing for two wheels, filled with that pre-test longing when any bike, every bike, even shit bikes are desirable. I took to hanging round bike parks, cooing at commuters. 'A GT550, you say? Boy, that baby must really fly.'

And now I'm back in the saddle, King of the Road, Cock of the North,

Silly as Areolas, I want to play. First set of lights I pull up next to a dolphin-coloured Audi, woof the pipe and give him a nod. I hear 'Love Is a Battlefield' and an expensive click as the central locking clunks down and a hand cannon pops up. It's like staring down a well. Guess that car-jacking's done away with Traffic Light GPs. Chill out, mate, I'll let you win.

Back on the bike, back in control, knowing I'm on my way out, I start enjoying not-enjoying Durban. The gaff's got St-Tropez's climate but Clacton's class. Not exciting enough to feel African, not sophisticated enough to feel European. It takes me three days to find a restaurant where the chairs aren't glued to the tables – and the food still doesn't smell of anything. I go looking for a bookshop but there's just porn shops, pawnshops or chip shops.

Durban's all about the beach and the beach is all about cocky bottle-blond surfers, boards parked up like scooters outside coffee bars. The scene's very white. For the first time in Africa, race is an issue. The whites-only signs have come down, but old prejudices remain and segregation's still the norm. The Rainbow Nation still looks suspiciously like a pint of Guinness. The white attitude seems to be 'not in my backyard' reluctant tolerance. It's hard to know what the black attitude is – no one will talk to me. I try drinking in black bars, but people think I'm taking the piss or looking for trouble.

Eventually I meet Sipho, and yes, he'd be happy to talk. He tells me he's an ANC man. Tells me of the joy of receiving the vote when Apartheid collapsed in '94. Worries that too many people hide behind the excuse of racism to avoid being constructive. Applauds the role that Mandela played humanising South Africans, black and white. Supports hard-working successor, Mbeki. Wishes that more people from his community would work equally hard for progress. 'It is the responsibility of every South African to make this country great again.' I tell him that his fine words are only slightly undermined by the fact that he's just tried to sell me a wrap of Nigerian coke and a discount ticket for Sergeant Pecker's Strip Club. He laughs. We go for a drink.

The bars off Smith Street are very cheap and very cheerful, staggered happy hours mean hours of happy staggering. We end up in Buddies – empty coffee tins for ashtrays, floor littered with lotto tickets and teeth, bar swaying with randy and raucous old-timers drinking each other beautiful. Someone's put 'Lady in Red' on the jukebox a dozen times. I'm the youngest drunk in there by a bad twenty years, and that includes the hookers. Classy girls – their tattoos are spelt right.

Sipho palms me a Minolta SLR camera and the mobile number of a Moscow Mafioso in Mozambique. I don't know why. 'You should get out of the city,' he tells me. 'Have a look around. This is a big country.'

South Africa may be a mess, but it's a beautiful mess, the best of the rest of the world in one convenient cape. Pack up the bike, hit the road and within an hour it's another country – or several different countries. A sweeping Spanish highway swept clean of traffic and trash whistles through English meadows watered by Scottish lochs and streams, kissing up to Scandinavian pine forests with perky upturned needles, framed by dark and distant Utah hills. All under a childhood-perfect summer-blue sky – a sky so damn big it's dizzying. Feels like God's lifted the top of my head off and let the world in. For the first time since I've been in the southern hemisphere I feel like I'm upside down – feel that if I let go of the bars, I'd fall up. I try it. I don't.

Never try to impress a South African with British roads. It won't work. 'Yeah, we've got some pretty big cats in England, too.' Tiddles, meet cousin Simba. What the map shows as ordinary rides as extraordinary, up and down, round and round, and even overloaded on well-scrubbed sand tyres, the XT's bending like a reed. It's no R6 and I'm no racer, but go into a corner too fast and funny is funny and fear is fear whether at 50 or 150 miles an hour.

The last half-hour is dirt. Nothing too demanding, the kind of dusty road that Clint Eastwood's stuntman tears up on a Harley chop, into a sunset that reminds me that dusky pink isn't just a lipstick. And reminds me that I miss kissing.

The hostel is basic and basically perfect. Half a dozen whitewashed bungalows and a common room. No TVs, no Howard Jones hits, no telephones. No guests 'cause it's cold out of season. Just silence – the proper silence only found in mountains, deserts and oceans. It's profound but not precious – too thick to be broken by the occasional clatter of plates, a dirty laugh or the crunch of gumboots on gravel. I spend an evening in front of the fire and over the sink, watching the water go down the plughole the wrong way.

Only thing better than falling asleep in the mountains is waking up in them. The room's so cold I can see my breath, but in the outdoor shower the sun's hot enough to tan. It's all about contrasts. Kinda like skiing. But without the twats.

Yesterday was just the trailers – today's the main feature. I'm here to ride the Sanni Pass, a 30-mile piste that climbs from the valleys of Underberg to Lesotho, an independent land above the clouds on top of the Drakensberg. Drakensberg – the Dragon Mountains. The Zulus call them Quathlamba, the Wall of Spears, the Brits called them the Devil's Knuckles. These aren't romantic Alpine peaks but dark, snarling escarpments. And I've never seen anything like them anywhere else.

The road leads to the Drakensberg, the piste leads up them, through them, inside them. The rocky track's demanding enough to keep me occupied concentrating on where the wheels are, simple enough to let me look up and around. This is why I'm here – to get me some of that inaccessible natural beauty and space and warm my cold soul. It's just me, the bike and Africa, shuffling, bluffing and duff-duff-duffing our way up, standing on the pegs to give the springs a break, not 'cause I think I'm Showtime McGrath. This is skipping across a stream, not white-water rafting. It's lazy rambling, two-wheeled shambling. It's piste, perfect piste.

Breathe. And stop. Try not to smoke. Drink from a waterfall. Drop a pebble into a stream just to hear it plop. Then feel bad 'cause it's upset the wriggling tadpoles. Stop the engine and listen to the birds – someone's singing a rising-pitch glug-glug-glug-glug-glug that sounds like he's chugging on a bottle of wine. Sing 'King of the Swingers' to a nosy baboon. Dance to the intro of 'Voodoo Chile'. Wish I'd brought some acid.

I'm distracted by whale song. Maybe I shouldn't have eaten those berries. It's not a trip but a tipper-truck, creeping down in low-low, brakes moaning and straining but just about braking. I watch the driver tackle a jagged hairpin. In, nose over the edge, stop. I think he's overcooked it. He hasn't. For the wagon, it's a three-point turn. Reverse out (I hope that's reverse), down and round. We wave.

Back on the piste again, chasing the dragon again, doing the Devil's Knuckles Shuffle again, splashing through fords with a thumb over the kill switch, looking down on the peaks I was just squinting up at, stopping to applaud each new valley vista, wolf-whistling at Mama Nature's big-assed curves – yeah, baby, you know you got it.

The Lesotho frontier is 3000 metres above sea level. I don't really know what this means, but it's windy, clear and cold – frozen ponds wink like signalling mirrors from across the plateau. The border post's packed with sheltering soldiers watching Lionel Richie on a black and white TV. The walls are plastered with wanted posters for escaped prisoners and horse rustlers. There're a lot of horses up here – grazing in stone corrals, tethered outside shebeens, elegant and sure-footed, trotting along distant paths. The poncho-wrapped riders look like African Mongols. I've never seen anywhere like it.

When you're up, you don't wanna come down. The ascent was thrilling, the descent is worrying, sloping hairpin after sloping hairpin, slippery with shale and loose-loose gravel that make the brakes lock, not stop. The bike's not bothered – it loves the leap from road toad to dirt squirt – but I feel like a small boy being taken for a walk by a big dog. The bitch just keeps running away with me. I engage my own chicken-shit version of four-wheel drive – first gear, clutch out, feet down, Alpinestars toes dragging in the dust. Not stylish, but effective. Back to the base, turn around and do it all again. Because I can. Because it's there.

It's too damn beautiful to familiarise and too damn chilly to hang around, so the next day I get gone, heading for the ocean. I pick a town from the Lonely Planet and pluck a route from the Michelin map — something squiggly with lots of contours. It doesn't get any better than this — waking up with no plans, just ideas, spending ten minutes working out an unknown route, then making it real.

Every day something new to rinse clean my stinking thinking, scrub away the bad words and feelthy peectures that have haunted the last couple of months. Load up the bags, oil the chain, pull on my lid, adjust my goggles. Nod at the busload of squids with their itineraries and packed lunches. And drift.

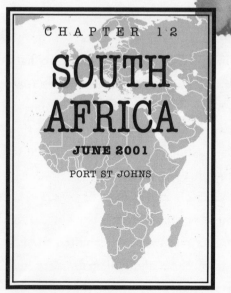

CHAPTER 12

SOUTH AFRICA

JUNE 2001

PORT ST JOHNS

'Hey, Danny,' says Layin Bricks, passing the popcorn and leaning over the bar conspiratorially. 'You know why I stay here?' He smiles up at the happy punters. Empty Vessels is telling his favourite joke – 'Why are people more likely to be run over by small cars than big cars? Because when they see small cars coming they think they are big cars that are still far away.' Fishin Rod's talking to his guitar – 'There's a song in here somewhere. We know all the notes, we're just not too fucking sure of the order.' And Bobbin Dylan's swaying like he's in a crow's nest, complaining to his shoes that one of his legs is shorter than the other – 'I'll tell you why, Danny. Because I can't stand living in the real world.'

Welcome to Port St Johns, a one-cop town at the mouth of a hippo-fat river where the mountains meet the sea on South Africa's Wild Coast. Four streets, half a dozen shops, couple of bars, couple of motels, and a laid-back population of runaways, stowaways and stayaways. Protected from the Real World by 20 km of dirt road, it's a sanctuary for the kind of people who turn hobbies into trades – stressed school teachers become reiki healers, chippy carpenters become fly-fishermen, porcine bank managers flee messy divorces, cultivate Jesus barnets and make jewellery out of beads.

Ride to work, work to ride, eh bro? I convince the editor of the local rag (sample headline 'Sardine Phenomenon') to give me a job. As offices go, the beer garden of the Lusikisiki Inn takes some beating. Got the recently revived Holy Hairy Palmtop (died and rose again over Easter) set up on a picnic table surrounded by eggs and pepper, coffee and Camels, and rhythm and blues – Chicken Shack and Muddy Waters strumming over the swish of sprinklers and the hissing roar of the sea kissing the shore. And Sweet Jane, the hotel manager's 21-year-old daughter, Lolita-lounging by the pool in a high-cut, low-cut swimsuit, lying on her tummy, idly kicking her legs, reading Wilbur Smith, smiling up with her baby-blue eyes, through her beach-blonde fringe, over her button-brown nose, through her rose-tinted shades. Er, you're staring, Humbert Humbert. It's no good. I have to move to the cybercafé.

Unlock the bike from the boat trailer, kick the tyres, think about oiling the chain (sorry, I'll do it tomorrow), think about not roostering the gravel drive (sorry, I'll not do it tomorrow) and hit the high street. Pass the colonial town hall flying an African flag, pass the post office and its queue of tie-dyed pensioners, pass the Boxer Superstore with its bargain-barking loudspeakers ('Maize down two rand a kilo. Only while stocks last'), over the footbridge, round the Bottle Store and into the groovy.

May the road rise with you. It's only five miles but it's got all the right moves. Five miles of gravel and potholes that just bends and bends and bends. Up past the smoking rubbish tip, down round the valley farms, up past the township; now warm and close, now cold and fresh, rising and falling through climate quick changes; whopping the throttle and jerking off the brakes, skipping between third and second, second and third; leans exaggerated as only a big trailie can, tyres raising a knobbled eyebrow as they hop, skip and jump.

Just before the beach there's a straight, but even that's animated by two speed humps, sharp ramps and table tops, me and the XT catching stupid air, further and further every time, funnier and funnier every time, despite and because of no lid, flip-flops, shorts. Dumb is fun.

At the Pothole Cyber Café it's dodgy business as usual. I can't work out whether it's run by drug dealers who like to surf or webheads who smoke too much gear, but the gaff is a green haze of Swaziland Poison and Mos Def, the lagoon-side garden full of hippies working for grass. XT Lee passes me a spliff and asks me if I heard about the time the Aids bandwagon came to town. Apparently they brought a box of educational leaflets and a box of condoms to be handed out. 'Nothing wrong with that,' chuckles Lee, 'except some bright spark came up with the idea of stapling the condoms to the bloody leaflets.' We laugh. I ask him to come to town for a drink. He laughs. 'Danny, this may be Port St Johns, but they're still Dutchmen and I'm still a coloured boy.' The ride back into town doesn't seem so much fun.

Back in the Lusikisiki, it's bawdy brandy business as usual. 'Strip her naked and slap her tits,' shouts Bricks. 'The orgasms are real but the jewellery's fake – or is it the other way round?' roars Vessels. 'I said I won't be spoken to like that by a kaffir,' says a plain-clothes cop. And I'm very glad that XT Lee didn't come with me. Maybe I won't stay here after all.

The next morning I pack and leave. On the way up the hill, I meet the road builders coming the other way. Guess you can't outrun the Real World.

But you can keep drifting.

CHAPTER 13

MOZAMBIQUE

JULY 2001

MAPUTO

Crazy like Sunday morning. Meet the Breakfast Club – Chico, Loco, Bruno, Paulo and Coco, aka the Maputo Mofos. I met them last night on Whisky Street, the place the sailors call the Street of Trouble.

Now they're back again, sitting on a wall outside their workshop, cursing as they squint into the too-bright sun, wincing as they slug on breakfast beers, chuckling as they slag each other's bikes in rapid-fire Portuguese. I'm not entirely convinced they've been home.

Portuguese – looks like Spanish, sounds like Polish, yet it's easy to work out who's the Crazy Guy, who's the Tough Guy, who's the Funny Guy. It's the usual café racer mix of crash-tatty Blades, Yoshi-piped ZX9s and blue-bolted R6s with matching Mad Max jackets, Versace jeans and Nike trainers. The joker in the pack's on a Desperado low-rider with fringed, lace-up leathers, Bob Marley wig and skull-motif Zippo in a pouch on his snakeskin belt. You know the score.

'You are Daniel from Inglaterra?' he growls. Yep. 'Then I shall call you Elton John.'

He laughs. Everyone laughs. I pretend to laugh.

'Right. So, has everyone got a funny nickname?'

'No, just you, Elton. Now, vamos. We ride.'

Ride or die. Damn these boys are ruff. Five or six abreast, no lids, through red lights, right up pavements, wrong down one-way streets. Stupid speeds, stupid overtakes, clever wheelies, clever tricks. As we approach the out-of-town péage, I'm given the nod. We split into twos and file in behind cars. It's like jibbing the Tube, but much, much more obvious. When the cars pay and the barriers lift, the trick is to nip up the sides. A couple of the boys can't help smoking the tyres on the way through. They motion for me to join in. I manage a pathetic off-the-throttle first-gear wheelie that's really half a bunny hop. They look away.

I feel like a prospect. I feel like I'm letting the side down. I feel the need to do something stupid. All I can do is backfire – could be worth a smile. Under a flyover, click, twist, bang, echo. The kid on the Blade gives me a thumbs up. I'm in. Er, no. He's looking past me. The Desperado pulls alongside, reaches into his tasselled jacket and pulls out a gun. A real gun. Click, whoop! Kwoff, kwoff, kwoff, firing into the air. Jesus. Call me Elton John? You can treat me like him, too. Just put the fucking gun away.

We're heading for a bar but the first stop's the butcher's to buy meat for the barbecue. Pull its horns off, wipe its arse and serve it with chips. Buy a slab, no two, no three slabs of Castle lager and plot up. It's not really a bar, just a yard on the beach, walls covered with faded revolutionary murals and adverts for cement. 'In the Portuguese days, this was used for executions,' hisses the Desperado. 'No, it wasn't,' laughs everyone else.

Beer, bikes, bullets and beef but not overbearingly butch. They're a good-natured Wild Bunch. They spot a very straight family celebrating a birthday and send over a bottle of champagne. The 21-year-old birthday girl sashays over in a silk gown and offers us some cake. She's not intimidated, they're not intimidating. I'm transfixed. She appears to have a slinky for spine. Chico takes advantage of the distraction and snaffles my steak. 'This is Africa,' he winks. 'You must be careful with your meat.'

I ask if I can take some pictures. 'Does your magazine come out in South Africa?' asks a feral-looking kid with funky dreads and a kung fu tattoo on his neck. Yeah, I think so. 'Then don't take any pictures of the bikes. We don't want the owners coming looking for them.'

The Desperado interrupts: 'You can take a picture of me with my bike, but make sure you can see my cannon, huh?' He opens his jacket and spins round with his gun. All across the bar, people duck, a reverse-rippled Mexican Wave. He laughs. Er, are all the bikes stolen? The Desperado calls up the table, the gist of which is 'Whose bike is legit?' No one answers.

The bikes are stolen from white South Africans, the old enemy. There's no guilt. The Apartheid regime funded, trained and armed the bad guys in Mozambique's thirty-year un-civil war. Bad guys who killed at least 100,000 people, mainly civilians, destroyed the railways, burned down hospitals, ran the country into the ground. As in Ghana, grand theft auto is small potatoes.

Last year the Johannesburg cops launched a cross-border operation, snatching and returning snide vehicles. The Mozambican government complained to Mandela and got it stopped – officially 'cause they considered it an illegal intrusion. 'The real reason,' explains Bruno, 'was that if the South Africans reclaimed all the stolen cars, buses and scooters, the country would stop. No one would be able to get to work in the morning.'

That reminds me. I've got to hit the road tomorrow. I make my excuses and leave. They're heading for the shooting range. Too rich for my blood. 'You go to bed, Elton, you look tired,' jeers the Desperado. 'Yeah, and your bike's shit,' I respond when I'm at least a mile down the road. That showed him.

'Park it next to a burst mattress and you'd swear it was a landfill site...', Departure Day, Chippenham Rd, London, December 2000

'Morocco is the closest faraway place I know' – running from Tangier towards Erfoud

Sandy ruts, rusted tanks
and salty wrecks — West African
roadkill in Casamance and Bissau,
January 2001

Corporate branded view of the Bay of Tangier

'Cool, fine, nice...' –
taking it Senegaleasy in St Louis

Todra Gorge,
Morocco

'Thank you lord for
another day, my belly's
full and my pocket's ok'
Accra, Ghana, March 2001

'The only thing
better than
falling asleep
in the Sahara
desert is waking
up in it...'
Riding the
Atlantic Route,
Christmas Day,
2000

'What a man can do, a man can do'
If this shuffling shambolista can cross the Sahara, anyone can

'Excuse me,' husked the Portuguese girl, arching a Brooke Shields eyebrow and cocking a salsa-sharp hip. 'Is that your beeg motorcycle?' Gosh. Lazy Sunday afternoon in Maputo, Mozambique, and I'm

CHAPTER 14
MOZAMBIQUE AND TANZANIA
AUGUST 2001
MAPUTO TO DAR ES SALAAM

about to get grifted. The open-air Café Mimo's easing its way out of Saturday's hangovers to the tune of espresso-machine hisses and welcoming air kisses. Mwah, mwah, mwah. There're a couple of tables of middle-class Mozambicans sipping South African whites' wine and flirting into mobiles. There's a happy Indian family chuckling at each other's spaghetti-stained chins. There's a table of Scottish aid workers getting student-union giddy on over-strength African beer. And there's me, a stray dog with a wagging tail and 'I've not spoken to anyone in days and I'm a sucker for a pretty face' shining out of my eyes.

'Can I sit down?' Every word is perfect, loaded and suggestive. 'Didn't I meet you at the UN building?' Respectable, charitable. 'I'm sorry to be so rude, but I seem to have lost my lift.' Polite, vulnerable. 'Would it be possible for you to take me home?' Take. Me. Home. 'I live in the suburbs with my sister.' Family-orientated, a hint of quiet nights lounging around in underwear painting each other's toenails. 'We moved here when my mother died.' Look after me. 'Also, she has all my money and I've eaten.' Here we go. 'Could you lend me the money till we get back?' Hook, line, sinker. 'I'm just sitting round the corner.' Hooked, blinded, blinkered. I hand over twenty bucks. 'I suppose there's a fifty–fifty chance you'll come back,' I half laugh. She smiles and disappears.

Outside a man with his feet on backwards wearing a 'Will Work For Sex' T-shirt is holding up traffic, ranting like Mussolini. Two street kids in baggy grandad shirts are swinging off a lamp post. I eat a plate of prawns fried in chilli and ginger. I drink another cup of scalp-tighteningly strong coffee. I know straight away, but it takes an hour before I burst out laughing and admit it. 'You've been grifted.'

Maputo, baby. A place to fall in love, a place to fall in love with. The Portuguese certainly knew how to build – beautiful not beautified avenues lined with red flame trees and long cool shadows, full of faded colonial elegance and modern stainless chic. It feels like a mythical revolutionary dream, the streets read like a fantasy leftist dinner party – Avenida Karl Marx next to Patrice Lumumba next to Ho Chi Minh.

It's an easy city where every day is like Sunday. No one's ever in a hurry. No hassles, no hint of violence. But not stuck in a time warp – there's Visa ATMs and internet cafés. They just don't work very often.

I run into Werner, a German Jeremy Hardy lookalike on a DR650. You have a scrambler, I have a scrambler, let's be friends. We go for a drink. He's living in Cape Town, ridden up here to sell his bike. I produce a map. I've got a vague plan about heading straight up the coast to Dar es

Salaam. Most overlanders go west via Malawi 'cause the roads are so bad. 'What roads?' he laughs. He's ridden it before. 'It's passable – just.' He reckons it will take three weeks to cover the two thousand miles. He's bang on.

Three weeks, two thousand miles. Werner rides with me as far as Vilanculos. He speaks Portuguese. That's helpful. He's quicker than me. That's not. We pit-stop in Maxixe (rhymes with hashish) and have lunch with a family of German Methodist missionaries. I just can't help myself. 'So you're a missionary? That's a great position to be in.' They stare blankly as I shudder uncontrollably and splutter soup out of my nose.

During the civil war, this was the front line. For three days we ride past broken bridges, torn-up railway lines, burned buildings and bullet-scarred ghost towns. And mines. There's an estimated million still lying around, waiting. It's a shock to find the rope cordons and death heads so close to live villages full of curious kids, horny teenagers and blind old folk. The war's been over since 1994, but no one's told the mines. According to the UN, every time one goes off it kills 1.47 people. How do you kill 0.47 of a person? Ask the double amputee begging by the roadside.

In Vilanculos we're stopped at a roadblock. It's just outside a bar. A convoy of Save the Children Land Cruisers zips past. Who's that then? 'Princess Anne,' says Josef the bar owner. I wave. She doesn't wave back – mustn't have seen me. 'God shave the Queen,' shouts Werner. We laugh and go for a drink.

Three weeks, two thousand miles. And an awful lot of luck. I met a Chinese guy who pointed out that a belief in luck is the same as a belief in fate. I pointed out that 'Fatalistic' Luciano doesn't have the same ring. Just outside Beira, just after dark, I'm waved down at a sentry box.

'Jabber jabber,' says the grim-faced cop, stabbing at me with his trigger finger. Passport? 'Jabber jabber.' Driving licence? Head shake. I'm stumped. A geezer in a Newcastle shirt intervenes. 'Oakleys.' What? 'Oakleys,' stabbing at my goggles. Yes, Oakleys, what of it? 'The officer says he prefers Ray-Bans.'

I smile and get back on the bike. I should have kissed him. He'd just saved my life.

Two klicks down the road there's a level-crossing sign. I dunno whether it's live or dead. I slow, the van behind impatiently overtakes, hurries onto the level crossing and gets hit by a very dark, very solid train.

The next bit doesn't make any sense. My eyes aren't expecting to see what they see, my brain doesn't know how to process it. I get off the bike and walk to the ticking, twitching van. The bike light shadows as much as it shows. 'You'll be all right, amigo, I'll get help.' The driver's side has been ripped off. 'Can you move, amigo?' The driver's right arm's missing. 'Can you hear me, amigo?' The driver's right leg's missing. 'Wait here, I'll get an ambulance.' The right side of his head is missing. 'Are you all right, amigo?' He's very dead.

A Land Cruiser stops. We look at each other. I'm waiting for an adult to turn up and tell us what to do. The train driver's walking round in circles, mumbling. We coax him back into the cab and he moves the train. We attach a rope to the wreck and drag it into a field. Then we spot the passenger. Motionless, apparently unhurt, staring straight ahead, deep shock. Smart suit, clean shirt and neat tie, trying to ignore the fact that his mate's brains are all over his shoulders. We turn our lights off.

We can't open the passenger-side door. The chassis's too twisted. More cars stop. It's been maybe fifteen minutes. I get back on the bike and return to the police post. There's another cop now, and he speaks English.

'Quickly, sir, a train has hit a car.'

'Ah, you are from England. London?'

'Er, no Manchester, but that's not important. Sir, there are dead people, we go now.'

'Manchester? Manchester United? My team is Sporting Lisbon.'

'Right. Er, there are dead people. Is there an ambulance?'

He shrugs and walks away. It's not apathy, it's resignation. There is no ambulance. He is not a doctor. A minute or two will make no difference to a man with half a head. He gets on his bicycle. I get on my bike. When I pass the level crossing I don't stop. There's blood on the tracks.

By the time I get to Beira, baby, I've decided that I'm dead. *I hit the* train. That's why the passenger couldn't see me. That's why the cop ignored me. I'm dead and Beira is the City of the Dead. The streets don't match the map. Screeching faces lurch out of the darkness. I can't get my bearings. A drunk takes a swipe at my tankbag. I can't find the sea. The dead man's wife will be here, somewhere, waiting for him. I know. She doesn't. A car pulls up – no bonnet, no windscreen, driver wearing a balaclava and welders' goggles. It's the Devil. 'Hey Dan, are you lost?' It's a taxi. 'Follow us.' In the back are George and Margot, Belgians I met in Vilanculos. Next thing I'm in Biques bar listening to pint pots clunk and stir-fries sizzle and pool balls rattle.

'I thought I was dead, George.'

'No, Dan, you're not dead.' He smiles. 'You just smell like it.'

Three weeks, two thousand miles, about half of it off-road. The worst is from Beira to Inhaminga. Slowest damn piste I have ever ridden, a narrow squeeze that's a river in the wet season and a bitch in the dry, a steeply cambered, granny-knuckled finger covered with slippery sand and jaw-clunking rocks. The day is lived through blistered feet on jarring footpegs, through aching wrists on slapping bars, through a not-quite-numb-enough bum that's on and off that bucking seat. The bike winces 'eeesh' as if it's banged its knee on a coffee table as we clip a pothole and ding the rim. I suspect the rear shock's burst. I know my kidneys have. Every time we hit a bump, I groan and the bike creaks. We sound like Steptoe doing star jumps. This is not sexy off-roading.

And then it rains. Proper tropical wet rain. I'm bone-dry and sweaty. I count to seven. I'm soggy-wet and shivering. It's like riding through a car wash. The sand turns to muddy clay. I spend an hour sitting in a puddle the size of whales, smoking soggy cigarettes, stuck behind a stick-in-the-mud truck.

Suddenly it's dark, I'm a wreck, there's still at least an hour to go and the track's getting worse. Get off the bike. Relax. Eat toothpaste. Try to conjure up an appropriate deity. Papa Legba, Lord Shiva or St Jude? I settle for the Ghost of Future Dan – picture myself up the road with a belly full of food, mouth full of beer, ears full of soap. It works. An old man wobbles past on a bicycle burdened with palm oil. If he can make it, I can. An hour later I shuffle into Inhaminga's oil lamp-lit sandy streets. I find a pensão. The cook's just about to go home. She says she's not killing a chicken at this time of night. The chicken looks relieved and clucks off. Two hours later she returns with a plate of undercooked chips and a bottle of beer that stinks of mutton. I eat and collapse. Kid next door's playing with his radio. Just as I'm about to bang on the wall, he finds 'King of the Road'. I drift off. Ain't got no cigarettes.

Three weeks, two thousand miles and a lot of good people. I couldn't have made it without them. I have always depended on the kindness of strangers. Two hours out of Inhaminga, heading for the Rio Zambezi (Zambezi, zam), it occurs to me I haven't seen another soul all day. No one know's I've left, no one's expecting me. If I bin it and break something out here, I'm in serious trouble. Just as I'm about to start crying, a bus pulls up. The driver asks if I'd like to ride with them. Says he'll look out for me. He didn't have to do that. It completely changes the day. Suddenly I've got a guardian angel and everything's all right. The piste levels out. The view opens up. I get a chance to look around and see the helicopter shot, little blue bike on a swooping red track bouncing through a palm-green jungle vastness under a sky so big it makes me dizzy and so blue it seems to stain the distant mountains. I can see for miles.

I stop for a perfect picnic. Boiled eggs and custard creams. I'm teased by a circus of cheeky monkeys. 'The only reason we don't speak is so we're not obliged to work,' says one. 'Shush, here comes the farmer,' warns another. 'If he hears us chatting he'll make us pay for all those bananas.'

I wave goodbye to the bus when we reach the Zambezi (Zambezi, zam). There's a queue of trucks a mile long. 'What time's the ferry due?' I ask a driver. 'About two o'clock.' It's midday. 'On Friday.' It's Tuesday. Arse. A couple of kids stroll up. They'll take me across in a canoe. No problem. But I can't get the bike in on my own. Half a dozen drivers jump up and help out.

They didn't have to do that.

It's an awfully big river and this is an awful little boat. And it's leaking an awful lot of water. But it feels awfully good to hand over responsibility to someone else – even if it is a grinning teenager in an 'I heart Lady Diana' T-shirt. Between the banks, this is his world. I feel decidedly feminine. Lie back and think of England. Wonder what I was doing this time last year? Que sera. I can swim, and if the bike ends up at the bottom of the Zambezi, would that really be so bad? I ask him if his name's Charon. He says no, Nelson. I pay the ferryman and get off.

Just outside Nampula I stop for a smoke. A pickup stops and a smile hops out. 'Hi. That looks hard work. Fancy a cold Coke?' He didn't have to do that. His name's Shari and he works for Coca-Cola. He's been on the road investigating cooler abuse. 'If we catch those boys selling anything but Coke out of our coolers they are in big trouble!' He insists that I follow him to a hotel. He insists on taking me home to meet his mother and wife. Before finally insisting that he takes me to dinner and introduces me to his friends in his favourite bar. I'm ashamed to say that I'm looking for an angle. I'm happily humbled when there isn't one. Why, man? 'Hospitality to travellers is an important part of Muslim culture,' he winks, sinking a large Johnnie Walker.

Three weeks, two thousand miles. A lot of sanctuary. The rougher the day, the softer the relief when it's finally over. Unload the bags, take off my boots, retch, relax. Tension and release. Really can't beat a hard day's night. A dusty mouth makes any beer taste wetter. A hungry stomach makes any food taste hotter. And an aching body makes any bed seem comfier. Night is part of day.

'Let me guess – a cold beer, a hot shower and some warm tucker. In what order?'

After another twelve-hour day I hit Pemba beach campsite. Aussie Russell greets me with a real smile and a big handshake. There's a coconut-mat bar swaying with English, French and Uruguayan overlanders, in from Zambia, Zimbabwe and Malawi. There's a barbecue licking tandoori chicken and garlic squid. Sky Sports on the telly, Massive Attack on the stereo, all muffled by the roar of the Indian Ocean. And paradise is enow.

Three weeks, two thousand miles. And one big off. Why do they always happen like this? A stretch of cement-powder-fine sand, get on the gas, repeat the mantra 'I have never fallen off in sand when going too fast, only when going too slow.' Next thing I'm slip-sliding away, still holding the bars, lost in a cloud of dust. Eventually we stop. I hear a voice murmuring, 'You're OK, Dan, you're OK, kidda,' while my shadow groans, 'Get off me, you fat bastard, I can't breathe.'

Odd moments. Lying there in the dust, moving my parts. Yep, all there. The kit did its job. Get up. Check the bike. No damage. The only thing that's broken is my bottle. Suddenly I'm terrified. A truck stops. The driver asks me if I want to put the bike on the back. He didn't have to do that. I almost say yes. A woman walks past with a 50 kg sack on her head. If she can do it, so can I. The truck drives away. I instantly regret my bravado and want to cry. I ride off with both feet down. I get overtaken by a Land Rover full of nuns. This is both humiliating and odd. Nuns shouldn't drive butch Land Rovers with Tonka-toy chunky tyres and jacked-up leaf springs down adventurous pistes. They should ride bicycles. Down cobbled streets.

The sisters herald a miracle. The map says fifty miles to Kilwa, the next town. That's about three hours at this speed, and it's getting dark. Ten minutes later I reach a magic roundabout, incongruous tarred traffic circle fed by sandy tracks. A sign says, 'Kilwa 15 km'. But? Another ten minutes and I'm plotted up in a truck stop eating fish heads out of a tin tray and watching *Kids Say the Darnedest Things*. Thanks, sisters.

Three weeks, two thousand miles. Just outside Dar es Salaam, just after dark, I stop for a smoke. Burning hayfields set the night on fire. I'm alive. And I'm happy. Properly alive and properly happy. Somewhere out there, between the sandpits and the potholes, the monkeys and the leopards, the shipwrecks and train wrecks, the shredded tyres and campfires, the death heads and the fish heads, somewhere between the Beira Devil and Pemba's deep blue sea, I kinda found what I was looking for. A self-contained, self-fulfilling journey. A great escape.

I ride into town and find the seedy Hotel Shirin. There's an English kid in the lobby. He asks me where I've come from. I tell him. Says he's just ridden the same route. I ask him what on. He points to the push-bike locked up outside. We laugh. We go for a drink. In the bar I'm approached by a camp Somalian waiter. 'Excuse me, sir,' he simpers. 'Has anyone ever mentioned that you look like Elton John?'

Keep drifting.

It doesn't last. It never does. I wish there was a way of holding onto that sense of auto-achievement, that feeling of self-generated self-worth, but I always fail. Maybe that's the secret of success. I try to put it in my pocket but it curdles quick as milk in the midday sun. Takes just two weeks to turn dusty Dar's wide-open circle delights into just another drunk's triangle – flophouse for a cry and a wank, internet café for long-range abuse, bar to get bed-wetting drunk on a school night with the usual crowd of lost expats and ambitious hookers. And Mocambique's deep wilderness magic drowns in the smell of fighting and onions.

Email home –

"Wake up. Cold shower in a brown trickle that doesn't even disturb the mosquitoes. Flip flop downstairs, pay the surly concierge and walk out into the chicken market. It smells. Walk round past the mechanics to the internet. Drink a coke, have a smoke, message you.

Today I went across the city. Sometimes it all looks very familiar. Today I saw it again.

This is a city where most people live on less than a dollar day. Imagine that in England. I woke up and walked past a chicken market where the entrailed-stained, white-coated chicken-chokers sit in car seats. Imagine that in England. I saw a cop with an AK giving his mate a backie on a pushbike. Imagine that in England. I was held up by a man who earns his living walking around selling nail varnish, dreaming of a stall in the market ('one day . . .'). Imagine that in England. I skipped past dungareed mechanics welding an exhaust on a crowded pavement. Imagine that in England. I ate spaghetti bolognese in an open air café while a Casio synth churned out pre-programmed sub-Kenny G with a shop dummy sat behind the keyboard. Imagine that in England. I avoided a crippled woman walking on her flip-flop-ed hands, dragging her wasted legs underneath her, carrying her shopping on her head. Imagine that in England? You can't. It can't be done.

Sometimes I think Africa is the same. Other times I think it's very different. Tonight I'll get drunk with the imported Indian belly dancers in Bombay Knights. Gods make it easy on me."

The trip's starting to unravel. I see the signs, but hide my face. I don't want to climb back into that crusty cocoon, deluded that only the devil or a dick would try to turn this fragile butterfly back into a maggot. But in less than a month I'll be on my way home, ambushed by bosses, kidnappers and a best friend's funeral.

First, I get fired. Decommissioned. 'Message from the boss – we're not taking anymore Africa stories. Where next?' I have no real clue, but I go through the motions, pack up and head north with a vague idea of shipping, chasing a 'worked my passage from Mombassa to Bombay' punchline. I ride out through a riot. Muslim youth protesting about police brutality are burning tyres and smashing mouths. A kid in a headscarf stops the bike. 'I have a sister in Leicester'. So have I.

The teargas keeps my crying all the way to Tanga. I spend the evening with a Kiwi nurse and hit the Kenyan border. Plot up in Diani Beach, watch the Twin Towers burn and wait for another fall.

Lou flies in. We lie on white sand so soft it squeaks, play in the blue-green ocean, eat crab claws the size of sweet pigs' trotters, laugh at the palm trees full of cheeky monkeys, fuck on this 15 mile paradise beach that's been empty of tourists since the Nairobi embassy bombing warnings, and tear each other to shreds. What secrets silent stony sit in the dark palaces of our hearts?

Bad moon rising. The sun sets on the Indian ocean, colouring the moon Welsh gold then Sterling silver and painting the palm trees inky black silhouettes. I sit on a typhoon-downed casherina tree, watching a fire-imp born on the road dance round a crackling charcoal pit, watching my ex best girl fly a kite, chatting knuckleheads with a German Harley mechanic, arguing politics with a shifty Rhodesian, talking designs with a South African tattooist, and wonder how the fuck it all went so wretchedly wrong. A distant affair turned this paradise into hell. 'It's better to dwell in the wilderness alone than with a contentious and angry woman'. It's time to make a split.

Real life intervenes. While we're at the beach, the room gets cleaned and I get cleaned out – passport, palmtop, credit cards, camera. The thief used a key to open the door – clever. Then used a key to lock the door behind them – stupid. It had to be an inside job.

I complain. Nothing happens. I go to the cops. Nothing happens. I waited a patient week, then went back to the cops 'So, have you caught the thieves?' Er, aren't I supposed to say that, not you? I went back to the hotel. I lost my temper. I overturned tables. Someone in here stole my stuff. Who was it? Was it you? Was it you?

They rush me – manager, bouncer, couple of beach boys. Drag me and Lou upstairs, talking all kinds of Mau Mau shit. It's violent and tense. 'Get out of this hotel now!' It's 2am. Fine. But when we try to leave, they've locked the security cage that surrounds the stairs. We're locked in.

It's a zoo. Drunken punters, hustlers and hookers from the bar start rattling the cage, running machetes along the bars, spitting through it, throwing beer through it, cursing through it. Open the fucking door. 'Yes, open the door, let us at him. He calls us thieves'. Lou tries to call the embassy. We're being held by force. That's kidnap, isn't it? She gets the ansaphone.

A night of this shrieking shit. Then the cops turn up – that's good.

They arrive in the manager's Merc – that's bad. 'You're under arrest'. You're kidding. He's not and there's nothing funny about Kenyan cop shops. Unless you're tickled by cockroaches and blood stained floors. Pay compensation to the hotel for disrupting business, or you and the girl spend some time here. He winks and rubs his crotch. I pay. We move hotels. Lou leaves. And for some reason, I don't.

Email from home –

'Hi Dan,

Sorry mate but Mo asked me to get in touch. It's some really shit news. Will died on Sunday. A heart attack in Police custody. He'd been on it all weekend and got nicked on his bike. Died while being restrained. Really sorry the first time I've been in touch and it's such shit news. The funeral is next Wed' in Wales.

Take care dude, see ya soon, Neil.'

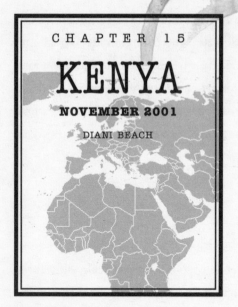

CHAPTER 15

KENYA

NOVEMBER 2001

DIANI BEACH

'Ehia obroni a, osane po.' When the white man is in need, he takes to the sea – Ghanaian Ashanti proverb.

When this white man was in need, he took to the road. December last year I jumped on the bike and ran away. I thought I could outrun death. Cancer in tired bones, needles in tied-off arms, sleeping pills in tongue-tied mouths – six gone in one sad, soiled spring. I turned six good reasons into one perfect excuse and ran for my life. Part 'get it while you can' opportunism, part 'don't need nobody' nihilism. Be quick or be dead.

When this white man is in need he takes from the road. Poor dirt roads lead through dirt-poor villages locked into the cyclical *Groundhog Day* monotony of rural Africa. From Mauritania to Mozambique, I've seen the same women carrying the same water to wash the same clothes while minding the same babies and pounding the same millet while the same husbands and sons work the same shifts in the same fields for the same subsistence wage, same day after day after same decade after decade.

'There is nothing to see in this village. It was the same yesterday. It will be the same tomorrow. What are you doing here?' I've come to steal your differences. I'm here to enslave your novelty. All too easy to worship landscapes while reducing people to cute but mute extras, an 'ooh, how exotic' backdrop to my selfish ramblings.

Of course they're not the same – people just seem that way because I can't be bothered stopping to find out. What would I say? And besides, if I stop, people will stare and ask me questions and it'll all become a bit of a hassle, man. Because although my imposition is taken for granted, theirs is taboo. Take from the needy. Give little, take the lot.

When this white man is in need, he takes to the liquor. Wouldn't you? It's either that or another night in another African flophouse, climbing its hospital-hued walls and whacking off into tennis shoes. Besides, it's in the bars that the overlanders meet. The overlanders need each other. Runaways of the world unite. No one else really cares that you've just ridden from Inhaminga to Alto Molócuè because no one else really knows what that means. It's like talking knee-down with your mam. 'Yes dear, that sounds lovely.' No one really knows what it feels like to hold your breath for the dozenth time in an hour when the bald front slides in sand and you're six days from a hospital. So we meet and drink and talk roads and try and work out what each other's running from. What's your story, man?

I grieve my death riff, and Backpacker Sean tells me how he lost ma, da and two brothers in one tragic sequence of accidents. 'Some nights that tent gets kinda crowded.' I groove my cuckold routine to Land Rover Lance, who shrugs as he says that he caught his wife in bed with his brother. 'I cried for months.' And so it goes in the overlander algebra of need.

When this white man is in need, he phones his da. And he sends money. Or he phones his boss. And he sends tyres. Or he phones Yamaha. And they send bike bits. Self-reliant independent adventurer? It's all a sham, kids. Ever get the feeling you've been cheated?

When this white man was in need, he took to the road. Despite or maybe because of the fact that someone needed this white man. The woman who loved me was reduced to a photo and imprisoned in a wallet. One day I looked at the photo and she'd gone. Her face was aching from holding that smile. While I was slouching towards Babylon, the centre could not hold. 'You wanted the best of both worlds. Instead you got the worst,' she said as she stepped out of the frame and walked away. Now I need to know whether it was worth it.

So. When this white man has new needs, he takes to the road again. Because the road works. Because of mornings like these – slipping into a safari suit (wouldn't you?), kicking over the XT and fanging out into the Kenyan bush. Brodieing around in those blue and yellow, purple Shimba Hills, chasing wild zebras, lassoing them with laughter while the bike plays barking sheepdog. Attaboy.

And because of afternoons like these – Aida, a hitch-hiking, top-knotted, ritually scarred Masai warrior motor mechanic with car-tyre shoes invites me back to his dirt-poor village – mud-brick houses in a reed compound, dusty floor wriggling with free-range chickens and children.

The village is known locally for its music. Paul plays a cracked-pipe melody as sharp as uncut coke, a sound so clear it feels like he's blowing into my mouth and playing my skull. Hassan plays a reeded horn that brays like a camel singing scales. Moses plays a shoe-box xylophone, blurring hands grooving the hand-tongued grooves. Clowning kids dance – a little 'un dives into a pair of oversize wellies that cup his little bum and laughs his way through a stiff-legged jig. Give a little, get a lot. A lift for a lift.

Ehia obroni a, osane po. All roads lead to home. I'm coming back. Gotta say goodbye to Will. Will was gonna come with me. Will was gonna meet me here, there and everywhere. Will was gonna come next time, definitely. Will died yesterday. Aged 35.

So I'm coming back to say goodbye. And hello. Gonna pick up that precious thing I forgot to pack and we'll hit the road together. Coast to coast across the States sounds about right. Let's leave in spring. Live the dream, take the myth. And keep drifting.

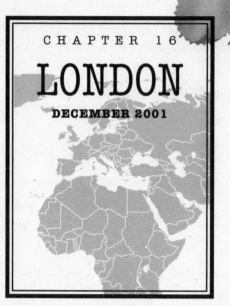

CHAPTER 16
LONDON
DECEMBER 2001

'Pull over.' Shit. Squintingly bright, refreshingly cold autumn afternoon on the A1(M), and it appears that I've been nicked. I was kinda expecting it – bald tyres, no baffle in the pipe, one indicator lens missing, one broken mirror – so I'm none too surprised when the Deauville pulls alongside and the white-helmeted, yellow-jacketed rider points to the hard shoulder. No flashing lights, must be an unmarked camera bike. Just my luck.

Bite my tongue. Best cop behaviour. Off the bike, off with the lid, bound over with a wagging tail and a 'we're mates' smile. 'Your luggage is dangerously close to the back wheel,' he shouts through his clear visor and steamed-up bins. Is it? How did that happen? So sorry. 'And your back tyre's bald.' 'So's your wife' mumble muffled by a buffeting artic.

Yes, officer, I smile. He looks confused. It clicks.

'Er, you are a cop, aren't you?'

'No, I work in IT,' in his best John Major geek whine. 'Just being helpful.'

Helpful? A heartful of wasted panic is helpful, is it? Pretending to be

plod is helpful, is it? It'll take me fifteen minutes to get back to traffic speed on this plodder. I dunno whether to laugh or lamp him.

Splutter. He shrugs and rides away to an indicated 58 mph. Guess I'll just have to laugh. Only in England would you hit running interference from a vigilante on a Deauville. Welcome home, kidda.

Two weeks ago I wouldn't have stopped for anyone. Two weeks ago I was riding from Mombasa to Nairobi with a head full of 'be careful' warnings. Kenya's main highway runs through a game park, but it's not the animals that everyone's scared of – it's the people. Favourite trick is for pedestrians to point at a wheel, shriek and wave the vehicle down. You'd be surprised how many naive tourists stop. The lucky ones are robbed at gunpoint. At least it's quick. The unlucky ones get taken for a longer ride – one grifter chats while another pours oil underneath a vulnerable-looking spot. Look, a broken rear diff. No matter that it's a front-wheel-drive car. Big problems, madam. It's not the parts, it's the labour. My brother's garage is just around the corner. Two-week vacation spent thumb-twiddling while Oily Olly dismantles the hire car. 'Luckily for me, he took American Express.'

I know this is my last ride – I know this is the end of the adventure. I stop and smoke and laugh at a gang of surprisingly fat zebras. The sharp black and whites seem unreal – nature doesn't do those colours. They don't look right. Neither do the giraffes. The lolloping gait and step-ladder necks are expected; it's the tongues that worry me – enormous spotted squid tentacles.

And damn, they smell bad. A jackal slopes past and gives us all a pimp squint. I wink and get back on the bike.

One last dusk, one last mosque ululating the evening call to prayer, one last wagon driver making tea over a fire, one last African night. I plot up in a game lodge – September 11th has sent hotel prices tumbling. $100 rooms easily talked down to $10. Breakfast thrown in. One last sundowner under a sky as pink as a cat's mouth listening to hippos grunt in a mudpit, betting on firefly races with Ben the Barman. Losing never felt so good.

Open a door and bang, all change. Geography as confused as in a dream, childhood corridors leading to sandy beaches. Riding down gently put everything into context – flying back is a shock. Nairobi to London in one woozy night. And suddenly I'm flushing a trolley past rows of suited chauffeurs holding laminated name cards. 'Dan Walsh?' Eh? Er, yes. 'Saw you in the magazine. Welcome home.'

I wasn't expecting that. Despite the flush of fame, the airport feels damn impersonal. Too bright lights, no this, no that, unattended baggage will be destroyed, smoke only in designated areas. African airports are all about people – emotionally charged extended families dressing up to see Mahmoud off or welcome Joseph back. In Heathrow, the people seem to be in the way – inconvenient clutter making the sharp architectural lines look untidy. Then someone slips an arm round my waist and kisses the back of my neck. Hey, baby. I'm home.

Next day I'm back to pick up the bike. Pocketful of bolts and a Golf tool kit – I had to remove the handlebars to squeeze the XT into an affordable-sized crate. And back into London. Damn, the traffic's fast and aggressive, the roads are damp, the bike's slow and I'm intimidated. First set of lights I heave on the brake and the bars loll into my lap. Maybe I should have tightened those bolts. Ever tried steering a bike with rolling handlebars? Ever tried filtering on a rowing machine?

Heathrow. Hounslow. Hammersmith. Not the most flattering side of London – 'I'm the same as him' semis, faux stone cladding and unleaded windows. Drives that lead straight into traffic jams – cars as extensions of the living room complete with comfy chair, remote-controlled enter-tainment and filthy snarls. Move over for a bike? But I'm taking part in a live radio phone-in.

So I'm back. Let's see how long I can treat England as another country on the list. A lot's changed since I've been away. Home's both fresh and freshly soiled. Time to work on the next Great Escape. In the meantime, see you on the Westway . . .

THANK YOU, THANK YOU

First, the kit. Yamaha UK for a lovingly prepped XT, Bracken MCs for the Touratech goodies, Bert Harkins Racing for the Acerbis tank and guards, Psion for the Palmtop, plus Arai, Aerostich, Alpinestars, Furygan and Giali for the apparel. Good eggs, all.

Secondly, the support. I snivelled for sponsorship, hoping to attract big-budgeted marketing departments – instead I found big-hearted *Bike* readers.

Enormous gratitude to – Barry Beamish, Sean Beamish, Andy Cushing, Ian Elsey, Miles Finch, Richard Fincher, Phil and Gill Flup, Dave Holmes, Naeem Hussain, Dave Lochhead, Nick McGivern, Alice Meacham, Sean Merrick, Patrick Norrie, Richard Pickford, Jim Pippit, Steve Read, Audrey Rodkiss, Speed Couriers of Manchester, Liisa Steele, Mark Stoddart and Grace Todhunter. And anyone else I've inadvertently forgotten. And my mum and dad. One love.

LONDON

☆ ☆ ☆

2002 – 2003

England? That's a dead end.
I never believed in it anyway.

TOM STOPPARD,
Rosencrantz and Guildenstern are Dead

I came back to London to bury my dead best friend. And to resurrect the rank corpse of our rotten romance. It's easier to forgive than to forget. Especially as I'd made the male mistake of dragging the dirty details of every sticky second from her not-so-secret box. Everywhere reminded me of them. Everyone reminded me of him. I just wouldn't let it die.

We should have made a clean break from the heart-ache. But we're trapped, fingers stuck in each other's hurting holes, deadbeat dependents. No love, just loss. No sex, just scorn. Our only intimacies are our insults – hollered and howled, horrible and honed humiliations that strike the same wounded weak-spots again and again, drink-driving us to despair, domestic violence and the deranged edges of dark mental illness. Good times.

Home no longer exists. So I stay in the pub. Where no-one cares where I've been or what I've seen. I never expected a hero's welcome, but maybe I had dreamed a little too hard of returning respect and recognition. Instead I get 'so what?' shrugs and blank-stared 'don't cares'. I sulk for a while, then remember I'm missing the point. Good travel should be self-contained. Some people will tell you that it's all about the stories. But they're wrong. Travel isn't about the told-tales, it's teleological, an end in itself. Good travel exists in those 'right here, right now' toasts on those best of all possible days, and never in the after-party anecdotes. Next time I won't make the same mistake. Next time I won't come home.

And while I sat at the bar and planned the next great escape, these weak words kept me in booze and fags. Froth and filler – less signal than noise. Even my ma's gonna skip this section . . .

Morning, Glory. What's the first thing you think about when you wake up in the morning? I hate alarm clocks. I'm late. She's late. Is that piss or sweat? I can't hear the kids. Have I got kids? I'm riding across the Sahara? How about 'Is the bike still there?'

Is the bike still there? Kettle, toilet. Garbage in, garbage out. Marlboro and morning music. Studio One reggae. Try to summon the sound of sand-floored sunlit shanties into this gloomy west London basement. It doesn't work.

Is the bike still there? Flip-flop upstairs, bang my shin on a pram in the corridor full of junk mail and leaves, stick my head out of the door murmuring the mantra 'steering lock, disc lock, chain through railings'. Bright and cold – eyes squint, coffee steams. Wink at Angie in the bathroom shop. Peer round the dustcart at the piece of pub pavement where the bike should be. Tension and release. Yep, it's still there. Good – that means I can go to work.

Not a lot of call for unemployed motorcycle adventurers these days, so I'm very odd-jobbing. She's prop buying for a film, I've ghosted onto the payroll as a gofer. Today's to-do list: 'Collect films from Portobello, count and measure beds in Greenwich, make a crack pipe. And don't forget to take back the videos.' Will do.

Mornin', bike. 'Mornin', Dan.' Eh? 'You talking to yourself again?' It's Tess, the pub landlady. 'That your new bike?' Yep, what d'yer reckon? 'Quite nice, isn't it?'

Quite nice. Did you enjoy that, darlin'? It was quite nice. Hardly uplift-ing. Every time I ask people what they think of the Fazer Thou, they say, 'Hang on a minute, I'll have a look.' 'Quite nice' follows 'looks like a crashed R1' and 'looks like a 900 Diversion'. Damn you and your faint praise.

Too many keys. Throw the disc lock in the courier bag, leave the chain on the railings, get things rolling. Key, choke, starter. Like all Exup engines, it feels alive, warbling and growling like it's chewing ball-bearing gum as the long pipe puffs damp smoke and we roll backwards off the pavement into the traffic and into the game.

First impressions? Fast. Picked up from the Peterborough office in the dark, the 90 mph run down the A1 to London showed that it was quick, light and kinda unremarkable. I almost understood why *Bike* colleague Hargreaves described its default position as 'sensible'. Only the engine hinted at a dark side – taut as a high-tension steel cable, waiting to be twanged.

And then we hit town's confined spaces and, hot tit!, the bike went mental, rearing away from lights, ambushing dawdling drivers, nose-diving into shellgripped pedestrian crossings, banging around like a trapped elk. I know I've spent the last year on a 33 bhp trail bike, but it seems to jump from one place to another quicker than is physically possible. Coming off a roundabout, I give it a little gas and suddenly I'm on the wrong side of the road. Spot a gap, open the throttle and suddenly I'm bouncing off the rear plate of a Speedfight. Pull out to overtake, some more gas, and suddenly I'm sliding past a 'Give Way', front and rear locked up. Laugh? I nearly rode under a Merc.

Looks bland, tastes dangerous. It's very peri chilli sauce in a ketchup bottle. Looks wet, plays rough. It's Ronan Keating pulling a Stanley knife or Paul McCartney kicking a cat to death. First impressions count for nowt when you're dealing with a two-faced liar. I pulled more shit power wheelies in an hour than in six years of riding. Guess what? I'm a born-again.

Could be a bit much first thing, but the Fazer also does lazy mornings. It doesn't like waking up any more than I do. At cold-start low speeds the throttle snatches, the carbs burp and the front buzzes. Then the screen rattles. It's like sitting in a transport café when a wagon pulls in. As it warms up, the buzz becomes a hum. By the time I hit Portobello I feel like a wet-lipped supply teacher getting the treatment from 5K. 'Who's making that humming sound? Will you shut up!'

Portobello Market to collect films – junk antiques at one end, vintage clothes at the other, everything from chirpy cockney fruit-and-veggers to pouting mockney vinyl junkies in between. Narrow street that's all shouting touts, barging carts, dozy tourists and local nutters tripping over kerbs littered with slippery cabbage leaves. On an R1 it would be all elbows, knees and boompsadaisies, slipping discs and clutch. The upright-not-uptight Thou's as gentle as a beach-ride donkey. And almost as smelly. I can't be doing with the boiling Windolene stink of liquid-cooled engines.

Where to park? Bike bay on the left but it's full of scooters and commuters. And a Renault Sprinter. White-van man pulls up, sticks it in reverse and dominoes a Superdream into a CBR into a couple of Piaggios. Third time I've seen that in a week and every time it makes me more uncomfortable about the responsibility of an eight-grand bike.

The XT has brush guards and folding levers – the Fazer's got brittle plastic and vulnerable plumbing. Gives me the willies. Anyway, that bay was too scratty. Parking a flash bike in London means playing the 'Which one would I steal?' game. The idea is never to have the most desirable bike in the bay. Avoid CX500s. Sniff down unlocked RSVs.

I gamble on a double yeller and swipe the films. Prop shots – sofas and bunk beds that will end up decorating a film set. Up to my elbows in a kitchen-sink drama, I run right into Tricky. Sorry, mate. Oh, it's you. I lisp one of his raps at him – 'They used to call me Tricky kid, I lived the life they wished they did.' He looks appalled then laughs.

Off again. Greenwich to count beds. Through knotted Notting Hill Gate, bustling Bayswater Road, hectic Hyde Park Corner. I pick up a crew – sure-footed courier on a GT550, brogue-footed commuter on a Triumph 509, and Adidas trainers scooter boy with a Santa hat taped to his lid. Ho ho ho. In London, you never ride alone. And the errand becomes a mission.

Game on. The GT's smooth, experienced, measured, always in the right lane, always thinking ahead. The scoot's erratic, enthusiastic and reckless, up the inside of parked buses, wrong way round bollards. The T509's hanging back, playing wait-and-see, happy to tag along. And me, I'm getting it all wrong, overtaking cars that are indicating right, undertaking cabs that are turning left, but absolutely loving it. Blame the bike – it outguns, outruns, out-stops and out-bops everything on the road. Its superbike potential and trail-bike usability combine to make the perfect traffic terrorist and it has me grinning like a Cheshire twat. And riding like one. 'You'll end up in hospital,' spits a cabbie as I charge up the bus lane. Er, that's the idea.

Queen Elizabeth Infirmary, Greenwich. I grab a bacon roll and laugh at the textbook Englishness of it all – half-empty Canary Wharf winks over a pub called the Antigallican, a tattoo parlour, a café that's advertising 'freshley made sandwiches' and a derelict hospital. This place has been shut for months – apparently there aren't any sick people in south-east London. The NHS have decided to sell the plot to property developers. In the (Greenwich) meantime, it's being used as a set for film companies.

'And on your left was the premature baby unit. Mind the puddles. Sorry, I forgot my torch.' Kevin the maintenance manager turned tourist guide leads me down miles of echoing, leaking corridors to a ward full of empty beds, burst blood-pressure gauges and discarded copies of *Bella* with the crosswords almost finished. It feels odd and bad and wrong. How many deaths and births? How many taxpayers' millions? 'Eleven,' says Kevin. What? 'There's eleven usable beds. With mattresses.' I write it down and get out as quick as I can.

Next. Bleak Woolwich High Road, bleaker concrete Blackwall Tunnel Approach, then the tunnel under the Thames which never fails to freak me out and has a couple of snagging bends that never fail to catch me out. I've clipped the wall before. High-rise Hackney becomes drizzly Dalston becomes gentrified Angel. Turn right onto the Pentonville Road, peek into Daytona's Ducati window display, think about popping into Shane MacGowan's local for a swift half and instead ride right into a wrong.

Priller Spiller. There's a Rossi rep RS250 on its side in the middle of the road, courier BM and a scoot parked up protecting the bike and rider from the ghoulish traffic. He's face down. He's lost a trainer. A passing

doctor has put him in the recovery position. The courier's calling the Old Bill on a mobile ('The fuckers put me on hold!') and swearing indiscriminately at cars. 'Why can't you wankers look where you're going?'

Us and them. I murmur at the sprawled rider. He wants to know if his bike's OK and if I saw what happened. It isn't, and I didn't. I lie. Jeans-and-T-shirt geezer with a toddler in his arms wanders up. 'Is he dead?' Nah. 'Thank fuck for that. We thought we'd killed him, didn't we, sweetheart?' The little girl nods her screwed-up head. The cops arrive just in time to stop a lynching.

Next mile is a subdued and nervous shiver past neon King's Cross drunks and sullen Euston commuters, heading for the Marylebone Road. Mary Le Bone – sounds like a Victorian stripper, all gold hoop earrings and gauze veils, immodesty hidden behind a whoreshair merkin, dancing on the tables of the Bucket of Tears for Dickensian draymen and Pickwickian pickpockets. Married to Simon Le Bone, 1880s music-hall star.

Will this light ever change? Something pulls alongside – just another glare in my mirrors. Red, amber, green and pootle away half-sharp. Glance back before undertaking a bus and the glare's still there. Eh? Half throttle is usually plenty to shake off a car. I wind it on a little too hard and, bang, it's gone, the wheel's up, we're veering right and there's nothing I can do about it. Once the power's on, it's on, and trying to rein it in is like putting a thumb over a popped bottle of champagne. Let's get fizzy. The front lands with a ball-clang as the Fazer sprays itself up the road, my eyes water and blur red tail lights, and we plummet left then right down the Euston underpass.

Don't look back 'cause I don't want him to know I'm trying, don't look down 'cause I don't want to know how fast we're flying. I'd guess at 90. In a 30. Which means the Impreza Turbo must be doing a ton, ton-ten as I bottle out and back off and he turbine-whistles past, a silver smear of squat aggression, polished alloys and UK garage, a boy racer in a ski hat braking hard as he jinks left and I thread through a gap.

The traffic's stopped. Slow below 30 to wriggle between a coach and a line of cars. Pop up at the front of the lights as if I'm coming up for air. And suck on a dump valve. Arse. He's slid up the bus lane and is right alongside. Here we go again. Red, amber, that'll do, go. Hairdresser in an MX-5 tries his luck and gets done on both sides. See ya. Scooby's good – better than me – faster, cockier, sharper. But he's not better than the bike. One more stop – red light at Baker Street. Whistle the sax solo through dry grinning lips. Whit whit whit whawahwah. Scooby pulls alongside. No begrudging manly nods but big cheesy grins and playground thumbs up. Nice car, mate. Nice bike, mate. He goes left to Paddington, I hit the uplift of the Westway runway. Taking back videos has never been so much fun.

First exit, down the ramp, take care on the roundabout 'cause it leads to a builder's yard and is always awash with diesel, under the flyover, filter between the lanes and gas it just as a car noses across from the right. Nowhere to go. Lock front and back. And stall it. Clutch is so light I keep thinking the cable's snapped. Hit the starter, nothing. Tap at the gear change to check it's in neutral, pull in the clutch, swing in the side stand, nothing but a quiet relay click. Bugger. On with the hazards, reach for the kick-start. Er, what kick-start? Guess I'm still too used to the XT.

A cop pulls up. 'Problem, mate?' Nah, just a dicky switch. 'That any good? I'm thinking of trading up from the 600.' Er, yeah. But it wheelies everywhere and makes me ride like a twat. 'I've noticed.' He grins and drives away. Inexplicably, the bike fires up. Home in time for tea. Bounce up the kerb to the pub, lock it to the railings. Tess waves and mimes the international signal for 'Pint?' I wave back the international signal for 'In a minute, just let me make a pretend crack pipe with a chocolate milk bottle and biro.' I'm not sure she got it.

Month on and it's all still good. Fazer Thous rock. What do you want from a bike? It'll country-lane hustle and roundabout rustle, it'll scream up and down motorways, it'll travel 160 miles plus to the tank, it'll carry a pillion (though it's quite keen on spitting them off), and it absolutely bosses in-town traffic.

Do I love it? Yep. Would I buy one? Nope. Why? Because it costs eight grand. Yamaha protest that it's not a budget-blaster, that it's a proper grown-up transport. 'We used the engine from the R1, not the Thunderace.' Ummm, but the Fazer 6 uses the engine from the Thundercat, not the R6, and that's hardly suffered as a consequence. London's full of them.

So. It's an awful lot of bike and an awful lot of money. I don't like the responsibility of expensive bikes, I certainly don't like the insurance premiums, and I'm not too happy about being the kind of person who'd spend eight grand on a bike. That'd buy me a year's worth of trans-African Tenere adventures. Or six months chugging round Europe on a guzzling Guzzi. Or XJR-13 cool and a lot of wild weekends.

But, right now, it is my responsibility. I can feel the key in my pocket.

If it's on the move, it can't get nicked or knocked over, right? Er, do you want to watch a video tonight, love? No, it's all right. I'll go. I fancy a quiet ride. Evenin', bike.

18 Pride comes before a stall. 'Er, shall I get off?' Bugger. Early evening, central London, heading for a party (Thirty-three? Christ, we're getting old) on the XT – best girl on the back, Brixton up front, six lanes of 'gotta get home to East Grinstead' traffic behind, Dominator and Gilera DNA alongside, happily catching a breath after the cluttered smother of Victoria. Then red, amber, 'Shall I show off with a daft wheelie?', green and, oh you little sod, I've stalled it. And, yes, you better had get off. Vauxhall Cross? Vauxhall bloody furious.

Start, you vicious, vicious bastard. The scoot sneers triumphantly, the Dommie shrugs sympathetically and chugs off, impatient cars tut and toot and swarm past. First kick, sheesh, forget about the pillion peg and put it through my calf. She's dodging teeth-clipping wing mirrors and toe-crushing tyres like an overdressed squeegee merchant while I try to paddle the bike to the central reservation, sweating like old cheese, blood seeping through my Levi's, cursing the delusional notion that kick-starts are cool.

Kick-starts – from a distance, they rock. They're an integral part of the motorcycling escape dream scene – 'Take this job and shove it/You'll be sorry when you see me stepping out with Madonna/It's my willy and I'll wash it as fast as I like' sneered over the shoulder through a haze of cigarette smoke, grab jacket and lid, slam the door on the way out, kick up the McQueen Triumph twin/desert racer trailie/teenage riot Elsie and roar/fishtail/wheelie away into the black and white night's drizzle, not looking back at the sobbing figure in the window calling, 'Look out, look out, look out!'

Marvellous macho nonsense – as long as the bike starts. In real life, the scene probably looks like this – storm out, jump aboard, realise you've forgotten your keys, plead to be let back in, try again, and while you're impotently banging away at the bike's highly sprung elbow, they've dried their eyes and sneaked off to the pub to meet that bloke who's always on time because he's got an electric starter, leaving you alone with thigh cramp and your 'Real men don't use solenoids' tattoo.

Solenoid. Two weeks ago I'd have made a gag about piles and shrugged – now I know that it's a magnetised coil that converts the battery's power into current and turns the starter motor over. I know this because Clever Mark the Clever Mechanic told me so. 'The solenoid's rotten – I'll pinch another off the next bent Yamaha that comes in – until then, you'll just have to use the kicker.'

The electrics have been playing up for weeks – the starter motor wouldn't stop starting and every now and then the power would just cut. I had a feeling I was riding on borrowed time – recent trips had been blessed by prayers to Yamahovah, Great God of Japanese Motorcycling – 'Just let the bike get to so-and-so and I swear I'll get it serviced.' He did me proud – the bike didn't conk out until I was actually on the mechanic's forecourt. 'Bloody hell, Dan, that was lucky. You'd better put the kettle on.'

Sweet tea, Rich Tea and a distinct lack of sympathy. 'Couldn't find any-one to adjust your chain for you in Africa, then?' Despite the jibes ('I reckon you've been in Hunstanton for a year. You look like you've got fatter.'), I'm damn glad to be here. The last garage stop was in Tanzania – I knew it was a motorcycle workshop 'cause there was a set of Showa forks cemented into an oil drum out front. I'd split my petrol tank in a

sandy wipeout – a smiley geezer who smelled of rum and Imperial Leather told me he could weld it tight. And he did – with the tank still on the bike, and still full of maybe twenty litres of gas. 'Sometimes in life you have to take chances,' he chuckled as I hid behind his wife.

Disappointingly, Mark didn't try to make the bike explode. Instead he diligently, systematically worked backwards – unscrewed the starter button and sprayed the contacts with cleaner, drained the float bowl, checked the spark plug. And laughed – 'Looks like it came out of my grandad's rotavator. Low-grade fuel has burnt the plug, and some joker's belted it up, maintained the gap by bending the earth.' Right – that's bad, is it? 'Bloody journalists. I think that kettle's boiled.'

Two hours and a lot of bad jokes later, it's ready. New plug, oil and filter change, rear MT21 knobbly finally swapped for a tarmac T66, new washer behind the inspection cover (I've no idea what that means, I've just copied it from my notebook), half a pint of oily gunk drained out of the bunged-up breather pipe and that's about it. 'Considering she's just come back from Africa, she's in surprisingly good shape. Good bikes these.'

It is a good bike – I'd forgotten how good, demoralised by a lack of confidence in my own ability to keep it rolling. Zen and the art of motorcycle maintenance sounds groovy and self-reliant, but it's always more reassuring to have a capable man in monogrammed overalls hand back the keys and say, 'It's safe to ride.'

And great to ride – I'd forgotten how funny the XT can be, especially in town, where it's as silly as areolas, all exaggerated lean angles, slalom lane swaps and free-breathing, gorgeous-sounding big-single wallop.

I'm even getting the hang of kick-starts. Which is just what I'd said to the pillion last time. Pride comes before a what? See you on the central reservation.

19

Carry on launching. 'I love crashing!' Rowdy Rob from *Fast Bikes* is jubilantly showing off his gravel rash and trying to pretend that the brand-new Beemer he's picking up isn't pissing oil mist up his legs. Sensible Tim from *Ride*'s executed a textbook road-craft mirror-signal-manoeuvre emergency stop and put on his hazard lights. Professional Kevin from the *Telegraph* has seen it all before and is trying to find the photographer, who's hiding in a bush somewhere, mumbling that he doesn't have to put up with this rubbish at World Supers and grumbling to the birds that there's not enough light. And I'm lurking around at the back, smoking duty-free Ducados and pestering Simon Pavey with irrelevant questions about mechanical bulls and Aboriginal hangover cures.

There's a squadron of BMW mother hens clucking around in matching waterproofs and cop lids, simultaneously trying to convince the journalists that they've never seen a rocker cover burst like that before, while trying to reassure the middle-aged Spanish landowners that there really is no need to call the Guardia Civil, and that it really would be better for everyone if they took their fingers out of their ears, stopped crying and went back inside. Welcome to the unreal world of the motor-cycle launch.

Whenever a new bike is released, there's an accompanying launch – the manufacturer flies the world's press to somewhere appropriate (Misano for Ducatis, Vegas for Harleys, Droitwich for Triumphs), puts them up in a hotel, wines, dines and generally lets them behave like spoilt rock stars for three days, in the hope that their product will get favourable coverage. Politicians would have to declare this kind of behaviour. In any other industry, it'd be called baksheesh. In motorcycling, it's just called good PR.

Days of bread and roses. Kevin Ash is rosier than most – he's been on pretty much every launch since '92, for *Fast Bikes*, for *MCN* and now as freelancer for the *Telegraph*. On the plane to Spain for the GS Adventure launch, he starts talking gifts – there's always a present with the press pack. Sublime? 'A silver ingot worth £400 on the 916 launch – about as subtle as an envelope stuffed with cash. I felt like Neil Hamilton.' Ridiculous? 'A mobile phone from Piaggio that only worked in Italy? A cactus from Kawasaki that was confiscated at the airport? A paddock jacket from Honda with "You've just been passed by a motorcycle journalist" embroidered on the back?' And the seediest? 'The ZX9 launch in '94. On the last night, the Japanese press officer interrupts the cabaret to say, "Problem with motorcycling – too many men. So Kawasaki provide the women." The curtain rises to reveal a comfort battalion of Malaysian girls, "for dancing", obviously. The response is regionally stereotypic – the Brits protest a little too loudly that it's "just not right" while the Italians grab two apiece and swish upstairs with jackets full of condoms and champagne.' And you, Kevin? 'In the finest tradition of quality journalism, I made my excuses and left.'

Gifts, free drink, someone else's motorcycles – this is where the air-brushed world of magazine covers is cultured, a land where the sun always shines, where knees are always down and the riders always look like heroes. Even riders like me. And after just one afternoon on the new GS, I was falling for it. Believing the bullshit. A year riding solo (i.e. with no other riders to show me up) across Africa had convinced me that I was probably pretty good off-road. Not just competent, but

properly tasty – maybe even kissing up to Dakar standard. No, really – that's what I thought. Properly good.

These Dan Quixote tipping-at-windmills delusions were punctured almost immediately – after a day on tarmac, Pavey took us for a refresher in a brick pit. You say 'refresher', I say 'rank humiliation in front of my peers'. Bloody hell, I'm absolutely rubbish. No, really – I ride like an absolute blouse. While Rowdy Rob's tearing it up sideways with 40 mph power slides and *Evening Standard* Simon's nonchalantly skipping up cliff faces, I'm wobbling around in never-decreasing circles, lurching and stalling and footing down, almost in tears 'cause Pavey keeps shouting at me, complaining to anyone who'll listen that I'm really much better on my XT and that the bigger boys are putting me off. I retreat to the bar to do something I'm good at – getting drunk on other people's money and sulking. Bastards.

The next day, it's even worse. When we ride ruts, I'm the only one who has to bail out and jump off. When we ford a stream, I'm the only one to stall and put my feet down (and obviously I'm the only one not wearing proper boots – at least it guaranteed me some space on the plane home. 'Hostess, I demand to be moved – this man smells like a damp dog.'). And when we hit a little bit of mud, I'm the only one who slings it away – I slide off the track, up a bank, think 'I've got away with that' just as I hit a bump, jar my throttle hand like the worst CBT novice and catapult myself into the ditch. All I'm missing is a rake to stand on, a ladder with a bucket on the end and a red nose. I make do with a dislocated knee.

Back in London I hobble off for a drink with Neil. Turns out he fell for exactly the same self-confidence trick after riding from London to

Nairobi in '92. Came back, sold the knackered Tenere and bought a CR500 – the nastiest, hardest motocrosser available.

'First time out, I vanned it to a track in Wiltshire. An old boy watched me unload and started laughing – "Evil bastards, those. This will be fun." It took me half an hour to start the sod. First lap, first time I put it in second gear, it spat me off and broke my foot. The old boy couldn't contain himself – "That's the funniest thing I've seen in years." I was like, "Right, good, anyway I'm just off to the hospital." The bike was left in a mate's garage. I never rode it again. I was so scared and ashamed of it that I used to take the long way round to avoid walking past his house.'

Time for another gin and ibuprofen. Carry on deluding.

20 Mission impossible. The cops have won. They're everywhere. They've got laser-gunning eyes and taser-stunning toes and an army of satellite-tracking technicians and shop-thy-neighbour civilian volunteers locked up in a Cold War bunker under Hampshire, and the only thing they care about, apart from Beckham's foot, is stopping you having fun on your motorcycle. Better get yourself a nice little car. Seen your latest insurance quote? Resistance is useless.

Resistance is useless . . .

'Biker jailed for speeding', 'Council leaders celebrate revenue increase at Spearmint Rhino', 'Speed bad, dope good, says Blunkett'. Defeatist headlines are starting to worry me. Anarchic London's the same as ever – the Met's too busy turning on sirens and tearing up pavements or filing paperwork and sickies in their high-tech fortresses to bother motorcyclists. But the news from the countryside is depressing – Victorian Father zero tolerance has apparently bullied the nation's outlaws onto step-thrus. Is it really that bad out there?

Time to find out. Get back on the road again. Nothing serious, just a three-dayer up to the lower Highlands with the *Bike* road-test team – and while they're testing second-hand tourers, I'm researching a serious question – is it still possible to ride like a twat and get away with it?

First indications aren't good – it is weird out here. The King's Cross train gets held up by a vicar waving a handkerchief, bleating 'cause he can't find a guard to help load his bicycle on board and the buffet car's bursting with silver-haired perms, Thatcherite twinsets and fold-away garden chairs – loud Lincolnshire ladies do love a good royal funeral, and the wall-mounted posters for two cross-eyed photofits who carried out a serious assault on a fellow passenger aren't going to puncture their pride in pomp. I've never been so glad to arrive in Peterborough.

Back on a bike, happy to be on a GS, cheered up to be teamed with Hugo on a Pan and his mate Steve on a Bandit 12, but it's just as sinister. First roundabout, first sunny evening of the year, and the first traffic cops of the trip are skulking in the lay-by, sole purpose stopping local surfers enjoying themselves. Good work, men – must make you real proud. We slink off, muttering. Tomorrow we'll head north.

Despite the sun and the big bikes, the A1's never gonna be anyone's favourite road, reduced to a single-lane sulk for mile after mile, clogged with traffic cones and wagons. One joker's stencilled 'undertakers' and 'overtakers' on his muddy flaps. Not that we're any classier – some mildcard's stickered 'Bad to the Bone' on the Beemer's number plate. I bet he was.

Thank God for the Land of the Prince Bishops. Stuffed with mince and dumplings, we hit the tremendous A68 through County Durham, and finally remember why we're riding bikes. The 68 is the textbook rural rollercoaster A-road, burrowing past Tow Law then Kielder Forest before rising across the border into Scotland and a shocking sequence of shellgripped switchbacks. Ruined by the law? Yeah, right – we ride it as fast as we like, whooping eyes-wide over blind summits with the bikes stretching onto tippy-toes, trampolining out of gullies with bikes compressed flat and our stomachs on the tarmac, chewing up and spitting out occasional pockets of four-wheeled resistance, easily spotting the dalek cameras and using them for braking and top-gear roll-on tests. The only thing that holds us up is, er, me. Damn, I'm slow.

We stop for a smoke at a loch north of Callander and watch the swans glide by. A couple of rough-and-ready kids have escaped the city and plotted up by the water, lazing on the shale shore with tunes, tinnies and spliffs, tents and campfire throwing two snotty fingers at the 'No Camping, No Fires' signpost. You not bothered by the 'No', lads? They look at me like I'm very old. I resist the urge to moonwalk away and instead head off to Glencoe for Guinness and bed. Blunkett will be delighted to learn that the obedient bar closed at eleven o'clock sharp.

Roaming in the gloaming – round and round the drizzly lochs and gloomy glens, larging it for photos – bellies in, knees out, heads down, chins up, fake it baby, 60 mph inches away from a Ford Focus, snapper Chip sat in the open boot ordering us left, right, faster, slower. It's hardly Hendon Roadcraft. Eventually we get spotted by the cops. Here we go? Er, no. 'Boys, boys, that looks terribly dangerous,' lilts a WPC in an inappropriately tight skirt and rather too much slap. 'Promise me you'll be careful?' Yes, ma. Sorry, ma. Airstrip One it ain't.

We head south, chasing the sun, taunting the daleks. Forget the Turner Prize, we've got our own high-speed version of *Light On, Light Off*, crossing the white line to trigger the cameras on the other side of the road, smug in the knowledge that all they'll capture are dark visors or sneers. Childish? Damn right.

Somehow we end up in a Mansfield tractor park. A Husqvarna barks past, spots our cameras and turns around. We know what's coming, but we're way impressed with the quality as he lifts up the front as easily as tipping a beer bottle, settles on the balance point and thumps past through first, second, third, fourth, five hundred yards of gloriously controlled motorcycle hooliganism. Husky do.

So have the bad guys won? Have they fuck. 'The level of cop has never been thinner, it's a runaway race where we're the winners.' So what if the daleks are spreading like foot-and-mouth? It kinda makes it more fun, more cat-and-mouse. Breaking the law is sexy, always has been. Cigarettes were so much more glamorous when we were too young to smoke, kissing always had that extra frisson when her parents were upstairs, and speed tastes better because it is illegal. Don't believe the hype. Worry less, ride more. And keep speeding.

21

'Hey, asshole. You look bored. Wanna race us wrong ways round this traffic circle?' Oh Jesus, no. Just another Saturday afternoon in central London, so why am I about to get nicked? The bored asshole? A motorbike cop. The roundabout? Parliament Square – yeah, that one. 'I think you'd better take your pillion friend away, sir.' The pillion? Crazy bastard himself, Pete Smalls. 'Chicken shit!' Will you shut up?

Pete Smalls – started out as just another busted crank caller on the *Bike* office phone, must have been May 1998. He was selling his story – 'Yankee in the Court of King Joey. I've been touring Europe on my Suzi 750, pissin' about in the Alps, now I fancy racing the TT.' I was buck-stopper and happy to chat – it beat answering questions from born-agains who couldn't decide between a Blackbird and Biposto. I tell him we'll be staying in the Empress on Douglas Prom. Drop in and have a beer. That was supposed to be that. But he did drop in. And he did have a beer. And he did enter the TT – on the roadbike GSX-R he'd been touring, on a circuit he'd never seen before, let alone raced. The moment he qualified for the Production Race was the moment people stopped sneering.

Of course he crashed. Spectacularly. Went straight on at the bottom of Sulby Straight, 140 mph take-off, landed in a field. 'Jefferies flew further,' sneered a disappointed marshal. Pete does the post-crash flex and is relatively happy to find that the only damage is to his balls – tank-splashed so hard he can't stand up. St John Ambulance rush over. What hurts? My balls. Your legs? My balls. Your neck? My balls. Your back? The marshal tries – I think it's his balls. While Pete's talking bollocks, the paddock sweats – all we know is that the rookie Yank has crashed on one of the fastest, least forgiving parts of the island, and the Noble's Hospital helicopter has been launched. An hour later he's in a nappy in the hotel bar, sinking whiskies and telling stories about Vietnam. Twelve hours later he's in his underpants in my hotel room, smoking a chillum and having flashbacks.

He calls every couple of weeks or so from his ranch in the Idaho boonies, full of life and death – near misses with deer, cross-border raids on the RCMP, his ever-expanding motorcycle collection: 'Turns out I've actually got four not three RC30s. Spare frame, spare engine, spare wheels, a whole spare fucking bike. Which is neat, 'cause I just smashed one up.' I was expecting more of the insane when he called last week. Where are you – at home? 'No, Mike's Bikes in Bow. Come and pick me up, will ya?'

Mike's Bikes – a neo-Dickensian backstreet garage rental gaff, hidden away from MOT inspectors in the East End's industrial cheapscape. Been there for years – I rented my first courier CGs and CXs from them. Different name now, same safe-house location, different Aussie mechanics, same snarling Alsatians, different bikes, same indifferent attitude. I guess that's the R1 Pete hired and slammed into the Continent – the one with the orange-peel tyre and no number plate.

He's in the café, glaring at an English breakfast. 'What is it with you guys and fried eggs? It's 'cause they remind you of the sun, right? Get real close and you'll get a tan, right?' He's equally unhappy with my bike. 'What the fuck is that? It looks like a duck.' It's a Bulldog. And no, it isn't very cool. I wasn't expecting guests. 'Where we going? Fighting at the soccer?' No, Brick Lane market – I've gotta buy a lamp.

Brick Lane market – a car boot sale for people who can't afford cars. If you want to know what Britain will look like after a nuclear war (pencilled in for third week in December), come down here and mingle with the economic, political, emotional, alcoholic refugees, native and distant, flogging the life out of dead houses. Ukrainians fence bins full of plaster-splattered power tools, Brazilians toss off bin liners full of hand-made porn, an old dear sells her late husband's early Leyton Orient programmes. Sometimes it's difficult to separate the merchandise from the litter. Slummed-down Shoreditch twats in deliberately filthy footwear haggle hard-faced over must-have rare vinyl and ironic trinkets. Pale-faced youths in tracksuits hunt Indians, looking for eyes to catch, spitting 'own country' and 'belong'. And a grey-bearded American in scuffed Daineses is talking all kinds of nonsense to the Chinese bicycle peddlers. What are you looking for, Pete? 'Monkey sweat and an electric hat.' Man, get back on the bike.

Pete Smalls rides pillion like, er, a TT-racing combat veteran. A builders' van strays across our lane on the Mile End Road – Pete's stood on the pegs, booting the door. 'I've got guns that'll make a hole in you so big you could throw a dog through it.' Red light at the Royal London Hospital, he's winking at a minibus full of student nurses. 'Wanna make little me's?' (Bizarrely, they flash their bras. I categorically will never understand women.) Pedestrian crossing on Charing Cross Road, clogged with peace demonstrators on the march. I toot my horn supportively at a gang of PLO flags, he grabs my throttle hand. 'Don't startle them! I hear one of them ticking!' Eventually I get him home. 'Where's the pub? Let's have pints, lad.' Next morning, he's gone before I'm up. There's a note. 'Always pull the cat's teeth out before pouring gravy on its vagina.'

A week later I get another call. He's heading to California for a month. Taking his son, the Gixer Thou and the R6. It's a business trip, buying South American gold, but there'll be time to ride the canyon roads and race a couple of tracks. 'Anyway, if I take the bike, I can't get followed and jacked. Colombians, man, trained in Bogotá, real pros.' Pete, by the way, is 56. Hope I die before I get old? Give over.

22 Get your motor running. The American Dream, the coast-to-coast — the motorcyclist's mesmeric mirage of big journeys, bigger roads and biggest skies, sizzling black bitumen scars snaking between cinnamon reds and cactus greens beneath a bright, denim blue; Cornish pasty-faced English rider transformed into pinched-eyed cowboy drifter, getting all tangled up in pan-fried diners and honky-tonk bars while heading for that heat-hazed horizon. It's *On the Road* meets *Hell's Angels on Wheels* meets *Wild at Heart*. And it's probably absolute nonsense. But I've decided to see for myself.

America, baby. It's all in the names — New York, New Orleans and New Mexico, Dakota, Sioux Falls and Cheyenne, Los Angeles, Los Alamos and Las Vegas. Just join the dots.

I'm looking at a different kind of coast-to-coast, suspicious that the old, clichéd Route 66 is just that, a dead-straight trawl through honking homogeneous cities and drive-thru monoculture, but inspired by the website transamtrail.com — fuzzy pictures and understated reports of a trail running from Nashville to Pacific Portland, four and half thousand miles of gravel, dust and sand, camping, cabins and creeks.

Sounds perfect — *On the Road* becomes Off the Road and a plan becomes The Plan.

The Plan — fly into New York, drift south on the tarmac to Nashville and hit the trail for a month of cross-country off-roading, then back onto the black stuff for the Pacific Coast Highway, North Cal to Mexico.

Maybe stop for a while in LA – grab some courier work or try my hand at B-movie scriptwriting. ('From the people who brought you *Thighs Wide Slut* and *Schindler's Fist* comes *Ben Hurts* etc.)

The Plan only becomes real when the bike is sorted. Nothing beats that 'What bike?' question, sat sitting on the khazi with coffee and mags, like a kid before Christmas hunched over the toy section of the Argos catalogue – 'That one, no, that one.' (Fast-forward five years, same kid hunched over a speeding fist and the underwear section of the Argos catalogue – 'That one, no, that one' etc.)

So tarmac and trails, maybe a pillion, definitely lumpy luggage. We're talking proper adventure bikes, dual sports, bikes off-road enough to be chucked confidently at sandy ruts, on-road enough to be walloped down freeways, and sexy enough to get me out of my tent on drizzly, hung-over mornings.

The XT will do all that – sort of. But I've fallen out of love with it – sorry, baby, it's not you, it's me. Always feels kinda odd replacing something that isn't broken, just because of glossy brochures, 'I reckon I'd be loads quicker on that' delusions and 'reward me' consumer vanities. But my head's been turned and, anyway, I've promised to sell it. Gorgeous George, an overlanding cyclist I met in Dar es Salaam, fancies the Great Silk Road and fancies swapping thigh power for horse power. He made me an offer I couldn't refuse and we'll be swapping keys and memories for money next month, inshallah.

So what next? Through a process that had very little to do with spec-sheet logic or sensible comparisons, and lots to do with groovy colour schemes, classy badges and implied ruggedness, I've narrowed it down

to four – red Honda, white BMW, yellow Suzuki, orange KTM, green Husqvarna. Five, then. Road tests that back me up get photocopied, greasy and dog-eared. Opinions that disagree with me get ignored – drooling over matt black supermoto pit bulls and lurid green enduro treefrogs in a Shepherd's Bush Husky dealer, I even end up contradicting the refreshingly honest sales manager when he suggests that these bikes might not be suitable. 'But look at them – and look at that badge.' The XT sulks through the window – 'How could you? I took you to Timbuktu and back.' Sometimes you don't get to choose who you fall in love with.

I consult another expert, Dakar rider Si Pavey. Turns out he's got two of the possibles in his shed – a BMW F650GS, plus his Honda XR650R rally bike. 'Why not come down and take them for a spin?' Get in.

First out is the Beemer, looking tough enough in worn Twinduros, without indicators or mirrors – Pavey uses this bike to instruct on BMW's off-road schools. And it's nice – nice engine, nice handling, nice styling. Nice. Maybe too nice – could I really own a bike called a 'Funduro'? As I said, logic's out the window.

And then he unzips the XR. Oh. My. God. Nipple-high, devil red, still sandy from its last desert race, packing more kit than a yomping marine, and, oops, oh my, I'm in love. Just another plastic dirt bike? The XR is the off-road FireBlade, make that the snarling original, not the polite contemporary. And this is a pukka race version – think popping down to Colin McRae's to borrow his Subaru WRX or bobbing round to David Jefferies to borrow his TT R1. Think underqualified jerk tottering round a south-east London housing estate on a bike capable of winning the Dakar.

I'm quivering. Throw a leg over, catch a lace on the rear tanks and, er, drop it. The brake light breaks. Pick it up quick before Pavey sees. No ignition barrel so no key, just top dead centre and give it a big kick. Christ, what a noise. And Christ, what a bike. Tall as a bus, fleet as a cheetah, crazy as legs, the next half-hour's a chuckling blur of short shifts, giant leaps and sawn-off backfires. Pavey waves me down – 'The rear lights aren't working. Wonder why?'

Er, I've no idea, Si. Anyway, gotta dash. Gotta get an XR. Gotta figure out a way to raise four grand. Keep scheming.

23 Cruisin USA
Milwaukee to Atlanta via Indianapolis and Nashville.

What made Milwaukee famous made a loser out of me? Not this time. Sat on a Vee Rod at a Tennessee pike crossroads watching the Christmas tree traffic lights swinging on a wire, reading 'Wrong Way', 'O'Reilly for Sheriff' and 'Reagan's Butchers – No-one Beats Our Meat' when the mirrors fill with grunting green. Lane and a half wide, horse and a half tall, it's an all-American Road Toad. It's a Hum-Vee. And it wants to play.

Let's go. Red green bite me, militia boy. Vee-Rod v Hum-Vee, Vee-twin v six litre vee eight, vee dumb v vee dumber. He woofs, I burble, we rear up and gallop away, arms stretched, teeth bared, corny as cowboys, so happy I could whistle through my willy as we tear past the Primitive Baptist Church, past Uncle Porky's Hickery Wood BBQ, past The Farmers' Bank and right past Officer Dibble.

Shit, it's Sherriff O'Reilly. Brown and white prowl car, blunt nosed Ford Interceptor with headbutting ram-bars screeches a uey across the road and pulls alongside. Pull over. A bullish cropped copper in slightly too tight brown pants lumbers out, hitches up his gunbelt and gives me his best John Wayne roll and drawl. I think he says 'Where you headed?', but it's difficult to tell through the chewin tobacco slur, all gurgle and lazy vowels – guess he saves up his konsonants for the monthly klan klavern kapers. Er, Lynchburg. 'Lynchburg? Hope you're goin there on purpose cause it ain't on the way to anywhere'. Right. 'Shaw is purty –

that big dawg pull like they say?' Er, yep. He spits, salutes and prowls off. That's it? That's it. Which proves either that Southern cops have gone soft, or just that good ol boys love good ol Harleys.

Harley's are officially ol'. One hundred years ol'. Happy Birthday, Harley. Or Happy Birthday, Davidson. The present president Willie G Davidson is son of co-counder William Davidson, father of Vice President Bill Davidson. Someone should get those Davidson women a book of names for Christmas. Ask what happened to the Harleys and people shrug and mutter something about a washerama in Des Moines. They've become the Andrew Ridgleys of motorcycling.

It's a family affair. Willie and Bill smile for the cameras and unveil the 100th Anniversary, extra-special, all-new, revolutionary, explosive, never before see on a motorcycle, laydees and gennulmen we give you, ta-daaaa – er, a new paint job. And redesigned badges. Sorry, cloisonnés. Only Harley would fly the world's press all the way to Milwaukee to admire a new spray job. And only the Harley press would respond excitedly with low-whistles and flash-gun pops. Can't imagine Ducati doing that. But then again, can't imagine Ducati selling sixty percent of the big bike market in the US.

We don't just get to admire the paint schemes, we get to ride them too. A thousand miles, from Harley's down-home hometown Milwaukee to Atlanta, via Indianapolis and Nashville. A whistle-stop tour of industrial, rural, cultural America. Starting right here on the edge of the Great Lakes, two hours north of sweet home Chicago. What made Milwaukee famous? Beer and motorcycles and Liberace. Let's drink and ride, pretty boy.

There's no such thing as a free bike. Before the ride, the PR schmooze and a factory tour schnooze. Try to look innarested, but it's hard – the monotonous repetition of assembly line mass production makes anything bland and soulless. Break Kate Moss down into her component parts, label them and put them on a bench underneath a 'Don't Mess with the US' flag and see how attractive she looks then. This is where we make the livers.

Lathes, robots, mullets and slogans stolen from Pol Pot. '2003 – The Year of Continuous Improvement' reads a sinister banner over the snack vending machine. No-one else thinks that's funny. Improve or be improved. Not improving enough, Walsh. Off to the Improvement Camp for six-sixty months. Let's get outta here.

Beer and bikes and Liberace. Add them all together and what have you got? The Vee Rod – the bike that redefined Harley in Europe from tart's handbag to man's dragbike – the Harley that it's okay to like – the Harley that's almost cool. The one with the Porsche-designed liquid-cooled lump and the future retro liquid metal styling. The Americans think it's Robo-cop brutal. I think it's Dan Dare comical. With its lava-lamp lines, spherical TV console controls and barrel-chested, superhero space ranger musculature, it comes on like a fifties view of the nineties. We'll eat pills instead of meals, holiday on Venus and Barberella will ride pillion on cycles that look like armoured robotic Weimerana hounds. KKK9.

And it walks the walk. All show, enough go. Harleys tend to flatter to deceive. Despite the babies-arms statistics, they've never really been able to get it up. But this one's got German performance lead in its pencil. Viag-ja. 'First time on a Vee Rod?' shouts snapper JC.

'Make sure I'm watching when you gas it. Your face will be a picture'. Damn, I'm excited. Paddle out of the bikepark, onto a wide, residential boulevard that's all tall, lonely wooden houses shadowed by tall, lonely wooden trees. Hang back to let the chromosexuals in front get away and wrench that fat throttle hard. And laugh and nod and whoop and brake and do it again, do it again, because fucking hell it works. It really works. It really goes. And it really stops. It's how we dreamed Harleys felt when we saw them in the movies, before we rode them and discovered they were as disappointing as a first beer. Gah – what was all the fuss about? But this is proper. A properly fast, properly daft Harley.

Onto Kelly Road, heading for Antioch and Lake Geneva. No-one else thinks that's funny. The Vee Rod's low and long. And supposedly heavy, but I never noticed till I looked at the spec sheet. The weight's there, but it feels appropriate rather than cumbersome, even at low-speeds. Kinda gives me hairy-arsed substance, anti-social big turd satisfaction, sitting in this dense, shiny bauble, feet forward, arms stretched, hands curled round the stubby beercan grips. Makes me feel kinda er mean. I'm a heart breaker, a lifetaker. A murderer. And at speeds, like a water skier who needs no boat or a windsurfer who needs no wind. Just plenty of hot air.

The murderous water-skier look is obviously big over here. Americans love this bike. It gets the kind of attention that would make Kylie's arse blush. Black kids with sloppy jeans and razor haircuts throw arthritic hand signs. I'm ghetto fabulous. A nu-metal girl with a face full of bolts and braces asks where the party is. I'm a freak. Greybeards with veteran's eyes throw thumbs-up out of pick-ups. I'm a patriot. And blond moms on school-runs start fiddling with mirrors and tousling their hair. I'm sexy. No need for Charles Atlas with a big bike and a dark visor.

Thirty odd Harleys pull into a dealers for a Fatboy breakfast. Sausage-and-cream-smothered fat steaks and skinny fries, bottomless coffees, top-heavy waitresses. A heart-attack on a plate. Drugs didn't kill Elvis, breakfast did. Our Road Captain, a shouting bear of a man who apparently withers and dies if everybody isn't paying him all their attention all of the time, tells us that in the state of Wisconsin helmets aren't compulsory but sunglasses are. 'In America it's illegal to be uncool,' splutters an easily impressed Belge. He's not being sarcastic. Dress like Will Smith or fall foul of the suede denim secret police.

Wisconsin's flat, Illinois is flatter, Indiana is flattest, but the traffic's a weird scream of weirder bumper stickers. 'Tough Guys Wear Bow Ties' lies a dog-faced kid in a Dodge. 'Keep Honking, Asshole, I'm Reloading' screams someone's rat-faced granny. 'Guns-save-life dot com' growls a pencil-necked suit geek (yeah, you tell the maniac that his grammar's as twisted as his politics). 'Breast fed is best fed' slurs a meretricious inflatable doll who looks like she'd give Baby a mouthful of silicon jelly.

American English doesn't mean anything. Even the sign posts are weird. We pass Bloomington Normal. No-one else thinks that's funny. We pass Ogle County, home of the peeping Tom, and Menomonee. That's not a place, it's an annoying song. That you'll now be singing. Bad language is contagious.

We pull into the Indianopolis Speedway. It's closed. Simon, another Brit, just been thrown off for wheeling a 1200 Sporster in front of an appalled marshall. 'You haven't missed much'. The locals call this India-no-place or The Brick House in the Cornfield or Naptown. I take their word for it and get an early night.

Freeways, interstates, motorways, autoroutes – alright, there's no bends to bend and they can get kinda tedious, but sometimes they're just right – feeling of big space, rolling roads, trucking travelling. We fuel up and I swap the Vee Rod for an Electra Glide Ultra classic, full-faired, full-fat, full-funny, stereo cranked up, cruise control on, lid off, brain out, sat on the pillion seat, steering with my feet, playing the 'how long can I go without touching the bars?' game. About seven minutes. Freebird never sounded so damn good. Love Will Tear Us Apart would've sounded even better.

Back on the Vee Rod and the sounds are just as fine. Standard American pipes are louder than ours. They have to be. Because Americans shout. ALL THE TIME. Jesus, settle down, I'm sat right next to you. This bike's singing through after-market Screaming Eagles. Loud enough to enjoy without being embarrassing – a bassy burble that becomes a guttural gargle that becomes a snot-thick arr-rrolling snarl as the revs rise, pitched perfectly as the soundtrack to Vanishing Point. Obvious but true – the Vee Rod is a two-wheeled Dodge Challenger – it's got lazy wallop, heavy v-shaped flutter and that big dawg charm, one arm out of the window style that lets you do slow and easy as well as fast and frantic.

Just as well – these highways are heavily patrolled, and these cop cars can zap you from in front, from behind, from the other side of the road. Old pros use big trucks as cover. 'The radar won't work if you're within a hundred yards of a semi' says the Road Captain. No-one else thinks this is funny.

Next stop Nashville. The Broken Heart of Country Music, the Darwinian end of Daniel Boone's Wilderness Trail, and the home of

Maxwell House coffee. We're booked into the Opryland Gaylord Resort. No-one else seems to think that's funny. The hotel has 2800 rooms. So large it has its own zip code and employs people specifically to help guests find their way to their rooms. My room is in the Cascades – an area recognisable by the three-storey high, indoor waterfall. I'm beat – better join them. Dress up like a rockabilly and head for the swinging door saloon for some Southern sedation.

'Objects in Your Mirror May Be Closer Than You Think'. Even with a hangover, that's the dumbest thing I've ever read. Cue Father Ted explaining perspective to Dougal – 'these cows are small, those cows are far away'. Closer than you think, and more intrusive than they mean to be. It's hard feeling adventurous with a 'please look after this bear' emergency phone number tag round your neck and a pair of corporate minders in your mirrors. Just outside Nashville I throw the dummies a dummy and ditch the interstate for some country lanes.

Flat Indiana's become green Tennessee, and as the traffic speeds increase, life slow downs. More I travel across the US, the more it becomes a collection of fifty different states, the less it becomes one homogenous country. People change, accents change, attitudes change. There's a stereotype of idiosyncratic laid-back, course I've got the time, southern hospitality, and folks down here seem keen to love up to it. 'Have a nice day, now get out of my face' Northern brusqueness and company-taught manners replaced by genuine 'hey y'all, how are you? Who are you? What you doing here?' interest. Shopkeepers smile and mean it – old boys doff hats and wink. Only thing missing are the animals. In three days, I don't see a single cow or sheep. They've all been eaten.

Warm summer rain makes the old road's over-banding twitchy and gives the Vee Rod a winker's tic. Time for a stop. Jack Daniel's Distillery, Lynchburg, Population 361. What made Milwaukee famous made a boozer out of me? Not this time – Moore County's dry. You can make it, sell it, distribute its peculiar Guns and Roses meets the Waltons image to half the known world, but you can't sip sour mash here. No problem. Plot up in its sleepy, timbered courtyard, pull up a chair and watch the old Tennessee squires whittle. Three hours meander by, lazy as esses. Rockin and a sippin. Shredded sweet pork, cowboy beans, washed down with icy real lemon-ade. Rockin and a sippin.

Back onto the bike. There's a couple more Harleys in the carpark, gently modified Lowriders. Girls in Daisy Duke denim, boys in Jack Daniel's cut-offs flirt with the Vee Rod. 'I seen one in pictures, but never in real life. Not round here,' says Jack. 'That costs more than twenty thousand dollars. Is it yours?' cooes Daisy Number One. 'Yep'. I lie. Money doesn't talk, it swears. I can't resist roostering gravel as I chip out. Flash and fraudulent on someone else's bike.

It's dry and close. The road messes about by the rivers, clatters across canyon bridges and sweats round brackwater backwaters and faux smugglers jetties. Even when the funk gets stickier, the Vee Rod keeps on dancing. Chasing my tail uphill, first a boot scrape then a peg scrape, but I'm a long way off the exhaust which will apparently lift the rear. Yeah it's barge-long but it's also rigid – that hydro-formed frame, crinkles blown out by high-pressure water jets when it's still blue-hot, isn't just polished it's pole-ish stiff. Give it the bum steer and sling that dawgie home.

Er, this ain't home. This could be anywhere. I think it's Winchester,

Tennessee. Two-room wooden shacks, verandas clogged with kids' bikes and who knows what, drives full of rusty pick ups and cheesy muscle cars, mailboxes full of 'You may already be a millionaire' junk and 'We have charged you $20 for this letter' final reminders. A graffittied mural in confederate colours reads 'Rebellettes'. Old boys in dungarees hang around outside pharmacies, selling hill-billy heroin prescriptions to bored country youth. I like it around here. It's worrying and poor and completely out of whack with the normal view of America.

Deliberately hit a red light so I can play again, show out again. I've got the hang of this. Walking pace, clutch in, big handful, clutch out, and feel it squirm and shiver and rev out and fuck off. Damn, this bike is entertaining, easy enough to be mastered by a putz but still slightly dangerous feeling, playing will-she or won't she spit or wallow with twenty three thousand dollars worth of motorcycle. Bikes rock.

Georgia's on my mind. Atlanta arrives at night, all lit up like a commercial Disneyland, scraper after scraper, blues and greens and twinkling aircraft warning lights. Home to Dr Martin Luther King and Coca-Cola and CNN. This town's big – bigger than anywhere I've been outside of New York, and brasher too – American capitalism at its brashest best or worst, build it and they will come, build it bigger and they will come and lend you money and buy your things. Warm air, short sleeves, oil money, feels like Saudi. And the bike makes me feel like a million bucks, just as brash, just as comfortable, pouting back at the waving commuters, as smug as a conceited nudist. What made Milwaukee famous made a cruiser out this me? Damn right. Happy Birthday, Harley.

A week in the wilderness
listening to the fire pop,
the crickets chirp and the
stars twinkle, and if this
isn't nice, what is?' –
Mali, 2001

MINISTERE DE LA CULTURE ET DE LA COMMUNICATION
MISSION CULTURELLE DE TOMBOUCTOU

DJINGAREY BERRE   UNIVERSITE DE SANKORE
GORDON LAING   DJAN TENDE
RENE CAILLE   NASBA MAROCAINE
TOMBOUT-KOY BATOUMA   AL FAROUN
D— BERKY   ES SBOLI
Dr HENRICH BARTH   ES SAHELI
MOHAMED BAGAYOGO   ES SAYOUTI
SIDI YAHYA   HOTEL BOUCTOU
YONDU BER   HOTEL AZALAI
OSCAR LENZ
MOSQUEE DE SANKORE   ITINERAIRE
EL ADIR   TOURISTIQUE

'You people think Timbukto
is at the end of the world.
But I am from Timbukto, and
I know that we are at the
very heart of the world'
Timbukto, Mali, 2001

To the memory of
MAJOR
ALEXANDER GORDON LAING
2nd. WEST INDIA REGIMENT.

The explorer who, at the cost of his life,
reached Timbuktu in 1826.

Erected in his honour by
THE ROYAL AFRICAN SOCIETY
in 1963.

You're never alone
in Africa...

Surrounded by
smiles at a smoke
and coke stop by
the river Niger,
Mali

Niafounke market -
note '24 hour
bitch' t-shirt

Southern African
seaside shanty

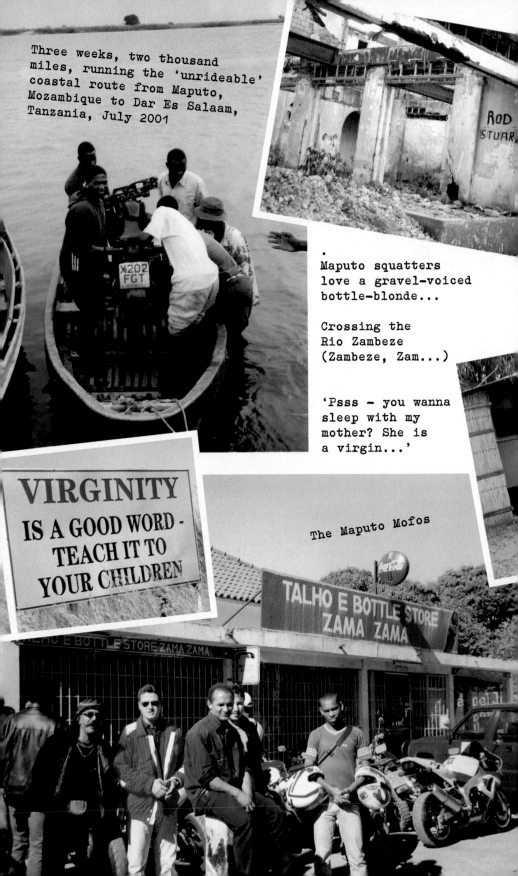

Three weeks, two thousand miles, running the 'unrideable' coastal route from Maputo, Mozambique to Dar Es Salaam, Tanzania, July 2001

Maputo squatters love a gravel-voiced bottle-blonde...

Crossing the Rio Zambeze (Zambeze, Zam...)

'Psss - you wanna sleep with my mother? She is a virgin...'

VIRGINITY IS A GOOD WORD - TEACH IT TO YOUR CHILDREN

The Maputo Mofos

TALHO E BOTTLE STORE ZAMA ZAMA

ADULT

GIFTS ... OVIES

STOCKISTS OF HUSTLER MAGAZINES

South African
synthetic smut peddlar

Maputo's Corniche

Looking for
coffee outside
Maxixe

Port St Johns - a one cop town at the mouth of a hippo-fat river where the mountains meet the sea on South Africa's Wild Coast

It doesn't get any better than this – waking up with no plans,
spending ten minutes working out an unknown route, spending
ten days making it real – Sani Pass, Lesotho, August 2001

'I've gotta pick the boy up from school. Wanna come with me?' Damp December twilight in the crumbling concrete badlands of south-east London and Simon Pavey's gearing up for some serious errand running. Wallet, keys, goggles, kid lid and, er, £20,000 worth of desert racer? That should do it. We could take the van? 'Nah, I need to grind the wax off my knobblies.' This should be a hoot.

I skip over to the XT while he nudges that blue rhinoceros over a tip of muddy tyres, round a red-dusty XR650 and into the yard. It's a BMW F650 Dakar, wearing an outsize Touratech Rallye kit utility belt. It's bloody enormous. 'And it's bloody loud.'

He didn't actually have to tell me that. I'd noticed. Felt my teeth rattle, seen the curtains twitch, heard the car alarms trigger. And almost been knocked sideways by the back-blast – every blip of the throttle makes the end can explode and belch out a fistful of gas so strong it feels like I'm riding into a flock of seagulls. Not the first time this week I've been hit by a bird. 'Why don't you ride in front?'

I would if I could get past. Quiet man, noisy rider. Off the road, on the road, Pavey's as raucous as his race pipe, yomping through commuter jammed sandwiches, walloping past startled school-run mums, wheelying past the Woolwich Catholic Club, Belmarsh Prison and the Antigallican pub in a bellowing, blue Beemer blur. I give up trying and just enjoy it, revelling in the madness of a rally bike lighting up the Blockbuster and KFC high-street mundanity. 'Incongruous' doesn't really cover it. Apparently 'heavy' does. 'That is well heavy,' coo Pavey

Junior's midget mates as eleven-year-old Llewellyn, already a tasty motocross rider, takes a running jump at the pillion seat. 'Dad, you're a nutter.'

Pavey is a nutter. Must be, this is his third Dakar Rally. 'I know I always say this, but it is the ultimate off-road challenge.' He shrugs and bites into a cheese toastie. 'The racing's the easy part. Getting the sponsorship is harder.' Somehow too-tall thumpers and flat-twin Beemers racing across the Sahara is duller than multi-million-pound concept bikes flashing round a closed circuit in Malaysia. In the universe next door, Stéphane Peterhansel tattoos outsell Foggy books, and a radical race rep means a Gauloises paint scheme, three feet of suspension bounce and a tank and seat big enough for a Manchester wait-and-return. On this side of the looking glass, we have SP2s. Hurray.

The good side of all this ignorance is that the Dakar has maintained its core of keen amateurs (cue Roger Atyeo's best joke – 'There are no hookers on the Isle of Man, but plenty of keen amateurs'). A rash of dilettante entries in the eighties by goofy minor European royalty and Mark Thatcher-type arms dealers gave the rally an ugly image of soiled rich kids taking expensive adventure holidays in other people's misery, but the truth is more down to earth – passionate enthusiasts scratching around for entry fees and plunging themselves into debt. Which is why I'm interviewing Britain's brightest Dakar hope not at vainglorious Goodwood but in a Thamesmead council flat. That's a good thing.

'I guess I was just lucky.' The harder you work, the luckier you become. Pavey's always worked hard for his sponsors, suffered the meedja, grafted with BMW, and it's paid off – BMW GB are providing the bike and Touratech bits, and a punter from the Off Road Skills school with a big enough heart and deep enough pockets has weighed in with the rest. 'His name's Neil Miller, he's got a company called Dome, we got chatting after the course.' Viva Team Dome.

What goes around comes around. Ever since we've known Pavey he's been involved with a charity called the Archway Project. Based on his notorious estate, it gives local kids a positive alternative to dividing along racial lines and kicking each other to death round the back of Iceland by getting them involved with motorcycling instead. They take knacker's yard wrecks, learn how to rebuild them, and race round motocross tracks. Like the Dakar, that's just too good an idea to catch on. Nick Plumb, Pavey's Team Dome team-mate and fellow off-road instructor, started out in the Archway Project.

Three weeks, 6000 miles. How's the training? Chirpy wife Linley laughs. 'Bloody marvellous. Especially when he decided to play footy and got taken out by a chunky teenager. Knocked him into a barbed-wire fence and dislocated his shoulder. He's sticking to swimming now.' She chuckles and I say something inappropriate. Do you worry? 'No. He was doing this when I met him; it's what makes him happy. I wouldn't have married an accountant.'

There's a pause. John Deacon, Pavey's friend, riding partner, Britain's best ever desert racer, was killed last year in Syria. Get involved with Pavey, with BMW Off-Road, with the Dakar, and his presence is still there, lingering like cigar smoke, large as ever, not in a creepy way, but in a 'he'll walk through that door any second' way. 'For a time it was hard, but now I'm ready to race again. You gonna ride that bike or what?'

Damn right. I can't wait to strain a leg over this angular sled. First impressions? Tall, noisy, solid, rigid, and surprisingly easy to ride. Looks and snorts like an armoured warhorse, rides like a dainty dressage pony. I've wankered around on all of his previous rally bikes, and compared to those lurching savages, it's positively urbane. Definitely BMW. Though once it hits sand it will be the same as any other overloaded rally raider – aggressive, twitchy, like steering a cow by the tail. Which is what Pavey will be doing when this magazine hits the shelves. Bonne route, bonne chance, Si. And Viva Team Dome.

'Dan, phone.' Yes, ma. 'It's an Australian girl called Kylie.' She does a mum dance, all pointing fingers and cocked legs, and starts singing falsetto, 'You just can't get her out of your head.'

But it's not the disco-dancing, puckered pop bum, it's better than that. It's Kylie from BMW GB, and that means one thing. 'Your bike's ready for pick-up.' Get in.

Cheshire to East Yorkshire, Knutsford to Doncaster, my ma's house to BMW's main distribution centre, should be a dreary, mundane chore. Instead, it's a cheery, exciting mission. There's still nothing better than that new-bike feeling, that unfulfilled potential excitement, those 'this time I'll look after it and learn to ride proper' slate-cleaning, self-deluding fibs, even it does mean riding an increasingly geriatric XT along the country's most dismal motorway in typically tragic January weather.

The M62 in the rain. Christ. Out of Manchester, it's downhill and up moor all the way. Past Oldham and Bolton's dark satanic mills, across the naturally bleak and inhumanly cruel Saddleworth Moor (trying not to remember what makes it unforgettable. And failing), grumble two lanes of shit-spraying wagons, swaying in the canvas-flapping side wind, and one lane of aggressively impatient 'gotta get to Hull by 14.15' tailgating Vauxhall drivers. I never thought I'd be so pleased to get to Doncaster.

Donny – home to Brian Blessed, Diana Rigg, Thomas Crapper, the

Flying Scotsman and BMW GB. I'm led through plastic door flaps, across a dazzlingly clean warehouse full of box-fresh executive toys (is that the new Z4?) and clipboard ticking white-coats. In a corner, a man called Ray is fitting knobbly tyres to a jacked-up 650 Dakar. My new bike. Hello, baby.

Surprisingly, it looks kind of tough. Surprisingly, because F650s are not cool. Maybe it's the daft name ('Funduro – a funny cross between "fun" and "enduro", ya?' No. Now piss off, Hans), maybe it's the 'like a GS but for midgets or girls' tag, maybe it's that inescapably middle-class, golf-club badge, but they've become the kind of bikes that middle-aged dentists pick for 'me-time' sabbatical trips from New York to Patagonia, born-again bourgeois beatniks with meticulously detailed websites meticulously detailing their packing arrangements and vaccination schedules. Practical, urbane, worthy, smug. *Hello!* on wheels.

But this looks different. And decidedly second-hand. It's a rescue dog, liberated from a bad home at the Off Road Skills school, its short life full of muddy puddles, low-speed spills and grassy high sides. The rear shoulder panel's been smashed up, patched up and lashed up with butterfly-stitched cable ties. It's an improvement – dicks dig scars. And it's lost its mirrors. This seems to help. A dentist who doesn't care what's going on behind him? Cool.

Ride without prejudice. Forget the old Funduro, this is a great, different motorcycle. Tall enough to give that big-bike feel to a big lump like me, narrow enough to be fired between seething Friday commuter jams with gay abandon, fast enough to whir happily at 90 with a fistful of swerving burst still in reserve, comfy enough for Donny to Manchester non-stop, easy enough to have me instantly dreaming of rocky pistes down Mexico's Copper Canyon. I like this bike. The only downside is it's cross-eyed – Ray reckons the bars are bent, I know the cockpit clocks are out of whack with the fairing. At low speeds it means aim right to go straight. It's like talking to a man with a glide. You looking at her or me?

Three days on, I like it even more. I love the upright, rigid balance and exaggerated sense of lean that only comes with a flick-flacking big trail bike. I love the rugged, Tonka-tyred, big-wheeled stance. I love the metallic, mechanical substance that makes it feel more like a Steve McQueen Triumph scrambler than a plastic Mike Metzger moto-crosser. And I love the perennial potential – I've always wanted a bike that I can keep for ever, ride around the world and around the clock, rebuild and redesign and eventually retire into a front-room place of pride. This could be the one.

First, some changes. Nothing serious, just tweaks to cope with the next few months' jaunt across the States and Central America. The bent bars will be replaced with stand-up, elbows-out, high-rised Renthals. A Laser pipe will lose weight, bin the green but impractical cat (low-octane bush petrol will ruin it anyway) and, muy importante, change the sound and feel, swapping grunting flat vowels and barking glottal stops for its nasal estuary whine. On advice from men who know better, the front springs will be replaced with more boing and less dive, and the rear sprocket swapped for more punch off-road and easier wheelies – though I can never remember whether gearing-down means more teeth or less teeth. Thank God for mechanics.

And it'll need luggage. BMW have offered aluminium boxes, but they're just too damn, er, German. Alloy panniers on an F650? So you're a

German dentist? Not a good image in darkest Central America where octogenarian Nazis still hide out in safe houses from Simon Wiesenthal's hunters. Is it safe? Yah, und vaterproof, too.

Best of all, the adoption of this baby Dakar has made The Trip real, transformed from just another beery fantasy into a metal and rubber reality. Now I've got the bike, I can book ships, plan routes, dream dreams, spend sleepless nights arguing with myself about Pirellis or Contis, cash or travellers' cheques, peyote or tequila worms, Colombia or not Colombia.

I can't wait. And I can't wait to see what the Yanks make of the bike, especially its Dakar Rally 'hooded man' logo. It's a stylised, stencilled Tuareg – but I'm opening a book on how long it will take for a third-generation incest creationist to decide it's actually a picture of Bin Laden and try to pump me full of poisoned shotgun love. 'Look what's writ right there on his sickle – BMW – Bin Must Win.'

Game on. Just as soon as that Nigerian email deal pays out . . .

THE
AMERICAS

☆ ☆ ☆

2003 – 2006

Que el cielo exista, aunque mi lugar sea el infierno.
JORGE LUIS BORGES

THE AMERICAS: PART 1

NORTH AMERICA

☆ ☆ ☆

**MARCH – SEPTEMBER
2003**

*No matter how slick it looks on
top, it's a hobo jungle underneath.*
JACK DEMPSEY

So I rock up to the US border and wait for the shit to hit the fan. Like all chancers, bluffers, wankers, I take to borders like a cat to water. Three days ago I was holding up the queue in Toronto airport, throwing my cheekiest duck's whiskers 'I'm a good guy' grin, pretending I wasn't irritated by nicotine needs, bewildered by portraits

CHAPTER 26

CANADA AND USA

MARCH 2003

TORONTO – NIAGARA – ALBANY

NEW YORK CITY – CAPE MAY

CHESAPEAKE – JACKSONVILLE

CHARLESTON

of the Queen or freaked out by every flunked 'Why don't you have a return air ticket? Why don't you have a credit card? Why don't you have a hotel reservation?' question. Every shrugged 'Dunno' took me deeper into the immigration maze and further away from the exit. I really didn't think they were gonna let me in.

That was chirpy, British Commonwealth Canada. This is the edgy, just-about-to-get-its-war-on USA. And this could be the world's least convincing trans-American trip. 'So where did you go?' Er, Canada, mostly. Just for the weekend, like. I'd be a lot more relaxed if my paperwork was slightly more legal (maybe I'll tell you all about it at the end of the trip. Or maybe I'll just let lying dogs sleep).

I love the smell of anticlimax in the morning. The snowy bridge frontier is guarded by a friendly salt-and-pepper beard. 'I rode a hand-change Harley to Rio in '65. You'll have a blast.' Thank fuck for that – I don't think I could have coped with another night in Niagara.

Niagara Falls are beautiful – Niagara Falls town is beautifully tacky. I don't know what I was expecting, but it wasn't this – the Hanging Gardens of Babylon at the end of Blackpool Pleasure Beach (think Coney Island Boardwalk but with less class and worse weather). No romantic park surrounds, no leafy picnic tables buffer; instead a cheesy neon strip of freak shows and ghost trains, burger joints and sports bars, family Thriftlodges and US teen-drinker novelty casinos, and then a dual carriageway, and then the Falls.

And then the Falls. The Falls frozen. A river wider than the Thames or the Irwell forever throwing its hissing self over horseshoe cliffs into a steaming, frozen lake. Frosty snowmen the size of blue tower blocks chill nature and climb back upstream. Damn, it's beautiful. I stare at it for five minutes and wander off, wondering how long is enough to give a world wonder. I've got a border to burgle.

Welcome to the States, baby. I've ridden here before, three maybe four times, but only on nannied Harley press launches. Kinda hard feeling adventurous with a 'Please look after this bear' emergency-number pack round your neck and three corporate-liveried minders in tow. Kinda hard feeling reckless with prebooked hotels and place-card dinners.

Now I'm on my own, I'm excited and nervous – excited 'cause it's the beginning of an open-ended, unplanned road trip; excited about seeing the hazy Mojave Desert and drunken New Orleans and kooky California; and nervous, nervous because it's the beginning of an open-ended unplanned road trip; nervous that this big country has been ruined by Homeland Security paranoia; nervous because Bush and Blair are just about to ruin the international reputations of two mostly progressive nations by plunging them into an illegal, unnecessary war; and nervous that I'm gonna get my clock cleaned 'cause I can't keep my pinko faggy mouth shut. When did modern motorcycling become so damn complicated? Man, I need some calming miles. Woman, I need the reassuring rhythm of the road. And God, I need to ride south out of this March cold.

The New York State Thruway (bloody Webster) chilly-whistles south past a day-long polluted scar of rusted stockyards, deadheaded railheads and coughing chemical mills, broken only by Bakelite Buffalo's Frank Lloyd Wright charms. It's snowing, so I stick to the filth-gritted interstate. I'm happy to be On The Road, giddy about being away from home, but this is not sexy riding. Too many bulky layers make me sumo-clumsy but don't stop my nose running down my red face into my snotty scarf. And knobbly-ish tyres, raised bars and wobbly bags may give me gravel-drive-cowboy cred in the bike park, but they make the Dakar a flapping sail for the gusting slow-lane semis I'm using to hide from the laser-zapping cops.

Police paranoia's nibbling. It took all of fifteen minutes on the Canadian road before I got my first pull. Apparently getting a spanner out of the toolkit in the courier bag and swapping wing mirror from right to left grip is frowned upon in Toronto. 'Only if you're doing 75 mph in the passing lane at the time, sir.' Who knew?

No cops out today, just me, the trucks and frightening fast-lane exits for petrol and pudding stops. I've never seen signs before that tell drivers just how far they are from the next Hot Fudge Fantasy. Run that through Google and see what you get. Answer – Japanese girls pooing into their tights. Probably.

New York City just kinda happens. Coming down from the north, from an anonymous night on Albany's Applebee's-arcaded Wolf Road, there's no dramatic build-up, no looming Manhattan skyline, just a couple of bridges, a thickening of the traffic and next thing I'm passing signs for Yonkers (Well, hello, Dolly!) and Queens (peace, Jam Master Jay), and sitting at lights in the crumbling Bronx. I don't really know where I'm going, but it doesn't really seem to matter.

Excited. Throw a right across Madison Avenue Bridge because it's there, throw a left onto Malcolm X Boulevard, past Marcus Garvey Park and, ace, this must be Harlem. Throw another left–right and I've got the Guggenheim on one shoulder, Central Park on the other, eyes full of steaming manholes, mirrors full of yellow cabs, and start spreading the fucking news, man, I'm in New York!

I head for the Hotel Riverview in the Lower West Side meatpacking district because at thirty-five dollars a night it's the cheapest gaff in town. Posh street, rough block, rougher brownstone building. According to the guidebook, the ground floor's a cinema. 'Tonight only – *Debbie Does Dallas*.' Oh, I see.

The lobby's polished-grubby, muffled-noisy. A bored West Indian takes my money from behind bulletproof glass. A Puerto Rican busboy in du-rag and knife scars takes me to the fifth floor. I've never seen an elevator slouch before. He hasn't even unslammed the grilled gate and I can already smell the piss and bleach. I'm led down a prison-grey corridor to a room that's barely wider than its door. Lumpy camp bed, broken green-screen TV, opaque greasy window. It's perfect.

Back in the lobby, more guests are checking in. He's straight out of

Rikers, everything he owns in see-through prison bin bags. She's on the game, everything she owns in pay-per-view red leatherette. I suggest this is a happy coincidence. They pretend not to understand what I'm talking about but next morning I see her scuttle out of his room. I consider asking for a matchmaker's fee until I realise what that makes me.

Hit the streets and just laugh, goofing off the almost familiar visual signifiers, mostly fictitious cultural references of a foreigner's New York cocktail mix of the Velvet Underground and *Midnight Cowboy*, Public Enemy and *Mean Streets*, Sonic Youth and *Last Exit to Brooklyn*, James Brown at the Apollo, Black Flag at CBGBs, Marvelous Marvin Hagler at Madison Square Garden. It's perfect New York.

Perfect New York mornings – hot salt beef, fresh coffee and the *NY Times* breakfasts in sunny Bleecker Street Park. After three days I'm a regular and regularly expected to share my crumbs with the birds and smokes with the bums. The paper's the only thing I get to keep to myself. A copette saunters over. 'It's great to see a homeless person paying attention to the news.' Eau d'Hotel Riverview must be lingering. Maybe I should have a shave.

Perfect New York days – when I'm not hanging with the Lime Squeezers at 6th Street Specials in Alphabet City, I'm riding and walking up Lexington, down Broadway, across 42nd St, along the Bowery. Riding New York couldn't be easier – obvious Aztec grids, logical one-ways and, like all big cities, no one cares how you ride as long as you don't hit anything. Filtering's not allowed, but that doesn't stop the few bikes I spot, so it doesn't stop me. Without the touring fat suit, the bike's a traffic-violating hoot.

Perfect New York nights — unconvinced by the faux paddy-whackery of uptown St Patrick's Day (there's something not right about cops singing Irish rebel songs), I crawl back down, to project-block-shadowed Farrell's, a long dark bar in a long dark bar, where men in hats sip bourbon and play chess at one end, while kids in caps drink long-necks and shoot pool at the other; to the traditional White Horse, an oak and ale and fiddling inn where Dylan Thomas sipped his last whiskey sour; and to fashionista Finally Freddy's, where wet-drunk photographers and sniffing models get their nod on to Jurassic 5 and NERD while the greatest of all cities asks, 'Who do you want to be tonight?'

Answer — someone slightly drunker. So one more drink. The Corner Bar on Jane Street. A buck a beer and the juiciest burgers around, served with a side order of Coltrane and conversation. I slide in between Brian, a construction worker from Hell's Kitchen ('Not Clinton'), and Sally, a grad student at Columbia University. 'My nephew wants to join the marines,' says Brian with a *GoodFellas* growl. 'I told him they don't recruit kids with broken legs. If he's gonna fight for oil, he wants a contract guaranteeing his share.' 'They're walking the elephants tonight,' smiles Sally. 'Down Broadway to Madison. Wanna come see?' And the greatest of all cities asks, 'Who do you want to be with tonight?'

I leave town on the New Jersey Turnpike, trying not to sing Simon and Garfunkel, heading for Atlantic City and the Ocean Drive, 1300 miles of coastal two-lane that runs from the Jersey shoreline to the Florida resorts. Oranges and summer seem a long way away — up here it's all seabirds and lighthouses, sandy grasses and salty winds, the road a wild, wintry Atlantic, and Lucy.

Lucy's a six-storey-high tin-and-wood elephant. She doesn't do anything, charge anything, sell anything, market anything. She just is. Philosophically perfect. And even better than that, she makes the passing, slowing traffic smile and laugh at her and at each other. Good work, Lucy.

'Follow the gull.' Over fifty-cent toll bridges and soaring concrete causeways, past out-of-season seaside towns of pointy-roofed, white-washed-slatted wooden houses with their whipping yellow ribbons and snapping flags, Ocean Drive slowly swoops through 55s, 45s, 25s. It's in no hurry, but neither am I.

At least I don't think I am until I get caught behind a school bus. These things are harder to pass than kidney stones – illegal to overtake when parked, impossible to overtake when moving because the cop-proof drivers hit 60s in 30s. A cod-fisherman in a Camry (strapline 'America's most stolen car') winds down the window. 'Times like these, I usually just pull off for ten minutes.' I suppose that might help.

Instead, I bail out in chintzy, contrived Cape May, a town that's just a little too pretty-in-pink for its own good, so picture-postcard that it's impossible to tell the butcher's from the bank. Somehow I find the only open bar in this closed town and watch the war roll in. The Fox News clock counts down like a death-watch beetle. The first bombs drop. The first humans die. The bar cheers this Baghdad snuff soul fry. I feel sick. Call me old-fashioned, naive, but I think that war's a national liberation/international emergency last resort, not a knee-jerk, first-choice crusade.

Bush addresses the nation. Seems I'm the only one in here who can see his devil's horns and forked tongue. 'Won't be held to ransom . . .

evil-doers . . . nine-eleven . . . democracy.' Swill for swine. The pigs grunt and squeal and bang their trotters on the bar. It's devolution, regression into stupid brutalism. I guess I shouldn't have said that out loud. Fortunately PigBoy throws a punch like my ma throws a cricket ball. 'Bleedin' heart liberal.' Yeah, and now you're a bloody-nosed neo-con. I slink back to the hotel and talk conspiracies with the Bulgarian receptionist but go to bed when he starts blaming the Jews.

One night's enough. Escape on the ferry to Lewes, parked up next to a different kind of road trip – a mothership RV the size of a Zeppelin tour bus, towing a run-around Blazer SUV bigger than most British vans, carrying a Thunderbird 4 Kwak crosser. 'What do you think?' beams proud Pa Brady. I think it looks like the old woman who swallowed a fly. 'I know what you mean,' he lies.

Delaware becomes Maryland but I miss them both because of the rain. Next thing I'm passing a 'Welcome to Virginia, Welcome to the South' sign. The south? I stop at a diner to drip-dry and clarify with a waitress and a meatloaf. I thought this was the east? 'No, honey, this is the south.' So where's the east? 'That's west of here, honey.' Oh, I see.

Back on the bike, past farms, tobacco plantations, mansion homesteads, community churches, chuckling at the differences. 'Virginia is for lovers', according to the bumper stickers. Virginia is for lovers of ham, fireworks and peanuts, according to every shopfront. 'Pull over, darlin', I got me a powerful hankering for pork products, salty snacks and colourful noises.'

The rain comes down, the wind picks up. How cross does a crosswind have to get before it snatches away that front wheel? I'm in no hurry to find out, so call it a night mid-afternoon in a cosy Holiday Inn some-where near Chesapeake. Drape my socks on the heater, wring my long johns in the sink, fill my belly with KFC and turn on the weather channel. 'Tornado warnings in eastern Virginia' makes me feel better and worse. And means cancelling the Outer Banks' Kitty Hawk Beach and Blackbeard's Lair and cutting inland.

Don't fear the detour. Across the brilliantly named Great Dismal Swamp I pick up the backdrop I'll be following from here to Texas – marshes, bayous, trees up to their knees in oily black crocodile ponds, shotgun shacks, shabby motels. Kitschy diners and always-friendly faces.

Sometimes a leetle too frennly. North of Charleston, SC, slurping aeroplane-trolley miniatures in a motel-diner-bar freeway rest-stop, I get chatting with Harry, a cowboy-booted bounty hunter with a twinkle in his eye and an endless supply of travelling-salesman jokes, getting flirty touchy tipsy with Trudy, his younger, prettier fiancée. I need company and they let me join in. It's nice and easy, funny and fuss-free.

When I leave, Harry follows. He shuffles and coughs. 'Son, can I ask you a question?' Yes, Harry, you can. 'Are you bisexual?' No, Harry, I'm not. 'Well, can I blow you anyway?' No, Harry, you can't. 'Why not?' There's the awkwardest silence while I try not to blurt, 'Because you're a man, Harry, with a man-tache, Harry, and man-boobs, Harry.' Good night, Harry. 'Nice bike,' he calls through the closed door. Next morning there's a heel-crushed cigar on the stoop, one end still stained soggy from sucking saliva.

Next stop, Savannah.

CHAPTER 27

USA

APRIL 2003

SAVANNAH – DONALSONVILLE

PENSACOLA – BILOXI

NEW ORLEANS – NATCHEZ

GIBSLAND

Rainy night in Georgia. Warm spring rain slowly soaks Savannah's old south squares, gently spatters green-bronze Confederate general busts, softly showers cobble-clopping drays patiently pulling the day's last tourist trolley, and soaks soggy the girl with the mad red hair and matching eyes who just won't quit rap-tap-tapping at my window. 'Hey, mister, can I borrow another dollar? I must have lost the other, I guess.'

Welcome to Savannah. I was formally greeted by a fast kid on a rude R1, tricked up and chilled out, race pipe and beach shorts. Picked me up on the interstate intersection, popped it up on the downtown exit and didn't let it drop till we'd chased round-down the apple-peel corkscrew off-ramp and hit a red on Martin Luther King Boulevard opposite the Visitors' Centre, where two sweet old dears, pomaded and pancaked, fussed me real lemonade and no-reservation recommendations. I'm looking for the cheapest kip in town, ideally run by a bald man with a hairy back and gravy stains down his vest. 'Vest, dear? We call them singlets. Or wifebeaters. You should try the Thunderbird opposite the Greyhound Station.'

The Thunderbird – Red Indian motif, Gujarati Indian manager, thirty bucks a night, 'and don't open your door to anyone after dark'. I think he's talking about my neighbours. He's reedy, sly, and I hear through the wall that he likes to underline insults with slaps and lasts about twenty-five seconds. She's ginger and wired and can't be bothered faking. And she's knocking at my door. Yes? She fumbles a cigarette packet and drops a glass pipe. You smoke a weed? 'Some. But mostly rocks. Can I borrow a dollar? My name's Nikki. Like the Prince song. Been living that down all my life.' Or living it up. 'I guess. Can I get a dollar? Did I already ask that?'

A tale of two cities. Heads we win, tails you lose. Downtown: white-town, tourist town, 'America's Grandest Little City' town; the mood's set by antebellum architecture, shady-park walking tours, vacationing grandmothers, field-tripping girl guides and sketch-book-clutching art students. And behind it, uptown: darktown, the literal other side of the tracks; there's barber's shops, auto shops, vacant lots and project blocks, screen doors buzzing to hip-hop.

And an island. Tybee, eight miles out across the causeways, and behind the beaches and the holiday homes and the fishing village, a bar called Café Loco where a girl called Hope serves up smiles to 'forget the food, just get me another Margarita' leathery locals, and fat prawns in spicy vegetable stock with Buds and suds to me, and as Uncle Kurt said, 'If this isn't nice, what is?'

Heading west on Highway 280, dodging the dead dogs and tyre carcasses, the eastern shoreline's marine bases and favours for sailors, stinking plough mud and puffing paper mills give way to the wet-kneed trees and one-crossroad towns, one-post office towns, one-school, one-store, one-Baptist church towns of the Dirty South.

This is easy riding – low speeds, quiet routes, little traffic, no danger. It's motorcycling without the fear – I haven't had a moment in 2000 miles. Away from the interstates, it's just me, the muggy heat and the occasional pickup, thin white kids topless inside the dark cabins, their girlfriends with their bare feet on the dashboards.

Between the towns, the shotgun shacks, run-down enough, poor nuff, to look like reluctant recompense for the emancipated black families that maybe still live there. Nowhere. Mailboxes for draft papers, tax reminders, 'Regret to inform that son/husband KIA' notices. Seems improbable that these isolated, rural, poor folks get to vote for the most powerful man in the world.

Just outside Waycross, I pull into the perfect diner – chromed stools, Formica'd booths, harassed faded-pretty waitress juggling hungry customers, a restless son and a call-in-sick phone: 'This is the last time, Marcy – you better bring me a doctor's note or just not come back.' I chat with the chef, a capable ginger kid with a smile full of braces, sweating over a grill the size of a snooker table, cracking an egg in each hand, casually flipping pancakes ceiling-high, giggling about my Austin Powers accent. 'What's a wanker?'

A trucker sits down, arms sleeved in faded road tattoos, sunglasses perched Rommel-style on his mesh cap peak. 'Brother-in-law had one of those Kawa-sarkis.' Don't tell me – broke every bone in his body, wife carries him around in a Thermos, talks through a straw, eats through his arsehole. 'I guess.'

Peckerwood follows me out. His perfect Peterbilt fills my mirror. There's a poster of a missing child on the side. That's common enough, but it seems like this fella is showing off, not helping out. I decide he's a jinx and give him the slip in a town called Enigma, home to the Mona Lisa, Gregorian trance chants and smiling cats. God throws his 'Rays of Sun through the Clouds' trick. I run over a snake. A butterfly lands in my mouth.

The next town's called Climax. I stop to take a picture of the sign. 'What's so funny about that?' straight-faces the Sheriff. A nine-hour, five hundred-mile day and I'm still in the same state. Georgia on my mind? Georgia tattooed onto my rosy-cheeked arse. I collapse in Donalsonville. When I close my eyes, all I see are black-on-white road signs.

Sweet Home Alabama and the morning's glowing with primary-school colours – wet-grass green, fluffy-cloud white, happy-sun yellow, sticky-tarmac black. I stop for gas before the next state line 'cause the petrol station's called El Cheapo. Three fat, funny, friendly Stooges in bowling shirts take it in turns to throw me lines. 'Best thing about Alabama is Mississippi's worse,' yucks Larry. 'In Mississippi, pumpkin is something you do, not something you cook,' clucks Curly. 'You know how they court in Mississippi? Sis, you awake?' mocks Moe.

As smiles go, the one generated by watching the mile numbers tumble on the run into New Orleans will always be hard to beat. Faceful of warm wind, eyeful of morning sunshine, pocketful of greenbacks, mouthful of 'Baby, Please Don't Go', 'Bobby McGee' and 'House of the Rising Sun', hammering the Hammond solo on the brush guards. Sing it, Bob.

New Orleans, the big N-O. I find a hostel on Canal Street. It's clogged with faux Hindu murals (Ganesh in a bikini?), patchouli-steenking joss sticks and attention-seeking kids, but it's stumble-able from Bourbon Street. I dodge the hippies and stroll, looking for Ignatius J. Reilly and Dr (and Doctor) John.

Bourbon Street, the French Quarter, New Orleans' hiccupping heart. The brochures show the colonial facades and the wrought-iron balconies, but miss the smell of bleach and sick, the cackle of the tramps, the crooning down-but-not-outs busking for beer, singing blues for booze. 'You must be a mirror, baby, 'cause I can see myself inside of you.' Guess this is what happens when the gigs dry out but nothing else does.

There isn't a sanitised, sober option available – New Orleans demands you get your round in. So I do. The beers become rum, the afternoon becomes evening becomes neon-light night, Bourbon Street bounces with staggering, slouching, swerving, singing drunken drunks. I bump into a barker outside a strip joint. He's from Peterborough. I ask if I can take a picture of his advert cooch dancer. He says no. I take one anyway. He demands the film. Yeah, right. He'll call the cops. So? I'll be gone. 'Hey, Officer.' A cop peeps round the door – he's inside the bar, just out of sight. A five-foot-nothing midget with bottle-blond streaks. I probably shouldn't have said that out loud. 'You're under arrest.' For what? 'For being an asshole.' Fair enough. 'Get in the car.'

The car's hot, smells bad, lurches worse. Stop, start, jerk, squirm. Wee Jimmy Krankie (ah, just google it if you're bothered) lets on to door-men, barmen, other cop cronies. I know I'm gonna yak and there's nothing I can do about it. Cuffed hands behind my back, windows up, doors child-snatcher locked. I've never tried to say 'Can we stop?' through cheeks puffed with puke before. It's not especially easy. I laugh and hit the door, my knees, the back of his seat with a chunky, coughing spray.

Sorry, buster. 'You dirty, dirty bastard.' He stops the car, gets out, gets back in again, gets out again. Lets me out. I spit in a bin and wait for the shoeing. His 'If I ever see you again' threat is drowned by door slam and tyre squeal. I catch him up at the next red light. Er, any chance of taking the cuffs off?

I wake up in a bunk bed back in the hostel dorm, fully dressed, sneakers stained with sick and dog eggs. 'You snore too much,' says the Russian student who's shaken me awake. 'And that's my bed.' He's right – I'm not staying in a dorm. 'It's been the ruin of many a poor boy, and God, I know, I'm one.'

After a bad drunk, the fear, and the need to repent. In my world, miles mean industry and distance means redemption, so I slink away and hit the highway, trying not to look like 'that guy who puked in Bud's Interceptor' every time I pass a cop. I keep getting distracted by flashbacks (the cowboy dad in Oakleys urging his country-singing teenage daughters to grind their embarrassed hips, the girls on the balconies showing their tits for Fat Tuesday beads, the fight in the liquor store, the nice couple from New York drawing me a road treasure map on a napkin, the bald man in a turtleneck goofing the Benny Hill theme on a trumpet) and end up riding east instead of west, then south instead of north. Takes me four hours to cover sixty-five miles and finally find the Great River Road, Muddy Waters' Blues Road, Dylan's Highway 61. 'How does it feel?' Pretty damn good, thanks, Bob.

A nothing night in Natchez watching the TV tell lies (Basra 'liberated'? Again? Isn't that four times this week?), then a leafy, rambling detour along the Trace Parkway, an Indian trail turned slave trail turned trade trail, and so what if it's going in the wrong direction? Highway 61 heads north to Memphis. Elvis was a hero to most but he didn't mean shit to me. Instead I cut west on the 80 and pay my respects to the Barrow Gang.

Sex and death, boys and girls, cops and robbers. In fedora hats and flapper dresses, with stolen cars and scatter guns, Bonnie Parker and Clyde Barrow deliberately created the perfect American Nightmare when they cut loose on that two-year fuck-you smash-mouth, that bank-raiding, jail-breaking, cop-killing, press-taunting road trip across the South's Great Divide, living and killing and dying out of the back of a Ford V8. 'For sustained speed and freedom from trouble the Ford has got every other car skinned,' wrote Clyde to Henry Ford. While on the run.

The last outlaws faced the last ambush here, this quiet, backcountry byway south of Gibsland, Louisiana. The busters put 167 rounds into their mobile 'Home Sweet Home'. I sit smoking on their weathered stone marker, kicking at bottle caps, trying to hear the sub-guns rat-a-tat-tat, watching the sun set over the rolling hills and strolling meadows, then do the one thing they never could – ride away from Gibsland.

'They don't think they're too smart or desperate, they know that the law always wins. They've been shot at before, but they do not ignore, that death is the wages of sin.'

From 'The Ballad of Bonnie and Clyde', by Bonnie Parker.

Next stop, Texas.

CHAPTER 28

USA

APRIL, MAY, JUNE 2003

LONGVIEW – SNYDER – ROSWELL

SANTA FE – LOS ALAMOS

HOLBROOK – OATMAN

JOSHUA TREE – HOLLYWOOD

SANTA CRUZ – SAN FRANCISCO

VENICE BEACH

Everything's innaresting the first time. Even Texas. Any town's exciting the first night. Even Longview. Even in the Horseshoe Pit, the breeze-block and busted-neon pick-up joint between the 'Closed Due to Extreme Vandalism' Mexican cantina and the 'Open 24 Hours' tattoo parlour on a strip so clogged with 'Larry's Discount Guns', 'In-n-Out Burgers' and 'Abortion – the Forgotten Holocaust' signage that it looks like it's subtitled. I've never read a street before.

The bad ole boys in the ten-gallon hats and ten-pint bellies pay me no mind – they're too busy thinking up more 'Darwin is the Devil – I ain't no chimp' graffiti for the restrooms or singing along to the 'I got friends in low places' jukebox. So it's just the Fat Marilyn barmaid and me. 'This ain't my real job. I design tattoos. Lesbian fairies mostly. Bikers sure love those lesbian fairies. Wanna play pool? It's either that or watch the flies crawl up that wall.' Rack 'em tight – and call me Fat Arthur Miller. At midnight a man called Earl rides a Z650 through the bar.

Why Longview? Because it's there, here, at dusk on the old US 80 in this part of northern Texas that looks like a hand-painted Protestant Paradise, a picture postcard from Jehovah's Witness Heaven featuring uptight white folk in slacks and shirts relaxing uncomfortably in a naive landscape. This is Bush country. Somewhere round here, a village is missing its idiot.

Perfect, pointless drifting, day after dawdling day, down bumbling backwater byways. Since leaving New Orleans, I've been switching directions like a dropped fire hose. I know I'm heading for California, but via where? The un-plan changes by the hour, with the weather. San Antonio ditched for Galveston ditched for Dallas, ditched 'cause of rain. Watching the pastoral panhandle become drained oil country, red dirt, nodding-donkey derricks, rusty ranches and a sky so overwhelmingly clear and cathedral-cavernous that I feel like I'm peeking at it through a letterbox. With heavens this impressive, it's easy to see why so many grown-ups in this Bible-belt buckle still believe in Sunday-school fairy tales.

Suppose it beats believing in aliens. After a chance conversation with a trucker (Where's better, El Paso or Santa Fe? 'Santa Fe.' Thanks.) I cut north into New Mexico and into Roswell, extraterrestrial ground zero for the Desperately Seeking Somethings who claim that a UFO crashed here in 1947, complete with little green men. The locals view it as a goofy gimmick but play along 'cause it brings in the odd tourist and who ever heard of neighbouring Carlsbad?

There's even a UFO museum. It's free, but after five minutes I still want my money back. Until a nipper runs past and right into the perfect gag. 'Did those aliens come from Mars?' All together now – No kid, they came from Uranus. I've never been thrown out of a museum before.

Britain has climate, America has weather. I leave Roswell with a greasy sweat on. An hour later, the dazzling desert sunshine turns purple then turns horizontal white. Snow? Snow, and wind, wind so fierce it has the bike slapping like a sail as we dodge car-chasing tumbleweeds the size of scribbled thorny dogs.

I stop for a smoke and a snivel. A cop pulls over. To check I'm OK? Er, no. To throw a cheap gag. 'Know why it's so windy in New Mexico?' Go on. ''Cause Texas sucks and Arizona blows.' Right. Thanks.

Another hour later and the sun's shining on higgledy-piggledy Santa Fe's peach adobe beehives and its downtown plaza mix of native Indians selling traditional crafts from shaded sidewalks and yuppie hippies, rich enough to wear beads and beards to work and turn hobbies into loss-making businesses, selling artsy crap out of air-con arcades. The jingoistic flag waving's all but disappeared, replaced by 'No War' placards and 'Impeach Bush' bumper stickers. 'Hey, we're not all warmongers,' grins a kid in a mint, muscular Chevelle SS. He's right. They stay up the hill in Los Alamos.

Los Alamos. This is the place where the scientists walked away from the philosophers and bent over for the military. This is the place where the hazy line between combatants and civilians was scorched out for ever. This is the place where Robert Oppenheimer invoked the Upanishads and cursed 'I am become Death, the destroyer of worlds' as he hit the button and let the genie out of the bottle. And this is the place where Scott lives.

Scott's a fireman. He rides a Fazer Thou. Reason enough for him to invite me into his home and introduce me to his family. We throw chilli steaks on the barbecue, stuff fresh limes down a dozen cold Corona long-necks and watch the worst punk rock band I've ever seen appal the local saloon, and if this isn't nice, what is?

Best of all, he shows me his favourite mountain roads. After 3500 miles of going straight, it feels damn good to corrupt a few bends, get that big trail-bike pendulum swing on through this tickled-pink landscape of pink sand, pink cliffs, pink mountains and, when the sun's right, pink clouds and pink skies.

Scott waves goodbye and points me down the highway towards the Jemez Pueblo museum, a ruined Spanish mission built on a ruined Indian village. Get off the bike, walk, try to get a sense of the old continent beneath the new tarmac. 'When the Anglos came, they asked us what we called ourselves. We told them "Walatowa", which means "people".' I cross the state line into Arizona and check into a concrete wigwam motel.

The only thing better than falling asleep in a concrete wigwam is waking up in one, especially when it's on old Route 66. America's Main Street, Steinbeck's 'Mother Road', 'It winds from Chicago to LA.' As different from the interstates as a sleazy funfair is from a corporate theme park, it's like riding along a seaside pier, past plastic-dinosaur playgrounds, wooden ice-cream shacks, mom and pop motels, past puffing diesel-train railroads, past a stick-naked fool driving a wrecked car full of rubbish, and past a Palm Sunday Parade in Winslow, Arizona. I stand on the corner and get pop emotional reading the Eagles fans'

graffiti. 'Don't say maybe, Betty n Hank, lovers 4 ever, June 16, 1974.'
God, I hope they're still together.

The longest remaining stretch of original 66 runs 160 miles from the
railhead at Kingman into the California desert; 160 back-switching,
tight-turning, over-band sliding, Black Mountain-crossing miles,
peaking in Oatman, a boom town that stopped booming when the gold
mines stopped mining. It's named after Olive Oatman, a fifteen-year-old
pioneer girl kidnapped by the Mojave. When she was rescued by her
brother seven years later, she had a tattooed face and someone else's
eyes. Now her town's just one ramshackle street, a couple of bars, a
couple of souvenir shops, but I see more wild donkeys than spending
tourists.

I check into the only hotel. If it was good enough for Clark Gable and
Carole Lombard's honeymoon night, it's good enough for me. Wash up,
settle down, drink a beer with the roughnecks – cowboys in the style of
Dr Hook not John Wayne – and listen to them lullaby ghost-town
ghost-stories. Seems this place is haunted by William Ray Flour, an
Irish immigrant who worked the mines and saved the money to send for
his family, who then drowned during the crossing. He drowned himself
in here with whiskey, stumbled out back and died. They found him two
days later and buried him where he fell. Slan, Willy, ar dheis Dé go raibh
a anam.

I'm the first person in the town to wake. That's never happened before.
Even the burros are still snoozing, long-lashed lids twitching with
sugar-cube dreams, tails swishing in the fresh morning breeze. I ride up

and back down, without the bags, without a lid, with a smile and a whistle and eyes full of wind-rush tears. Then I pack up and start California Dreamin'.

I cross the Colorado River and the state line and cut into the horizon-wide, salt-white Mojave Desert. It feels more nature reserve than Saharan wilderness, more tranquil than adventurous, but that's OK 'cause it gives me the chance to talk to a tortoise and clear my head before jumping onto Interstate 10 for the eighty-mile trawl through Valley mall sprawl that leads into LA.

Los Angeles, La La Land. This is where they make the stupid movies, the lying TV shows, the fraudulent adverts for a world that doesn't exist. This is where the 'soft bigotry of low expectations' is created by swine whose blow- and blowjob-addled imaginations can see no further than porn-star chicks and wanksta rides. This is where the mundane American lifestyle is cosmetically enhanced into a dishonest dream.

'No matter how slick it looks on top, it's a hobo jungle underneath,' said gentleman boxer Jack Dempsey. Two and a half million jobs lost since Bush stole the election, and the human face to the dry statistic lies just south of Hollywood Boulevard, in the original downtown Skid Row. Hundreds of ragged shadows live on these streets, in cardboard shelters, in shopping trolleys, out of mission soup kitchens, in Dickensian poverty. 'Give me your tired, your poor, your huddled masses yearning to breathe free' is just too easy to quote.

I'm all right, Jack. Despite the faux-nies, LA still manages to throw up a perfect evening. A decorator from Oxford turned actor from Santa

Monica picks us (Us? Mind your own business) up in his tinted-window Jag and whisks us along the bright-night Harbor Freeway to a fashion par-tay full of gay guys in mesh caps and tweaking 'rexic chicks in ironic T-shirts, to a bar run by a Welsh Clash fan where a Latino cholo shoots himself in the foot trying to pull his piece, and on to an all-night pizzeria where a busker sweet sings Muddy Waters' 'Rollin' Stone', standing on Claude Rains' star, and if this isn't fiction, what is?

Two months later, I'm still there, stuck in a hostel on Venice Beach, a place that contrives to be less than the sum of its parts, manages to be just the clichés and nothing more, a place that creates soft memories as indistinct as dreams, where the ocean doesn't smell of anything. What the fuck am I doing drinking in LA?

Just that. Sit at the bar in the Townhouse and watch the world come in, new characters sliding along the bar like bottles in a Wild West saloon. So there's William, the Liberian trying to break into the stand-up scene, and Andre Philippe, 'Of course it isn't my real name', a septuagenarian bit-part actor betting 'Hope or Pope' with Steve the barman, and the unnamed girl who sits down next to me and sings 'Diamonds and Rust' in my ear so clear it would have fooled Joan Baez's mother.

And there's Larry. Larry lives on the beach, when the cops let him. Larry came from Chicago with big ideas that hit the rock. Larry tells me stories of Soledad and the P. Stone Rangers for chump change. Until he meets this guy, a working stiff, who asks him why he's on the streets. Larry tells him if he could just get back to Chicago, he's got a house and job waiting. This guy returns the next day with a plane ticket. 'You'll laugh, but seriously, man, I believe he was a angel.' We make so much noise celebrating that Anjelica Houston calls the police.

Larry leaves. A new hobo takes his place. Says he's from the tribe of Hell's Angels, and a doctor of theology. He looks behind my eyes and asks me who died on Golgotha next to Christ. Er, a robber? He winks. 'I'm older than I look. You ever need help, just call my name.' Which is? 'Quadrangle. Or Irwin. Or Lynn.' Los Angeles, City of Angels.

Next stop, Mexico.

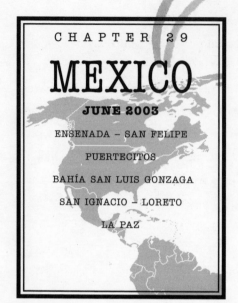

CHAPTER 29

MEXICO

JUNE 2003

ENSENADA – SAN FELIPE

PUERTECITOS

BAHÍA SAN LUIS GONZAGA

SAN IGNACIO – LORETO

LA PAZ

So I rock up to the Mexican border and, er, roll straight through without even stopping. No say hello, wave goodbye, just an 'International Frontier' sign, a rumble-strip slow-down and my last experience of the States is drive-thru.

Adios San Diego, hola buenos dias Tijuana. The change is instant, obvious, but less dramatic than Kensington to Stepney or Didsbury to Seedley. Older cars, brighter clothes, but best of all, pedestrian street life. In the States, no one walks. Try it and they stare like you're, well, Mexican.

Right or wrong, Tijuana has the kind of reputation for substantial abuse and dank sex that would make Bukowski blush. During Prohibition it was a watering hole for thirsty northerners and a cubbyhole for booze smugglers. Now it's a loophole for underage Yankee binge drinkers and a rathole for human-trafficking coyotes. Seedy sin looks a lot more attractive at midnight than at ten thirty in the morning. We ride past feelthy peecture temptation and 'Hurley Devidson' tattoos and hit Highway 1.

We? I've got company. Trys, both kinds of painter from Salford, first ran away to LA when he was seventeen, spent five years living in a burnt-out van, working the black market, attending AA meetings for the free

doughnuts and vulnerable women. He recently returned to California, got himself a driver's licence ('worryingly easy – they may as well ask you to throw your shoe at that wall') and a Honda XR650L (push-button Dominator engine in an XR-derived frame; so it's either a butch Dommie or a fey XR, depending on the size of your rooster). He fancies riding with me to Argentina. Let's see how we cope with Baja first.

Baja California, the desert and mountain dingle-dangle peninsula that droops over north-west Mexico. Outsiders know it for dune racing, but the first bikes we see are serious sportsters – an R6, a 955i, and a GSX-R something that's travelling too damn fast to identify. No number plates, big speeds, they appear out of the mist, make us jump and fuck off. We catch them up a couple of miles down the road, wriggling in a speed trap, and tortoise past into Ensenada.

Ensenada's a low-rise Pacific port town that makes its living catching fish and tourists. Twice a week the cruise ships spill their pigeon-toed passengers into two purpose-built shopping and drinking streets. By sunset, they're back on the boat, hair braided, pockets fleeced, clutching bags of discount Viagra and ibuprofen (if he's getting his first e-rection in fifteen years there's no way she's using the headache excuse), leaving the town to sweep up, count up and drink up in Hussong's Cantina.

'The bar that built a town', Hussong's is the textbook swinging-door, sawdust-floor saloon. No attitude, no posturing, just a bar full of Mexicans in white cowboy hats and heeled boots getting happy drunk while mariachi singers croon folk favourites. Sure beats feeding coins into a jukebox.

It's a locals' local. The first night we're tolerated, the second night we're welcomed with a wink and a half-understood dirty joke, and LA's twisted tension dissolves in another round of cold Coronas and another chorus of 'Guantanamera' and nobody seems to mind when we change the words to 'One Bryan Robson'.

We cut east on Highway 3 for the far coast. On these roads, where the tarmac's lumpy at best and gravel at worst, where blind bends hide wagons creeping along in low-low or dust-masked gangs of labourers slinging fresh bitumen at potholes, the Dakar switches from knobbly, bouncy 50-horsepower ho-hum to boomslanging weapon of choice, carrying speed but not crippled by its need, carrying luggage but not crippled by its sag. So far, across the States' double-nickel speed limits and too-tight-trousered cops, the bike's just been there, an anonymous, obedient platform. Could have been an XJR, could have been a Road King, could have been a car. (And in fact was – call me a punk traitor but I drove from LA to San Francisco in a Land Cruiser, seduced by the sound of the Stone Roses and the slap of windscreen wipers. Talk about claustrophobic. Never again.) But now, heading for foreign dirt, the generic becomes specific. How will this bike cope with this hole, this sand, right here, right now? Er, pretty damn well.

The mountains flatten into desert as we hit our first military check-point. 'Something drogas something armas,' says a small man with a large rifle. I nod and smile. I guess from the scowl it's the wrong answer. 'Drugs. Guns,' he repeats. Ah, right – good idea. These are difficult times. As soon as I score some, I'll let you know. This seems to reassure him and he salutes and waves us into San Felipe.

Weird to ride a day deeper into Mexico but feel closer to the States.

San Felipe is a fishing village turned RV service station for Winnebago warrior snowbirds. I sulk as we pass Century 21 estate agent boards, a 7-Eleven and a bumper sticker reading 'Ted Kennedy's Car Killed More People Than My Gun', but cheer as we find a seaside bar with chilli octopus tacos and a dartboard. No, *I'm* Bobby George.

Next day is D-Day, Dirt Day. For once, I'm kinda prepared. Mighty Mitch at *Motorcyclist* magazine had sorted me a service at BMW back in Torrance and Aerostich Andy had sorted me a throw-over of Ortlieb panniers – the BMW gear was commuter-fine but too zippy and top-heavy for dirty bouncy-bouncy.

Good dirt's faster than bad tarmac. South of San Felipe, the road disappears under an acne-pockmarked rash of rim-bending potholes before turning into smooth graded piste. It's the perfect off-road warm-up, loose enough for the back to snuggle down without the front slipping away, easy enough for wheel-spinning thumb-to-nosery, beautiful enough as it skips along the Sea of Cortez to have us both whooping 'Ohio!' into our lids.

We plot up while the going's good – the next stretch is supposed to be trickier. A couple of clicks past the mobile-home shanty hideout of Puertecitos is Bahía Cristina – a bay, a beach, a bar and half a dozen coconut-matted palapa shelters. So sling up the hammocks and spend an afternoon lolloping around in the sea and eating fresh fish with Hector, Maria and Ivan.

There's no electricity and they turn the generator off at nine. Sure gets

late early round here. Stroll back to the bikes, stretch out, one foot on my front tyre to gently rock the hammock, watch the yellow moon sparkle on the waves and drift into dreamy sleep.

Yeah, right. After an eighteen-hour watch in a wind-lashed, salt-stung crow's nest, fending off the amorous advances of a lonely bear from Portsmouth, I'm sure a hammock is heavenly. Otherwise, it's just sleeping in a rope bag. I feel like an old lady's shopping. I try to enjoy it, I try to concentrate on the lullaby wash of the waves, but you can't fake sleep. When dawn hits my cross-hatched, cross-patch face I give up, rub seawater in my eyes, pour coffee up my nose and get back on the off-road.

Arse – washboard. Ju-ju-juddering bastard washboard. Good dirt goes off quicker than warm milk; rain and truck shocks batter smooth graded piste into teeth-grinding corrugations. There's a sandy alternative running parallel, but I haven't got the energy or aggression to attack it. So I stay on the rough and keep it slow.

And I mean slow. When most moto-journalists claim to make like Harry and Potter, they're lying through their speed-stained teeth. When Dakar-riding mate Simon Pavey describes my off-road pace as 'crown green bowls on two wheels', he's being charitable. So it's especially weird that I'm the fast one. Trys is not without skills, and should I ever need help painting a mural, stealing a Ford Cosworth or deciphering a mumbled Joy Division lyric, then he'll be top of my list. But as a motorcyclist, he's novice-wobbly. Makes a change that it's me picking someone else up. Again. And again. And, Christ that looked sore, again.

'It's 160 kays to the tarmac,' said Hector. 'Maybe two hours.' Six sweaty

shaken hours later we're not even halfway there. We take sanctuary in a shop's shade, suck back Gatorade and lie to each other. Well, we've not been overtaken. Nobody could ride this stuff any quicker. Two XR650s thunder by, shower us with shale, wake a sleeping baby and slam sideways into the junction at maybe 100 mph. We sheepishly follow them into Bahía San Luis Gonzaga.

Another bay, another beach, another bar, plus company. The fast Yanks are Mick and Dale, trucked their tricked-out XR racers down from Venice for some serious Baja bashing. We settle down next to a submerged runway (seems that the easiest way to get here is with a private plane, though the roughneck neighbours look more CIA crop dusters than flying doctors) and get humiliated. 'Man, just attack the track – speed up and you'll float over those bumps.'

Float like an elephant. Shamed and inspired, I really do try to go faster. But at 60 mph the front-deflecting rocks and shock-crunching holes come far too quickly for me to cope with. And the bike starts to disintegrate – half the chain guard gets ripped off and the tail unit comes loose, swinging on its lead like an eye that's escaped its socket. Red-headed vultures stop picking the skin off a flyblown donkey and urge me 'Faster, Faster!' into a crash that'll be beak-sharp, talon-sharp, cactus-spine sharp. I'd rather be slow than punctured.

When it's bad, it's horrid, but when it's good, it's very, very good. Past Coco's Corner, a Baja 1000 staging post and ramshackle café run by a crude old man with one leg and a collection of soiled knickers and sun-bleached-silver beer cans, the piste smoothes into an absolute joy, swooping through cactus forests, past eagles' soar and farm girls' wave, stones pinging a Morricone soundtrack off the belly pan and I'm almost

disappointed when we ride back onto tarmac and into Loreto and a head-on collision with a bottle of tequila.

Tequila. Sounds cheeky, playful. Jesus of Nazareth, King of the Jews, this is some heap powerful cactus juice. After one, I like jazz. After two, I can speed-read Joyce. During three, four and five, I lose Trys and learn to play 'Comandante Che Guevara' on the spoons. After six, I can speak Spanish. After seven, I can speak Dog.

I get shooed out of the wrong hotel for shouting 'Where are the white women? Share them with me!' at the chuckling night porter. I climb over Trys's balcony and break into his room, carrying two stray dogs. I don't know who's more surprised – me, Trys or the nekkid girl from Stockport who's straddling him. I cover the pups' eyes and try to maintain some dignity by leaving through the front door, letting them get on with whatever it was they were doing. 'Playing pool with a piece of rope,' I think she said.

There was no tomorrow.

South of Loreto, Mex Highway 1 officially becomes the Greatest Road in the World. From shuddering goat track to Ducati-smooth superhighway, el camino sinuoso zigs the zag along the too-turquoise Sea of Cortez. No blink-and-you-miss-it beauty spot, this shit goes on for miles, long enough to do both kinds of riding, an hour at a time, first head-up gazing, then head-down monkey spanking, barrelling into yet another Armco-and-ocean blind-exit right-hander and into La Paz.

La Paz is the end of the road. From here, we have to jump the ferry to Mazatlán and the mainland. We should be shuffling paperwork, but instead spend a week riding to the beach in shorts and flip-flops, jumping about to Molotov rhymes and Pancho Villa ballads, and practising Spanish with Rainbow Hawk, a proper hippy, an original Bezerkeley Merry Prankster who's been hiding down here for twenty-three years. 'The sixties? All I remember is the taste of LSD and the smell of tear gas.'

I understand Baja after we leave. It's empty Mexico, Mexico-lite. The roads are easy, the towns pleasantly provincial, the people patient with stuttering monoglots. It's a dress rehearsal. The mainland's the main event.

Next stop, Mexico City.

CHAPTER 30

MEXICO

JULY, AUGUST 2003

MAZATLÁN – SAN FELIPE

PUERTO VALLARTA

GUADALAJARA – VERACRUZ

VILLAHERMOSA – PALENQUE

SAN CRISTÓBAL

Someone must have been telling lies about Mexico. Someone seems to have been spreading slanders that it's the States' sleazy, second-rate cousin, a fly-buzzing, donkey-riding, cactus-desert backwater of tequila-drunk cut-throats with bad teeth and worse breath slumbering under sombreros, waiting to ambush passing greeengos. But day-tripping zipping down the charm-smooth (and fraud-dear) superhighway from the cultured capital to glitzy Acapulco, sat sipping espresso on the rooftop terrace of the Holiday Inn, watching the sun set over the cultured capital's medieval cathedrals, happy sweating gazing over the step pyramids and sun temples of ancient Palenque, it's kinda hard to work out what the fuck those liars are on about.

Someone's definitely been telling lies about the cops. 'They'll rob you, set you up, sling you in a blood-on-my-knife-or-shit-on-my-dick prison wing. Stay at home and watch "shock and awe" on video instead,' oink the swine. The first real contact (there was a stop-and-search, late night in Ensenada, but being told to 'Spread 'em!' across the hood of a patrol car made me feel pleasingly Snoop) comes at the end of Baja. Travelling off the peninsula to the mainland means getting a Temporary Importation Permit – and that means leaving a deposit of $400. And despite my stuttering Spanish, it couldn't have been easier, more helpful, less open to abuse. The uniforms don't see the money – it goes into the State bank, the receipt's produced, the paperwork issued, the deposit returned with a smile at the next border. And that's it, ride as fast as I can, as slow as I like, as unconcerned as can be. There's double this cop-paranoia in England.

Until I hit Mexico City. Just as I'm congratulating myself for toasting the crush hour with 'old couriers etc' nonsense, I get pulled. Two smiley cops point to my number plate and say something like 'No circulo' and 'Jueves'. No traffic on Thursday? Arse. A speed-read, quick-forgotten by-law – to reduce congestion, they've set up a scheme to limit traffic based on number plates. No ones or twos on Thursday, no threes or fours on Fridays, and so on. And it's Thursday. And my number plate ends in a two. And arse.

Sometimes a little local corruption is a good thing. Truth is, I have broken the law. I am riding illegally. In England, corruption involves six-figure donations to the inappropriate election fund. Here, it's more democratic – it's chump-change figures, so everyone can join in. The cop gives me a lollipop and we haggle. 'One hundred dollars.' Five. 'Ten.' Done. Best of all, he gives me a receipt. Next set of lights, another cop points at the plate and blows his whistle – I flash my chits and, bingo, he apologises, smiles and waves me on. I think I'm gonna like this city.

Someone's certainly been telling lies about the cities. I was ignorantly expecting swarming slums and coughing, consumptive poverty. Especially from Mexico City, the biggest, most populous city in the world. The first impressions are odd – blurred flashes through a tropical rainstorm, 'El Punk no es muerto' graffitied on a bridge,

blue-tarpaulin shacks huddled under an overpass, blue-glassed banks looming over the financial district. Plot up in the city centre and try to work out why this particular valley has become the most attractive place to live on this planet.

Before the Spanish, the Aztecs built their capital here, at the spot where an eagle landed on a cactus and killed a snake. They believed it was the literal centre of the earth. And as the biggest city in the world, it kinda is. And an unprecedented centre – never have so many people lived together, anywhere. Officially, it's 25 million, unofficially, maybe 35 million. Guess it's difficult getting that many people to stand still and be counted.

The heart of the city is the central square, the Zócalo, 400 majestic metres a side of Gothic cathedrals, presidential palaces, parliamentary offices, swanky hotels. And people – this is a public space. From misty dawn to hazy dusk, the place rattles and hums with honking bug-green Beetle taxis, shrieking sirens, thumping Aztec drummers, and fat-faced, blond-tinted barrow boys hawking everything and nothing, from Goa trance CDs to Pierre Cardin shirts.

At the weekend, it's pop concerts and political protest. Mexican democracy is new, fragile, suspicious, but taken seriously – the modern nation was founded on the slogan 'Death to Bad Government'. In London's Parliament Square, there's usually a couple of scruffs hanging around the railings chanting something about bicycles and peace. Here there's radical trade unions showing guerrilla training videos to office workers on lunch break, gaggles of teachers singing about unpaid wages, while indigenous workers with the patience of peasants sell ethnic prints and Che posters to patronising tourists.

No one-square wonder, but street after street, plaza after plaza – forget Spaghetti Western preconceptions, think southern Spain, Cádiz or Seville. This shit's grander than Madrid, grand as Paris or Rome. Say what you want about slave labour, it certainly gets results . . .

Someone's definitely been telling lies about the people. Third world? No one's told them. The only thing third-rate about this country is its history of corrupt government and lack of international spending power, and that's just as much to do with its noisy, nosy neighbour destabilising the region as with internal inadequacy. 'Pobre Mexico, tan lejos de Dios y tan cerca de los Estados Unidos', as the crazy old dictator said: 'Poor Mexico, so far from God and so close to the USA'.

Everything else is first-class. Especially the funny filth. The Mexicans love innuendo like a Carry On grocer. I tell the waiter I'd like my eggs boiled and he has to step outside for air. I ask a street vendor if his corn-cob's hot and the queue chokes laughing. All right, all right, calm down. 'Coger' means 'to catch' in Madrid but, er, 'to fuck' down here. Where do I 'coger' the bus? 'Round the back, I suppose,' straight-faces the driver, tooting 'dat-dat-da-dat-dat' on the horn, which in England means 'I'm a good guy, not a burglar' but here shouts 'Chinga tu madre, cabrón'. I certainly will not – that's my father's job, and from what I hear he's damn good at it.

This isn't some 'Poor is cool, the slum's got so much soul, maaan' mouthwash. 'I've been to London, it was nice – small and quiet,' laughs Carla, manageress of La Gioconda, where she and English husband Liam serve up cold beers, hot pasta and warm music, from the Clash to Youssou N'Dour. What do you want to do today? Pay peanuts and wander round a world-class Josef Koudelka photography exhibition in

the Palacio de Bellas Artes? Eat popcorn and watch *Terminator 3* in English? Lose hours in the anthropological museum? Catch the underground to the Azteca stadium and watch Mexico play Brazil?

And what do you want to do tonight? Drink in the Plaza de Mariachis and watch the silver-liveried, bawdy folk singalongas delight local working-class drinkers while tubas parp the happy sound of fat folk fucking? Maybe smoke in a pavement café and discuss Houellebecq with coked-up cocky journalists? And then? Dance all night, but to what? Cuban salsa, Mexican punk, German techno, English new wave?

All this culture on offer, but I still celebrate my birthday with a new tattoo and a fight. Don't worry, this is no hooligan chest thump. In fiction, fights are always either preposterously dynamic, amplified single knockout punches delivered to bloodless noses, or graphically gruesome, teeth crunching on taps or cracking on boots. In my real life, they're clumsy and rubbish and no one ever seems to get hurt. Which is bad for the caveman ego, but good for the Catholic conscience.

So I end up in an alleyway with some dickhead from Donegal, cursing and swinging, hissing and missing. And giggling. I keep getting the giggles, 'cause I can't remember why we're fighting (I think it's 'cause I called him a tourist not a traveller), 'cause the Smiths' 'Bigmouth Strikes Again' is blowing out of the door we've just tumbled through, 'cause he's throwing old-fashioned, bare-knuckle Marquess of Queensberry shapes, but mostly because we can't actually hit each other. Eventually I connect and he collapses, more drunk-drunk than punch-drunk. Two cops stroll over. 'Finito?' Yes, finished. 'Bueno.' They gesticulate that we should shake hands. I almost faint. Mine's broken. At least the tattoo is poetic.

Someone's been telling lies, but here's two double-truths, Ruths. First, there is no better way to see the world than to ride the world. Riding a bike removes the need for clutter, toys, rubbish that other men have to take on holiday. If I want adrenalin, I'll rush a giddy overtake, not rent a jet ski.

Riding a bike means that a startling journey rubs out a disappointing destination. The man who said 'It's better to travel than to arrive' must have ridden to Puerto Vallarta. I had heard it was the classiest of the Pacific resorts, but it's as mundane as Benidorm – fine for a two-week break, but hardly adventurous. But the road from Mazatlán, gurgling down through wet green mountains, to sweat-wet jungles, to the sparkling sea, made up for my one lasting image of the town – a middle-aged taxi driver staring in lusty contempt up the cheek and thong-flashing miniskirt of a good teenage gringa pretending to be a bad girl by dancing on a bar.

Good travel blows bad blues away, turns dreary laments into songs of the open road. I leave Mexico City confused and bruised, wincing over a broken hand and a confused heart after another 'Dear John' email from London ('Still here I carry my old delicious burdens'). What happens if you find what you're looking for? Answer – ignore it and run away. See you, Grainne.

The space, the place, the bike all come together on the road from Palenque to San Cristóbal in the south. On my own again, On The Road again. Some things are meant for sharing – kisses, breasts, inside tips on outsiders in the Cheltenham Gold Cup. And others aren't – a girl-friend's kisses and breasts (I know, I'm being naive – again), gambling debts and maybe motorcycle adventures. Since California, I've been

riding with Trys, a good lad, but somehow things just don't seem that exotic when shared with a painter from Irlam o' th' Heights. So I've sent him to Belize to get lewd. We'll meet again in Panama.

Palenque to San Cristóbal. Before the Aztecs, the Mayans built the ancient city of Palenque, a complex of step pyramids and towering temples, that makes Stonehenge look like, er, a big pile of rocks, part of a civilisation that collapsed 500 years before Columbus reckoned he discovered America.

And San Cristóbal, the home of the Zapatista rebels. In 1994 this previously unknown guerrilla outfit took over town halls and government offices across Chiapas state, protesting against the appalling treatment of indigenous people. The army cut them in half and chased them back into the jungle, but clever use of the internet and their commander's poetic communiqués won an international audience. Their lack of military effectiveness seems to have helped their cause-célèbre status. Student union revolutionaries prefer their AK-47s to be edgy design icons, not shockingly effective tools for firing pieces of hot metal into other human beings' bodies at a muzzle velocity of several hundred feet per second. The town's now clogged with phoney-radical day-trippers goofing off balaclava chic.

In between, a summer's worth of spicy jungle mountain roads compressed into one green, dizzy day, buzzing on nothing but the bends' motorcycle emptiness and high on histamine after a giant wasp flew into my shirt and stung me like a taxman. Like a small boy on a swing, like a little girl dancing on her dad's feet, that relaxed, that happy, lolloping side to side, side to side, side to side for mile after mile after mile, and if this isn't nice, what is?

And the second truth. For many British riders, the US coast-to-coast is the biking dream. Which is good, but this is better. Beautiful beaches, belting roads, tasty trails, bouncing bars, punny people. Really. These are the days that must happen to you. Viva Mexico.

Next stop – Guatemala.

CENTRAL AMERICA

☆ ☆ ☆

SEPTEMBER 2003 –
MARCH 2004

A sunny place for shady people.
W. SOMERSET MAUGHAM

So I trot up to the Guatemalan border with no real clue about what to expect. Guatemala? I don't even have ignorant prejudices about the place.

CHAPTER 31

GUATEMALA EL SALVADOR, HONDURAS

AUGUST, SEPTEMBER 2003

HUEHUETENANGO – PANAJACHEL – ANTIGUA

EL TUNCO – SAN SALVADOR – LA PALMA

SANTA ROSA DE COPÁN – COPÁN RUINAS – TELA

LA CEIBA – WEST END

The Pan-American Highway switches nationalities in a misty, Mexican mountain market town. Both kinds of locals skip underneath the candy-striped barrier with a nod and a wink, with boxes and bundles of whatever's cheap here and expensive there. Bus passengers grumble and trudge and hump suitcases and flash ID cards as they get off, get back on again. Black marketeers slouch in the back of Policía pickups, counting bricks of pesos and quetzals with spivs' fast fingers and dirty nails. And I hop about, smiling, sweating, trying to catch someone's eye, trying to work out what the fuck I'm supposed to do.

We know everything about you, yet you know nothing about us. 'Manchester? Manchester United?' says a man in a jungle-warfare hat. 'Where is David Beckham?' He laughs and hand-holds me through immigration, customs and fumigation (the bike, smart arse, not me) and in fifteen easy minutes I'm plum-deep in the new.

Welcome to Guatemala. I've got the highlights of fifty (very) odd countries stored inside my baggy eyes, but I'm whooping into the wind, rushing off the uncut novelty of a fresh scene. I've never ridden hairpins through volcanic incisors before. And I've never known a four-lane highway atrophy into single-lane dirt track mid-corner before. This must be how the French feel when their high-speed bullet train pops out of the tunnel and hits creaky England.

An old boy in a construction hat on a DT175 takes advantage of the dirt and flashes past. Every time we hit tarmac, I cheat by; every time we scuff dirt, he dusts me. Ding dong, tick tock, thumbs up, all the way into Huehuetenango. Thank Christ for that – it's kinda tricky asking for directions to a town you can't pronounce.

A transit night in a transit town. Find a cheap hotel, park the bike in another lobby and familiarise. Check out the price of Marlboro ($2), the quality of the chicken chimichangas (juicy), whether my card works in the ATM (it does – ace) and if I have any money (I don't – arse). And finally, taste the local beer.

Ask the sweet girl for a cold one, take a swig and look at the bottle. 'Gallo.' And spray girl and bar with beer through my nose. 'Gallo' means 'cock'. And I just ordered a large one. That just gets funnier every time. I never claimed to be sophisticated.

Way-way (apparently) is a town that everyone's just passing through – usually on their way to Antigua. In the seventies, Antigua attracted hippies trying to put some space between them and The Man when Mexico became too obvious. It then picked up the backpackers, stuck on its faded colonial charm, crumbling chapels, pastel-walled villas and slow pace.

Now it's chock-a-block with gap-year undergraduates, round-the-world-ticketeers and Spanish-language students. Why? Because it's easy. Behind the cobble-clopping donkeys, the blind beggar singing for his supper, the indigenous women in patchwork shawls serving up sizzling street food, there's a whole other town catering for the gringos, who can drink gringo beer in gringo bars served by other gringos while listening to gringo music and watching gringo TV. Pinche gringos.

Which isn't necessarily bad, it just feels a bit insensitive. Awfully authentic and authentically awful Penny and Jenny and Zoe and Chloe remind me of the ongoing gentrification of English cities, of an increasingly voracious middle class that buys up council properties, chews up boozers and spits out gastrated café bars, and inflates the prices of everything from a pint of milk to a pint of Guinness.

I'm here to see an old friend, Chelsea Mick. Last time I saw him, he was dispatching round the West End of London on a Z650. Now he's married to a Guatemalan Indian woman, raising a trilingual family, running an internet café – roaring, laughing, loving proof of better choices beyond the mundane.

So Mick shows me around and I see the other side. Gringo bar staff, but Guatemalan owners. 'I've worked in a factory in England, I've picked fruit in Spain, I've delivered newspapers in Denmark, and it was hard. This is easy. The gringos have money? I'll take it,' chuckles former gang-banger Julio in his popular wine bar. 'Drink, gringo?' All together now – another big Cock, please.

These good times might not last. We open a bottle of rum and throw away the top, crack open the coke mixer and talk about Ríos Montt.

Looking like Mr Burns, smelling like Adolf Hitler, during an eighteen-month presidency in the early eighties, Montt was responsible for the murder of at least 25,000 people, mostly Mayans. After twenty years of exile, twiddling his thumbscrews, setting fire to cats and trying to keep the blood out of his clown suit, he's back and running for president again.

Most of the country's appalled. The Supreme Court banned him from standing. So he marched a mob of his old Indian Killers into the capital for a bit of mouth smashing and journalist stabbing. The Court backed down, Montt got on the ticket, and now nobody believes he has any intention of losing. And if he wins on November 8th? 'On November 9th I take my family and leave.' I laugh. Julio doesn't. Because he's not joking. Because it isn't funny.

I spend three weeks in Antigua. Sometimes it's good, maybe necessary, to get to know a place, have a look below the obvious. And then it becomes more necessary to build some momentum, ride for six, seven, eight days in a row, create contrasts, experience everywhere as a stranger.

Partner in grime Trys drops down from Belize on his XRL and we hit the road. Just before the El Salvador border, I stop for a last look. A well-groomed geezer strolls up. Used to work in London for Unilever. We share the view. 'This is a beautiful country,' he says, 'but with too many sons of guns.'

El Salvador. The only country in the world named after Jesus, The Saviour. Any meaning was drowned in demonic irony in 1980 when four US nuns were raped and killed by a government death squad. Carter withdrew aid. Carter lost to Reagan. Reagan increased aid exponentially. And the death squads got back to work.

Number-one target was Archbishop Oscar Romero, heir to the tradition of Latin American liberation theologians, radical priests who found inspiration in the Sermon on the Mount, not Papal bull. 'I'm sorry, Holy Father, but I've been reading the Bible again, and I still can't find the part that says we should kill the poor and steal their land.'

The ARENA government's twisted logic – the Church supports the poor, the FMLN communists support the poor, therefore the Church supports the guerrillas. And should be treated as insurgents. On 24 March 1980, an ARENA assassin shot the archbishop through the face while he was performing Mass in San Salvador Cathedral. Jesus wept and El Salvador collapsed into twelve years of unholy, uncivil war.

So I'm expecting black-eyed paramilitaries and weary victims. Dick. The war's been over since '92, ARENA and the FMLN share power as uneasily as snakes and mongeese, but people are rebuilding. What I find is a slow, friendly border ('Paul Gascoigne! Tony Blair!'), an empty free-way and then one of the most astonishing roads I've ever been lucky enough to ride.

Highway 2 runs along the coast from Guatemala to Honduras. There's more musty green volcanoes on my left, the roaring Pacific Ocean on my right, and a freshly surfaced road wriggling underneath me like an eel in hot pants. It's dusk, and we whistle past farm workers cycling home from the fields, through villages settling down for the evening, through the smell of dinner cooking. We hit the beach at El Tunco as the sun sets and turns the sky red raw over the black-sand beach. Settle in, order fresh ceviche, raw fish marinaded in lemon juice and chillis, and watch a tropical storm set the night on fire. In bed, through closed eyes, I can still see the lightning strobe, smell the ozone burn, feel the tin roof rattle in the thunder. Raindrops keep falling on my head. And my feet are too big for the bed.

I'm the first person in the building awake. A Dalmatian walks me up the beach to watch hardcore surfers tame a double-overhang left-break in waters violent enough to drown any swimmer, through rocks sharp enough to sink a ship. As I'm packing up, they're sipping Gatorade and talking tubes. And because I'm on a bike, these superstars give this fat twat big respect. Pop an all-right wheelie and head north for San Salvador.

All I know of the city is old news footage, jackboots and tear-gas clouds. So I'm surprised by the Périphérique-fast ring road that dashes past malls, KFCs, international banks. This emperor wears no clothes. Forget the swanky development-district ear grafted onto this mouse's back, the gaff's tasty rough. Rat-run stairways lead from the streets down to riverside barrios. Every shop and business is guarded by private security with pistol-grip pump-actions. Every wall's plastered with revolutionary murals or coded gang scrawls. Every derelict building's squatted by gang-bangers. I sneak past one crew, silhouetted in the smashed windows like a *Clockwork Orange* poster, hard bodies stained with sweat and Roman-numeral tattoos, their leader making a rocking hammock look as sinister as a swinging noose.

I'm on a pilgrimage to the cathedral to pay my respects to Romero. Take a pew, let the acoustics blur the traffic noise, enjoy the ecclesiastical quiet and light a candle for a good man. I'm invited to say a prayer, but I can't. I prefer people and ideas to gods and beliefs. And anyway, prayer makes me feel like a child talking into a toy phone. Hello? Can you hear me? Is that Santa?

I'd hoped to spend a week in San Salvador, studying Spanish in an FMLN school, presumably learning to shout 'Socialism or Barbarism!' while stripping down an AK. But I've titted away too much time and money in Antigua, so it's back On The Road and back into the rain.

It's wet season. I spend oven-hot, jungle-humid mornings sweating like a foreigner and monsoon afternoons getting drenched by sheets of fat, warm rain. Inside-out or outside-in, I'm getting wet.

I'm drowning but the bike's waving. Add webbed feet to its camel toes and racehorse hooves. The streets are flooded spindle-high, my eyes are full of grit splash, but the bike reassures me enough to laugh at a bunch of boys stood in their underpants by a pond-deep puddle, hooting every time a passing wagon soaks them. It would be really charming if it didn't smell like they were showering in cholera.

I give up in La Palma, a mountain village north of San Salvador surrounded by cloud forests and pines. A man wanders over. 'English? I love Dickens, but prefer Joyce. Have you read *Finnegans Wake*?' His name's Alberto and he studied English literature in Costa Rica when he was refugeed. 'This was not a good town to be an intellectual.' He draws a finger across his throat and gives me an FMLN beret. I give him too many bucks, because I can, because it makes me feel swell. A couple of hours later I pop out for smokes. Alberto's slumped in a doorway, eleven inches down a foot-long bottle of cooking vodka. And I don't feel quite so swell.

Bad borders are like welfare offices – incompetent, impersonal, obstructive. The Honduran border is the worst yet – all of the above, plus the sting of corruption. The straightforward procedure of tourist card for me, temporary importation permit for the bike, is clogged at every tedious stage by bent officials running interference. It takes three hours to reach the final form, the TIP. It's guarded by a fat man with tiny hands and a look in his eyes that says, 'Make like a sheep and prepare to be fleeced.'

Baa. 'Seventy dollars.' Yeah, right. Back of the queue. 'Seventy dollars.' Oh, my friend, that's not possible. Back of the queue. 'Seventy dollars.' Fuck you. Back of the queue. Closed for lunch.

Five hours later. 'OK, seventy dollars between you.' Scumbag. We pay up. Corrupt and gormless – according to all my paperwork, my name is now Daniel British Citizen.

As a first impression it's a cold kick in the balls rather than a warm handshake. The dull ache in my belly doesn't last. Ten minutes later I'm chasing the brightest rainbow I've ever seen across fields of tall corn. Two days later I'm whistling at the Mayan ruins in Copán, admiring the step pyramids of King 18 Rabbit and King Smoke Monkey (a direct descendant of King Smoke Beagle, the vivisectionists' mascot).

Eyes full of steaming
manholes, mirrors
full of yellow cabs –
New York, March 2003

'Man, I need some calming miles. Woman, I need the reassuring rhythms of the road....' North America, March 2003

Clifton Hill, Niagara Falls, Canada

Bloody-nosed anti-war protester meets deaf ears, New York City

Sand dunes and salty air on the Jersey shoreline

Paddywhackery, St Pats, New York City

Hotel Riverview's prison grey corridors, Jane Street, Manhattan

Niagara Falls frozen

Chirpy Americana, Myrtle Beach, North Carolina

DEAD END

Take your time like a tortoise –
prehistoric independent
traveller on old Route 66,
somewhere in Arizona

Don't fear the detour – happily lost in The Great Dismal Swamp's oily black crocodile ponds

'Solo los obreros y campesinos iran hasta el fin' — Managua, Nicaragua, December 2003

Hurricane season
sunset, Bocas del
Toro, Panama

Happy trails
run rings round
The Rock -
Roatan, Honduras

Lazy Baja beach
bend-swinging -
south of La Paz,
Baja, California

'A Year On The Road, transforming a monochrome map into a bubbling, laughing, loving book of waking dreams...'

Colombian cartels' sky-scraping, dollar-washing machines, Panama City

Trouser-dropping drunk on a school night, Players Bar, Panama City

Sweet Anna Banana, Players, Panama City

Five little men in a chest-freezer boat, Bocas del Toro

Hotel Dos Palmas, Bocas del Toro - home for 6 months in early 2004 and late 2005

The future looks bright - Bocas del Toro

And four days later I'm here, on Roatán, an island off the Caribbean coast. This morning was tanning and swimming, this afternoon was trail riding and wheelie practice, this evening will probably be spent with the saucy-as-sin staff of the Twisted Toucan pouring shots down my neck from the bottle and dirty dancing to Sean Paul and the Happy Mondays.

Next stop – here. For quite a long time.

CHAPTER 32

HONDURAS

SEPTEMBER, OCTOBER, NOVEMBER 2003

ROATÁN

Trouble. I knew she was trouble the first time I saw her reel across the bar, all oversize Gucci sunglasses, barely there Versace mini-skirt and legs from here to Cairo. 'She was the kind of blonde who could make a bishop kick a hole in a stained-glass window,' murmured Marlowe, somewhere.

An hour later she threw her drink in my face. A day later she met me for lunch. Two days later she was lunch. Caligula would have blushed.

Three days later she mentions she's married and I'm chewing on eggshell. He's back in New Orleans, right? 'No, he's here on the island.' Great. Doing what? 'Business. I guess you could call him a gangster.' Oh, fucking marvellous.

That should have been my cue to 'no thank you'. But 'thou shalt not' sounds a lot more convincing in a stone-cold celibate church than it does on this tropical beach, at midnight, barefoot, a tall rum in one hand, a taller woman's salsa-snaking hip in the other, as we dance real close, and she's got one hand flamenco-flicking the hem of her skirt and the other in my hair, and the warmth of her mouth's on my neck, my cheek, my ear as she drawls 'Dan, why don't you stay a little longer?', rubbing up against me like a hungry cat, and if loving this is wrong then I don't wanna be right.

Besides, this ain't real life, this is Roatán. I fell for the island when I read its history – originally populated by pre-Mayan Indians, it was depopulated by Columbus who decided the subsistence farmers and fishermen were actually cannibals and they'd be better off worked to death on the slave plantations of Cuba and Jamaica. Abandoned for a century, it was rediscovered by British privateers, buccaneers, including the legendary Welsh maniac (and inventor of rum, maybe) Henry Morgan, who used it as a base to launch noisy raids against the Spanish New World. At the height of its lunacy, Roatán was home to 5000 pirates – Friday nights must have made Salford's Barbary Coast seem like a Bournemouth retirement home.

Eventually the Spanish stopped torturing heathens for long enough to clear the pirates out. The island was empty again until the British abolition of slavery – although colonial landowners were forced to free their slaves, they certainly didn't want them living next door or marrying their daughters. So the Caribbean forced-labour force was shipped here. Where they stayed.

I can't blame them. Roatán's a place to fall in love and a place to fall in love with. I love this island because it's flawed, because it's not an airbrushed travel brochure. Sure, it's rum and reggae easy, but I still see sailors fighting on the dance floor, still see rude boys playing with knives outside the clubs, still see a taxi driver chase a colleague down the street with a gun (fortunately he shoots like these cowboys drive). Though it pretends to be as modern as tomorrow afternoon, with *Bowling for Columbine* on big-screen DVD and United vs Liverpool live on Fox Sports, though there's an ATM and internet access and satellite phones, when it rains the dirt roads muddy-flood, the power cuts out, the ferry stops and we're as cut off as the 19th century.

The beaches are beautiful but they bite back, alive with sandflies the size of blackheads with great whites' jaws. New arrivals get it worse and are easily spotted as they itch like the Singing Detective, picking at themselves like tweaking speed freaks. And it's hot. Damn hot. So hot that breathing doesn't refresh, just scalds and suffocates. Getting up makes me sweat. Cleaning my teeth makes me sweat. First smoke of the morning to last beer at night, I sweat like a fat bird on ecstasy. Or a fat man in the tropics.

The hottest place on the island seems to be the toilet in my almost-converted-container cabin on the beach. Going for a dump makes me feel like Papillon entering punitive solitary confinement. I emerge wincing into the sunlight, ashen-faced, fingers pruned like I've over-stayed a bath, soiled and appalled.

I'm not the only one. The toilet's off a terrace I share with two pretty Parisiennes. My guts aren't just bad, they're noisy. Try to sneak past with a discreet 'Bonjour', sit down, sweat, relax and, Jesus of Nazareth, King of the Jews, my bum turns into Brian Blessed bellowing 'He's poohing!' through my troubled, puckered beak. Again and again. I hear a noise from the terrace but can't tell whether it's a gag or a giggle. I gotta get a new room.

Five dollars more gets me air conditioning, cable and some private toilet dignity. After a week, I'm struggling to finding reasons to leave and dreaming of opening my own hobby bar. It's not just the island, it's the people too. Caribbean rather than Central American, English speaking (with a heavy Carib accent, me darlin') not Spanish, it's the kind of place where passers-by nod their heads to the mambos floating out of bars. The kind of place that attracts thirty-something gringos and

Euros who are a step beyond the usual teenage gap-year backpackers, a cut above the two-weeker holidaymakers who pollute the region's Ibizas with their vomiting and faux-MTV good-girls-gone-wild clumsiness.

Then the Blonde turns up. Summertime and the living is sleazy. Man, I'm living the dream – riding away on my bike to an island hidey-hole and scoring with a woman way out of my league? Big-grin happy, laughing-out-loud happy, making-up-songs happy. ('You put the ass into classy, baby, you put the hi into thighs.')

Nothing lasts for ever. I am happy, I just wish it wasn't at another man's expense. But it is. The drunk thrill of a secret rendezvous sinks into sober morning guilt. Sultry afternoons turn cold-sweat clammy as every car-door slam and gravel crunch startles her frigid rigid and me dish-rag limp. 'You just wilted like lettuce in the Alabama sun, darlin'.' Er, yes, thank you, dear.

Should I stay or should I go? Ride and decide. Drag the Dakar from under the palm trees, wipe off the monkey shit (cheeky monkey) and head out, past Sundowners beach bar and its alcoholic dive-master crowd, past the gym that's closed due to lack of Californians, past the taxi rank where 225 'The Seductor' and 003 'Night Stalker' still can't understand why so few female fares after dark, onto West End's sandy high street with its 'Cheapest in the World' dive shops, pink-legged tourists, pointlessly busy dogs and commuting crabs, and out onto the island's one road.

It's an up-and-down, left-and-right, storm-damaged single-lane that ripples up and down the green mountain from the tourist west to the poor east, sometimes empty, sometimes clogged with too many taxis

and too-large imported trucks. A month ago it worried me – now, it's a supermoto track, with humpback jumps, wheelie-practice slopes and slithery gravel slides. A month ago I always wore gloves and boots. Now I'm happy in trainers and shorts.

Past Anthony's Key, the $200-a-night exclusive honeymoon hideaway, past Parrot Plantation, the first pirate colony, past a bright green 'monkey lala' lizard sprinting on its back legs, past a gaggle of kids wobbling unpredictably on oversize bicycles as they race downhill, past the barrio shanties of Coxen Hole, riding as long and as far and as fast as I can, till I reach the other dead end and turn round and do it all again.

Five minutes from home, I hit a junction and decide at the last minute to swing left, up a road to nowhere but a beautiful view of both sides of the island. Park up, light up, watch the setting sun paint the scene fiery gold, baby blue, cat's-mouth pink. I love this island.

Decision made, I head back. The Blonde's gotta go – adultery's adultery even if the marriage is a sexless sham, an arm-candy for shiny bauble exchange. I wonder where she is? If she's at the Italian I can get some pasta while we talk and, bang, I crash hard.

The front wheel makes a tearing sound as it breaks free on a right-hander and, crash, I bang hard, wallop, I crash hard and the bike's heavy on my right side as my arms spread in front of me and we scrape down-hill, shriek downhill, and the tarmac tears my trainers and grinds down my toes and the tarmac bites at my hips and snags my elbows and the tarmac burns at my knees and rips off my clothes and the clock's still reading fifty and, fucking hell, I wish this would stop.

It stops. The stalled engine pings, my dizzy ears ring and every fucking thing stings. 'What goes around, comes around,' the spinning wheels sing.

A cab pulls over. The Spanish driver's taking his wife and son home. All three get the bike up, get me up, then coo sympathetically when I wobble and puke. 'Can I take you home?' I wish.

I thought I was abroad. I thought the people here were scruffy acquaintances, drunken partners, passing lovers. Turns out they're friends. Turns out I am at home. Patricio, the Argentine hotel owner, half-carries me to my room, strips me with no embarrassment and puts me in the shower with a Cuba libre and a bottle of Dettol. Alex, the Italian restaurant manager, and Julio, a local street hustler, throw the bike into a borrowed pickup. The Blonde turns up with a mouth full of kisses and a bag full of goodies. 'OK, we got rum, beers, juice, smokes and Valium. I gotta run. And by the way, first time I've ever seen a man with more holes than me.' Er, yes, thank you, dear.

She leaves, they arrive – the Sisters of Mercy. Lauren from Georgia snaps on rubber gloves and cleans the wounds, Danielle from Florida snips up dressings and tapes on bandages and Jeanine from Alabama sits on the edge of the bed looking purty and chirping about nekkid break-dancing and bikini downhill. 'Now that's what I call Southern comfort,' chuckles Trys.

Next day a doctor with kind eyes and cruel hands scrubs my wounds clean. With a soapy bristled brush. Scrubs. After he's run my cross-eyed body through the X-ray and confirmed two broken ribs and a chipped kneecap, he scolds me for riding in my pants. He's absolutely right – for

the past couple of years I've been posing for pics in sandals and shorts. Everyone crashes eventually – and without proper kit, it hurts. Really, really fucking hurts. For weeks. You try doing anything fun without using your palms, knees, toes or elbows. Boots and gloves, kids, boots and gloves.

Truth is, I've been damn lucky. I crashed minutes from a familiar hotel – it could have happened in the middle of nowhere, at night, somewhere genuinely foreign. And though I'm sore, I'm not broken. I'm useless, but not for long.

The bike's a bit battered but crashed well. Mainly 'cause I took most of the damage. Bent bar, scuffed guards, four popped indicators (apparently I hit both sides – I've no idea how); the only real problem came from the smashed switches – the right-hand cluster exploded and the kill switch is dead, Zed. Rob, a Florida mechanic, helps me bodge it back together.

I arrange to meet the Blonde for dinner. Her friend, the Brunette, turns up instead. 'She can't see you any more. He knows. You should leave.' Without even a bang and a whimper? 'Sorry, you're not my type.' Neither are you – gentleman hooligans prefer blondes.

Next stop – the 6 a.m. ferry to the mainland. Tomorrow.

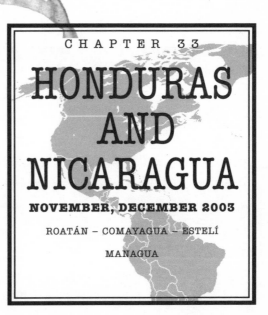

CHAPTER 33

HONDURAS AND NICARAGUA

NOVEMBER, DECEMBER 2003

ROATÁN – COMAYAGUA – ESTELÍ

MANAGUA

Beep fucking beep. Six o'clock in the morning. Last time I heard an alarm was March. Last time I saw dawn via sleep's cosy tunnel was Christ knows. What am I doing? Oh yeah – getting off the Rock before the Gangster shoots me for fooling around with the Moll. Chuckle. Very alarming.

Bare feet echo off cool wooden floors. Grab a Coke and a smoke, stumbling through early-morning clumsiness that fogs the room like shower steam. One last check under the bed, one last passport-pocket pat, and one last clomp down the stairs.

The monkeys are still asleep, but the taxi drivers are awake, yawning at the gate, hoping for an early fare, tinny ranchero music country-crooning out of battered Nissans. Push the bike out from under its palm tree, try to remember how to fit the bags, take one last look at the Caribbean bay and slouch into Coxen Hole.

Coxen Hole's the former pirate lair turned Island capital – grand name for a scruffy port with a couple of banks, a not especially super market and a cop shop on its one main drag. The ferry's already in and the quay's busy, with families in relative-visiting Sunday best, with puffy-eyed backpackers, with suitcase-slinging porters. I'm on last. There's no ramp, so five of us heave-ho the bike shoulder high and on board.

Gotta love boats. I really don't want to leave the Rock, don't want to leave my friends, my bars, my beaches, my Moll, but the waves' clucking slap, the wind's salty snap and the big diesel chug turn a sour so-long into the sweetest sadness. Roatán fades like a wake into the horizon's haze. You don't get that on a twenty-nine bus.

An hour later we reach the mainland. More helpful hands heft the bike ashore. An old boy wanders over. 'That bike is too heavy. If it falls, you will die.' Eh? 'This bike will kill you.' Will you shut up? He shrugs and smiles and keeps staring. Like some kind of Angel of Death. As I kick up the side stand, the boot loop snaps off. 'You see?' And I wobble away into the happy honking hell of a Honduran highway.

I don't like to generalise, but for these bastards, I'll make an exception. Hondurans are the worst drivers in the world. Shit and slow is one thing, but these maniacs are shit and fast. Their preferred road position is wheels on either side of the centre line. Which I suppose gives them a fighting chance of avoiding the children and dogs, cows and taxis dashing out from the verges with the fatalism of suicide bombers.

The road whistles through palm forests, industrial sprawls and dramatic mountains. I only know because I keep stopping to smoke and calm down. When I'm riding, I don't see a thing – too busy looking round oncoming buses for the inevitable head-on double overtake. By the time I reach the US garrison town of Comayagua, I'm a nervous wreck and decide to call it a night. Though it's only afternoon. A girl with 'Selfish' written across her chest shows me a room. Turn on the TV just in time to see the suddenly attractive Carol Smillie wrapping up *Changing Rooms*. 'And it's goodbye from Beckenham.'

Asleep by ten, up by six again. I've gotta deal with Tegucigalpa, the national capital, and a border today. Ride off with a worrying 'I've forgotten my head' bellyache. It's at least half an hour before I realise I've not forgotten anything, I'm just sitting on my plums. Damn those hairy boys. At least the driving's calmer. Maybe they're still sober.

Better driving, worse poverty. All through Central America, poor farmers use the narrow, unclaimed strips of land between field fence and hard shoulder for free grazing. Now I pass strips squatted with shanty shacks, washing lines, indigenous families. Half-dressed children play in the litter inches from the highway.

I stop to buy bananas from an old dear, force myself to look, remind myself that Honduras is not about self-indulgent beach holidays. Bananas, please. The old dear smiles, hands me a bunch and chirps at a little girl who nods and trots away, returning with a sloshing washing-up bowl. For me? I don't understand. The girl looks puzzled and demonstrates. Oh, I see. It's so I can wash my dusty face and hands before I eat. Thank you, darlin'. The old dear follows me back to the bike. 'Despacio. Hay más tiempo que vida.' Go slow. There is more time than life.

I ring-road Tegucigalpa's 'fear and consumption' combo of McDonald's and armed guards and head east. The sun's out, the sky's big, the mountains and valleys are green and soft. All good. Until the bike starts losing power, struggling despite an open throttle. What?

Pull over, though I don't know what I'll check. Oh, right. Even I understand that the rear brake disc shouldn't be, er, on fire. For some reason, the smoke and red glow don't completely convince me and I still feel the need to touch it, just to make sure. My fingers sizzle and stick to the caliper. Bugger.

Seems I've been watching too many History Channel stories about overheating machine guns. Why else would I decide to pee on the brake? I've got no water and I can't just sit here, nowhere. I start the splash, then panic that the heat will travel back up the stream and scald my willy, so pinch the end and this running interference turns the stream into a spray. Just as I spot the farmer. At a very basic level, there's something deeply wrong about saying 'Good afternoon' to a man with a machete in his hand when I've got the lad in mine. A lad that's pissing all over my boots, bags and bike. I guess from the look on his face that he agrees.

He sidles off, appalled. I resort to hitting the caliper with a spanner while trying not to cry. Maybe I should become a mechanic, 'cause it works a treat. Shame about the vinegary smell, though.

Wheel problems, like saline twins and those damn hairy boys, come in pairs. Several miles too far from the last town before the Nicaraguan border, I feel an unsettling knock coming from the front. Check the spindle (all right, I tap it with my lighter), check the tyre pressure (all right, I squeeze it with my blistered fingers), looking for Christ knows what, and spotting nothing. So I carry on.

Until the knock becomes a lateral waggle becomes a gentle but terrifying slap to the sound of rubber on metal squeak and then metal on metal grind. What the fuck is going on? Slow down, trying to stay off that tangy back brake, using the engine, a slight slope and my size twelves to stop. And flap.

The front wheel's all but seized. What to do? Ride back to what-was-it-called and find a mechanic? Thumb down a pickup piggyback? I smoke a smoke, wheel the bike back and forth, remember that my visa runs out tonight so decide to go for the border and sort things on the Nicaraguan side.

The border. Last thing I need now is a taxing encounter with two-legged customs rats. No problem. A badged tramitador guides me through the complex but honest process while we banter in pidgin English and turkey Spanish. Twenty minutes? That's the quickest since the States. I'm so relieved, I forget about the bike's bollocksed bearings. Oh, bollocks.

Welcome to Nicaragua. Between 1979 and 1986, the Sandinista revolution was romantic inspiration for European socialists, a living, breathing, fighting, voting progressive alternative not just to Thatcher's aggressively anti-working-class Britain, but also to the unhealthy, moribund, repressive Soviet regimes.

So I'm expecting the fluttering red-and-black rebel flags and the political graffiti, especially in this corner of the country that never lost faith even when they lost power. What I'm not expecting is the eye-widening, head-opening, worry-dissolving beauty. Dayum.

When conquistador Cortez was asked to draw a map of the region, he

just screwed the paper into a ball and said, 'It looks like that.' So they gave the job to more conventional cartographers who wrote across this land of lakes and volcanoes, 'Plenty of fantasy here.'

Just as it gets dark, my tail light packs up. And the front locks again. And again. And now I'm the suicidee swerving into the path of faster traffic. It takes two jumpy hours to crawl the twenty miles to Estelí.

Despite the bike, I'm excited to be here, so find a hotel and explore. And eat. Grab a pavement table in the main square under the cathedral and murals and scarf street food – grilled chicken, dirty rice, hot tortillas and a perfect spicy sweet chilli salsa. A lad in a Che T-shirt ring-dings past on a TDR250. Forget 'Bread and Work!' we want 'Hot Salsa and Saucy Strokers For All!'

Maybe not for all. A street dog with a snotty nose and a stray kid with puppy eyes compete for my leftovers. Mamacita shoos them away with a broom. Beggars are bad for business, especially guilty gringo business. I decide to buy him a takeaway. Because I can. Because it makes me feel swell. Some of that tasty dirty rice, please, señora? 'Gallo pinto. Te gusta?' I fall off the kerb, laughing and snotting kidney beans. Do I like your gallo pinto? All together now – yes, I very much enjoyed your painted cock, madam.

I give the kid the foil-covered plate. He eats a mouthful and feeds the rest to the dog. But he keeps the foil. Eh? He winks and runs a lighter over it. Oh, I see. And suddenly I don't feel quite so swell.

Next morning I email the boys at *Bike* magazine for advice. 'Yep, it sounds like the bearings; yep, it's dangerous; nope, you shouldn't ride,' says Stevie Westlake. I try to find a mechanic, but no one's innarested in helping this barely comprehensible anglo with a weird bike. Their advice – 'Managua'.

I have me a big decision. Should I stay or should I go? Managua's over a hundred miles away – not country-backwater miles, but Pan-American Highway miles down the main truck route from LA to Panama City. If it goes shit-shaped, if the buggered bearings crunch too hard against the spindle, if the disc gets jammed in the caliper, it could be sorta fatal. What's the alternative? Live in Estelí for the rest of my life?

Managua or bust. As stupid calls go, this is right up there with riding across a Saharan minefield and cuckolding a stone-cold killer. At least it'll give me something to write about. First, I'll change my pants – my gran impressed upon me the vital importance of always wearing clean pants in case of an accident. I guess it stops any confusion about which set of skid marks the investigating cops should measure.

Out of town, onto the highway, into the hard shoulder at a steady 15 mph. I spend an hour or so standing on the pegs, ready to jump off, looking over my shoulder for crushing eighteen-wheelers, crippled by panic attacks and images of my ma crying at my funeral. Comforted by Carol Smillie. Damn her insidious Scottish charms!

But as I calm down, as the wheel keeps rolling, the worst day turns into one of the most intensely lit, brightly remembered, slowly savoured, best days of my life, as I stroll past coffee plantations and tobacco fields, now riding alongside white-hatted gauchos on cow-herding horses, now beeping at the lads in the delivery vans as we leapfrog each other, now racing kids on grandads' bicycles. Speed is the enemy of reflection.

Eight hours or so later, I reach Tipitapa (say it again) on Lake Managua and realise I'm gonna make it. I'm not gonna die. Retarded maybe, but that rush of elation makes it all worthwhile. Clichéd maybe, but that fear of death made me feel more alive. An hour later I'm chatting with friendly bikers at the capital's traffic lights. Two hours later I'm showering soap out of my ears and watching *Seinfeld* reruns on cable. Six hours later I'm stood in the Shannon Bar, London Pride in one hand and a bodhrán in the other, belting out 'Dirty Old Town' with the Cork landlord.

These are the days that must happen to you? Abso-fucken-lutely, baby.

Happy Birthday, Jesus. Midnight in Managua and as Eve becomes Day, the city explodes in a celebratory salvo of firecrackers and skyrockets. I wander outside in my dad's pants and watch the noisy colours and colourful noises. The Immaculate Conception marked by fruity bangs.

CHAPTER 34

NICARAGUA AND COSTA RICA

DECEMBER 2003, JANUARY 2004

MANAGUA – GRANADA

SAN JUAN DEL SUR – BAHÍA MAJAGUAL

LIBERIA – PLAYA DEL COCO – ATENAS

ARENAL – PLAYA TAMARINDO

MONTEZUMA – JACO – ATENAS

I'm the only guest in the hotel and the staff have all gone to bed. Chris the Courier's mobile was off and the Ex put down the phone before I got past 'Happy'. The Blonde's not replying to emails and Home wasn't in. 'We're sorry, but the world you called is unavailable.' Life as a non-contact sport.

A fizzing bang plops into the pool and the talking macaws and kitchen chickens hoot a not-dawn chorus across the dark compound. I join in, throwing spastic mambo shapes to the Walkman's Radiohead. Wouldn't you?

Today we escape. Pack and get dressed. Three weeks I've been stuck in Managua, waiting, watching, drinking. Waiting for a new front wheel, watching more *Seinfeld* reruns on cable and drinking in the Shannon Bar. And drinking in the Shannon Bar.

Week one was all fresh fun, exploring a new capital, splurge shopping in the reassuringly bland malls, tracking down old Sandinista guerrillas. No bike, so I made 4x4 friends and day-tripped to the sulphurous Volcano Masaya and the perfectly preserved, perfectly beautiful Granada, the oldest colonial city in the Americas, and the only one to boast a piece of graffiti that reads 'Suck my Duck'.

The shopping splurge included new sandals. Took me five minutes to realise they were too small, non-returnable and, er, ladies' – high heels that cut and constrict and have me wincing baby steps, while trying to avoid the stares. A gringo is no big deal here, but a gringo who practises foot-binding is apparently quite unusual. The positive side is that Chinese men now find me curiously attractive.

Hobbled by shit shoes and change-the-channel familiarity, week two contracts into a lazy, limping triangle – hotel for sleep and TV, mall for internet and cinema, bar for shits and giggles and a sultry snog with a girl from Surinam.

By week three the triangle's become a single wobbly line between the hotel and the pub. Drinking till 3, 5, 7, sleeping till 2, 4, 6. Waking up fully dressed with blood on my trousers, a Viagra in my pocket, and dream-vague memories of naked bars and a soldier from Nottingham. Waking up undressed by a Finnish nurse, with embarrassed memories of 'I really like the way you are fondling me'.

The wheel arrives just in time. One more session and I'll be shacking up with the sodden old dear who sways at the end of every bar, crooning Patsy Cline's 'Crazy' into a glass that's more snot and tears than lager and lime. One more session and I'll never scrub off the smell of fighting and onions.

I enlist Miguel, a former logistics officer with the Nicaraguan Sandinistas and Salvadorean FMLN, to help me find a garage. 'Smuggling detonators across the border was easier than this,' he laughs after we lose ourselves in yet another featureless barrio's dusty one-way streets, littered with rusted-out cars and walled-off, low-rise compounds. We could ask for directions, but it wouldn't help – since the earthquake and the rebuild, there are no street names in downtown Managua. Attaching permanence to the new city would be tempting fate. And the locals give extraordinary instructions – 'towards the lake' or 'towards the mountains' rather than 'north' or 'south', and 'up' and 'down' rather than 'east' or 'west'. Made even less clear by reference to landmarks that no longer exist. Where's the garage? 'Two blocks to the lake, one down and turn where the cinema used to be.' Said in break-neck colloquial Spanish. Yes, thank you.

'Are you sure you need a mechanic?' Maybe not. I just wanted to swap that 'wobbly bike on a creaky chair and skinning my knuckles on inappropriate tools' nonsense for some 'capable man in overalls' reassurance. Round the corner from where the old cinema used to be, a teenager in phoney four-stripe Adidas props the wobbly bike on a creaky chair and skins his knuckles with my inappropriate tools. I'm not entirely reassured.

Christmas morning is my first test ride, and I'm nervous as a long-tailed cat in a room full of rocking chairs. I hope that odd turns of phrase are all I've picked up from my southern belle. Irish Paul, governor of the Shannon Bar, has invited me to spend the day with him and his Nica family down by the beach. Something's still not right with the bike – the front's loose, notchy, twitchy in corners, deflecting wildly off the smallest bumps. I'm damn glad to get off it.

And find some peace. Sitting smiling silently on the curve of this perfect horseshoe bay, toes full of soft sand, ears full of Pacific rush, eyes full of dusky sunset, I realise that this is what makes me happy – not noisy bars, not slurred insults, not jumpy hangovers. 'Coming for a drink?' calls Irish Paul. I'm just a girl who can't say no. 'What will you have?' Too much.

Noisy hours later, the Aussie hotel manager screeches, 'I don't care what time it is – I want you out,' as he holds back his Canadian crony. I pulled his leg, he pulled a gun, I swung a bottle, he hit the deck. 'Now!' No room at the inn. Only time in my life I'll ever feel like the Virgin Mary. I pretend I'm packing, lock the door from the inside and get my head down. I'm woken by the sound of bruised knuckles pounding on the window, the room filling with sharp morning light as my head floods with shameful memories of getting barred from the most beautiful beach in Central America. Cock-knocker.

It wasn't my fault. It never is. I throw my bags over the barbed-wire fence into the hippy campsite next door. 'You get barred, too?' says an Alaskan in a hammock. 'Welcome. Beer?' He smells of fighting and onions. Out but not down, I duck the Ghost of Christmas Future and spend Boxing Day on the beach with a book. The border can wait till mañana.

'No es correcto.' I've overstayed my visa. When I roll up at the frontier with a shrug, the Nicas think I'm taking the piss. I guess I am. Heads shake, lips purse and I'm pushed into a prefab office with plastic windows and an atmosphere clammy with bureaucratic procedure and unspecific threats. It feels like the Somoza Bad Old Days, sat sweating for an hour, two, three, under a photocopied portrait of an over-decorated general while plain-clothes customs officers drift past, sneering. Eventually someone taps his shoulder to indicate rank and shoos me towards the Chief.

The Handsome Chief, looking like Starsky and dressing like Hutch (or is it the other way round?), is having lunch. He eats flamboyantly, waving away obsequious intrusions with a plastic fork, snorting at my offensive paperwork, while the pretty secretary in the tight blouse throws me up-and-under eyes, asking me whether I'm married and how much I earn, as her pen slips from lip tapping to cleavage stroking. Good cop, bad cop? 'Fifty dollars,' says the Chief, just before she starts to undress. 'And your email,' smiles the Secretary.

Welcome to Costa Rica, Central America in sensible shoes. Nicaragua's the home of poetic revolution; El Salvador and Honduras once went to war over a football game (which makes a pitch invasion and a bit of bloodied Burberry look kinda tame); Guatemala has pyramids that would make Egypt blush; and Costa Rica? Costa Rica has an enlight-ened approach to conservation.

First thing I see is a Pizza Hut. Second thing I see is a Century 21 estate agent's board. Third thing I see is a daft dog scudding off my front wheel. Next town, Liberia, I dive into a hotel. And for the first time, I can't be bothered exploring – not because I'm too tired or too sick, but because I'm too indifferent. I just don't care. Grab a Burger King and slump in front of the TV. For two days.

What's up? Dunno. Maybe the beach will cure it. Maybe not. Two days on the Pacific coast and I feel worse, not better. Slouch back to Liberia, back to Burger King, back to the TV and back to an unpleasant conclusion. I'm bored.

Bored? Bored of border crossings, bored of bike worries. Bored of cheap hotels, bored of boozy bars. Bored of wearing crumpled clothes out of musty bags, bored of email friendships and virtual relationships. Bored of reducing my life to a series of tawdry anecdotes to be prostituted to motorcycle magazines. Bored of always having to worry about money. I'm thinking seriously about jacking, heading back to Roatán, Mexico City, New York, wherever, getting a job in a bar, on the buildings, whatever.

Whatever. Somehow, somewhere, the unusual became usual, the exotic mundane. Unremarkable. Boring. And the realisation that I'm bored angers me. Only boring people get bored, only shiftless wretches with no imagination get fed up On The Road. I don't feel that I have a right to be down living this spoiled twat's Life of Reilly. I feel duty-bound to puppy-bound everywhere, yapping 'I'm the luckiest boy in the world' with eager enthusiasm. But it can't be faked any more than sleep or wood.

I fire off sulky emails, blaming the innocent outside for my guilty insides. 'Costa Rica? Costa Shit. Beautiful but bland. You wouldn't want to be stuck in a lift with Costa Rica etc.' Seems I'm not the only one. Ian, in Honduras on his KLR, writes, 'There's a limit to the therapeutic effects of travelling and I think I'm approaching it. Funny as it sounds, I'm getting bored!' And this from Trys, in Venezuela on his XRL: 'I feel ungrateful when I get bored or waste days with a bottle of rum and HBO. I'm in South America, I should be doing something I can't do in Salford.'

I'm not really bored. But I am really lonely. I just can't tell the difference right now – too up my own arse to realise this, too convinced of my own self-sufficiency. While I still crave the approval of other men, I reduce friendly riding partners to dumbed-down sidekicks. Even though I still need the vindication of the vagina, I keep running away from loving kisses. And this demented, delicious double-bind is knotting my nap. Depression is rage turned inwards.

Out of the blue, a friend appears. His name's Chip, he read about my trip, he runs a dirt bike tour company from his hideaway home in Atenas, in the hills above San José. 'Pop in for a beer,' says the email. I'll meet him for a drink then get off. Other people's homes worry me – tippy-toes and pinched farts, smoking outside and asking permission to open the fridge? I can't be doing with it.

'Welcome, brother,' says Chip with eyes that mean it. He flashes his Paul Newman smile and introduces me to wife Gaby and daughter Andrea. 'Here's a key – you've got your own door and a separate toilet. The more relaxed you are, the more relaxed we are.' And he means it.

Comfortable as home, but with a better view. Cosy as a bath, but with a better library. Days in the garden with Seth Morgan, Dylan Thomas, Ted Simon, evenings on the porch with Chip and his stories, about his time in the submarine corps ('I joined because it was the only service that didn't do all that spit and polish crap'), about AMA racing ('It was four years before I won a race. Actually it was four years before I finished a race. I crashed a lot.'), and about King Kenny Roberts ('King? He and his boy are the Bushes of the racing world'). We gently toast the New Year with cold Coronas and he asks me again if I'd like to go on a tour. First time I said no – lied about limited time 'cause something inside was squealing, 'Guided tours are for tourists, part-timers, day-trippers.' This time I say yes, thank you. 'Great. The guys get in tomorrow.'

The guys – real people with real lives and real jobs, down on holiday to have a real good time. Real riders, too – more ex-AMA racers, Colorado 500 riders, cunning, experienced salt-and-pepper-beard riders. I know I'm gonna get toasted, but we're all surprised at just how badly.

'Could try harder,' says Paul, disappointed, after the first day's dirt. 'I overtook you with my engine off,' says Big John, bemused. 'Pathologically slow,' says Dr Ed, clinically. 'Slow as shit,' says his son Clay, appalled. 'You done great,' says JB, encouragingly. But because I don't care, they don't care. Because I don't whine about not being able to keep up, they don't bitch about waiting. Because I always turn up with a daft grin on my grubby face they smile back.

Man, I'm having a blast – five days of dirty nonsense, slithering through wet-as-the-Dales meadows, skidding down dry-as-a-desert jeep trails, splashing through deep-as-my-knees fords, chuckling over rickets-bent suspension bridges that tickle my ping-pongs as the boards ripple beneath the wheels. The DR350's wheels – the Beemer's on the operating table again, after Chip diagnosed buckled head races. 'Why not borrow one of my bikes while we order parts?' God Bless the Good Gringo.

Only one off, and that was 'cause I bottled and bailed. Loose-as-a-goose, steep-as-a-cliff downhill – I panicked, locked up, and when that didn't slow me down, jumped off the side. 'Momentum is your friend,' says ever-helpful JB as he stops to pick me up. I look so pathetic, he feels obliged to ride my bike down, then sweat back up the hill to collect his. Next water crossing, he gets his wet revenge – waits till I'm halfway across, then ambushes me with a soaking wake. Only time in my life I'll ever feel like Steve McQueen.

Back at base, there's one last group meal, one last ride in the back of Chip's truck, the Kia Bongo. The full moon's back-lighting low clouds and the lights in the valley twinkle like cats' eyes. 'Man, I feel free,' says JB. He goes back to work tomorrow. I laugh out loud and want to hug him. I'm cured like bacon. And can't wait to get back On The Road.

As we say goodbye, JB squeezes my arm and repeats his mantra, 'Momentum is your friend.' It takes me a couple of days to understand that what he really means is 'Keep drifting.'

Next stop – nowhere.

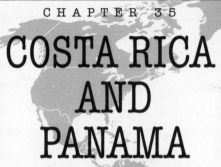

CHAPTER 35

COSTA RICA AND PANAMA

JANUARY, FEBRUARY 2004

SAN JOSÉ – PUERTO LIMÓN

PUERTO VIEJO – CHANGUINOLA

BOCAS DEL TORO

'No kiss and no chupa-chupa.' Saturday night in the New Yorker, San José, and Patricia's explaining that even the oldest profession has industry standards. Chupa-chupa? She laughs, sticks a tongue in her cheek, makes a circle with a French-tipped thumb and finger and ghosts a phantom menace into her pout. Oh, I see.

'You really know a town when you can score sex and drugs,' said Bill Burroughs. A block away from normal San José, a block away from the ped mall's glowing lights, open shopfronts, happy shoppers so festive they make every weekend feel like Oxford Street on Christmas Eve, lurks another market selling everything cheap and cheerless, fast and nasty. 'Pssss, hombre, wan' weed, coke, beautiful woomans?'

Or not so beautiful womans. A heavy dyke runs past, moulting earrings and sequins, high heels and loose change, as she bursts through a bus queue of shop assistants. She's being chased. She's being chased by someone I know, Kerry Jim from Managua. And he's not just chasing her, he's knocking fuck out of the back of her head. Jim, man, what are you doing? 'He's got my wallet.' He stops, panting like a puffed barrel of stout. He? 'Bloody transvestite muggers, Danny. They're an absolute menace.' Oh, I see.

Jimmy leads me into the New Yorker. 'You'll like it here.' The barmaids are all Nicaraguan, so tall, dark and lovely. If you find fits-where-it-touches black Lycra hot pants, miniskirts and boob tubes lovely. Put all the exposed bits of flesh together and it's possible to see a whole nekkid woman.

I guess that's what the guys are trying to do, older gringos from town's no one's ever heard of in states no one ever visits – Iowa, Ohio, Indiana. The older we get, the more attention men have to pay to our appearance to keep looking respectable. With patchy grey stubble, lank yellow hair and tired red eyes, these fellas have gone beyond seedy into seedier. I'm right at home.

'My name is Pat-ree-cee-ya.' I'd noticed her come in with him – mainly because she was strikingly beautiful and he strikingly wasn't. I guessed they'd just done business. Such a coy euphemism. Every time he tried to talk to her, she threw him a contemptuous look that could wilt wood through a bathroom door. He was being nice, but she'd eaten and now he was just a dirty plate. 'Can I buy you one drink?' she says to me.

Damn, she's good. Charming but not creepy, flirty not slutty, proper funny and very, very sexy. She looks like Shakira – if Shakira shopped in Costa Rican markets with dirty money she'd earned having sex with old men. If she wasn't a hooker, I'd be massively attracted to her. But she is. So I'm not. Just talking to her makes me uncomfortable. Because it makes me feel like one of Them.

Sort it. Sorry, señorita, you're very lovely, muy bonita, but I don't want to have sex with you. 'No sex?' No sex. 'And me no kiss or chupa-chupa.' She laughs. 'So let's get drunk, no?'

Yes. We leave, and I'm trying to look like a normal guy going for a normal drink with a normal girl. Jimmy follows with tonight's paid company. They look like a drunk and a tart getting a room. Until they climb into a police car. That she's driving. Er, Jimmy, I thought she was a, er, you know . . . 'Only by night. By day she's a police sergeant.' Oh, I see.

Patricia knows everyone and everyone knows Patricia. Taxi drivers shuttle us for free(bies) with a leer. Doormen wave us past queues and cover charges with a wink. Barmaids shoo away money for drinks with a shush. Strippers rack up rock-star lines in dressing rooms cloyed with hairspray and thrush. And every time someone nods my way and asks, 'You working?', Patricia says, 'Not tonight. I'm with my friend.'

Like everyone else, we end up in the Del Rey – hotel, bar, casino, disco, clip joint, cathouse. It's late, and the sellers outnumber the buyers maybe two or three to one. Which makes the girls especially desperate. Which makes the atmosphere especially unpleasant.

We sit at the bar and keep pretending. Patricia keeps predators away with a wild-dog smile and a flash of claws. For a while, we even fool ourselves, chatting easily, laughing tipsily, her hand on my shoulder, my balls in my mouth. And then I go and spoil it all by saying something stupid. How and why? She tenses up, but I'm too ignorant to notice. How and why? She punches me hard and looks through my eyes. 'Why? Why? Because is better they pay than my father takes it for free. How? How? Like this.' She slams a tequila. Oh, I see.

'I'm joking. It's just a job. Don't worry. I don't need saving.' I'm a clumsy amateur, but she's a slick pro, and with a flick of her hair, snaps back the atmosphere with a rant about Viagra. 'Before, many men, they could not . . .' She uncurls a finger and whistles. 'But still they pay. Now, every man can . . .' The finger again. 'Is too much work.' In the background, Clapton sings 'Cocaine.' The bar cheers, Patricia grins and slides away to powder her nose.

As soon as she leaves, I'm under pressure. Only time in my life I'll feel like a pretty blonde in an ugly meat market. I can't look up, look round without someone trying to make eye contact, thigh contact, sly contact. I hunch my shoulders, stare into my beer, pretend I'm not there. Every other man in here's loving it, riffing off this cheap monkey-spank-mag fantasy – 'I was in this bar, right, and every woman in there wanted to sleep with me' etc. But I can't see beyond the dirty money and the stupid lie. Besides, without the buzzing risk of rejection, seduction's no fun. Without that sweet-and-sour, girls-and-boys, will-she-or-won't-he, yes-or-no anticipation, it's just another commercial certainty. About as sexy as buying cigarettes.

I pop out to buy cigarettes. 'What's wrong with you, faggot?' sneers an ugly voice in my head. Maybe I am uptight, frigid. Maybe I should just go with it. She could use the money, I could use the contact. Maybe she really does like me. And maybe she can read me like a bad book. When I get back to the bar, she's gone. 'A kiss very strong, bye bye,' says the note on the napkin. I couldn't score in a brothel.

Just to make sure, I leave the next day, pack up the bike listening to the swirling sounds of an easy Sunday morning – 'On me 'ed' shouts echoing across the football pitch, sneaker squeak on a basketball court, the chug-a-lug of Harleys on the ring road. Sunday in the hung-over city, Sunday in the relative-visiting suburbs, Sunday on the empty freeway, Sunday in the chilly hills. That look surprisingly like Wales.

'Looks like Wales' is the lazy British traveller's equivalent of 'tastes like chicken'. Every country in the world seems to have a region that looks just like the Brecon Beacons. Low mist, rolling hills, a stone farmhouse, a tuft of sheep fluff snagged on a barbed-wire fence and, bingo, there's lovely. Though I don't remember Wales being quite so close to the Caribbean. Or so damn hot. As the hills sink, the fields dry, and chilly becomes scorchio. In the tropics, temperature changes with the altitude, not the seasons. Climb to cool down, drop to warm up.

The road skips along the coast, past the cruise-ship dock at Puerto Limón, through sweaty mangroves, across clacking wooden bridges with their gangs of little fisherboys, the so-blue ocean disappearing then reappearing like a conjuror's coin. Sun on my back, salty wind in my mouth, lively throttle in my hand. It's a beautiful day.

Last month I moped like Morrissey, this month I'm giddy as Tommy Cooper. Everything's exciting, innaresting, full of funny potential again. I hit a pothole hard and the tank plastics burst apart like a bad lie. So what? I make a wrong turn and add an extra hour to the journey. Perfect. I hit another pothole harder and knock the headlight so far out of whack that it sets fire to the lens. It's all good.

Plot up in pretty, touristy Puerto Viejo, smile at the phoney rastas, so-serious surfers, silly French hippies and rent a room on the sand from a porcine Fräulein. She smells of boobs and baking. And she's bursting out of her granddaughter's clothes like rising dough. 'My room's right next door,' she hiccups, unnecessarily. That night, I wake up and she's standing by my bed. Er, what are you doing? 'Sorry, I thought it was my room. A mistake.' Oh, I see.

Just to make sure, I leave the next day, pack up the bike listening to the swirling sound of the sea. I'm headed for Panama. And that means the bridge at Changuinola. I've been warned, but it's still a shocking surprise – a rotten, swaying railway bridge with more gaps than a tramp's smile, two or three hundred yards across and a dizzying don't-look-down drop below. No guard rail, slippery tracks, big holes – it's genuinely lethal. Sod it – I'll either make it or I won't. I make it.

And quick as I can say 'Amanaplanacanalpanama' I'm stamped through and waved down a bouncing dirt road that dead-legs me and the bike a merciless playground beating through green and yellow miles of banana plantations to the port of Almirante, where a banana boat ferries us to las Islas Bocas del Toro.

It's another backwater island paradise, wonky wooden houses wobbling on bow-legged stilts, fresh fish restaurants and cheap rum bars rocking decks over the water, and bay after bay of picture-perfect beaches only accessible by water taxi. Or a big dirt bike.

And that's how I met Anna, this sweet girl I'm desperate not to sour. A drink became dinner became lifts to the beach. Every time she sat on, got on, got off the bike, all I could think about was what was touching where and why. Three days later, sheltering under palms from a purple tropical storm, soaked with spray from the lashing surf and splashing rain, every drop of blood bubbling with that sweet-and-sour, girls-and-boys, will-she-or-won't-he, yes-or-no anticipation, I finally burst. Er, so do you kiss?

These are the days that must happen to you? Abso-fucken-lutely, baby.

CHAPTER 36

PANAMA

FEBRUARY, MARCH 2004

BOCAS DEL TORO

CHIRIQUI GRANDE

PANAMA CITY – ISLA TABOGA

Aitch-oh-mudderfucken-tee hot. Friday afternoon in Panama City, sat sitting at the lights on the Plaza Bolívar, laughing at a 'large-breasted pirate queen'- liveried bus airhorn-parping the theme from *The Godfather* as it jumps a red in front of heavily armed but barely innarested traffic cops, it suddenly occurs to me that I've been On The Road a year to the day.

And riding down Avenida Balboa, past the spot where that Spanish sailor became the first European to see the Pacific, mirrors full of the old town's crumbling charm, eyes full of the financial district's skyscraping Colombian-cartel dollar-washing machines, the Canadian Cutie on the back snapping pictures over my shoulder, it suddenly occurs to me that this has become normal. The Trip has become A Way of Life.

A year On The Road, a year from Canada to Panama. Slow as rust, easy like Cat Stevens. When I jumped out of the Girlfriend's Golf at Victoria Station, I swore I'd be back with her in six months. 'Yeah, right.' When I waved bye to my family in Manchester, I told them I'd be back for Christmas. 'Since the start, your weeks have been fortnights,' chuckled my da. I kinda meant it.

Three weeks from New York to Los Angeles via New Orleans was on schedule, but I stalled in Venice Beach, distracted by distractions. By the time I reached Mexico City, the Girlfriend had inevitably become the Ex. She won custody of the flat and the friends, I got the bin bags full of clothes I used to wear and books I never read dispatched to Chris the Courier's or distributed to the poor of the parish. And I got time.

With no reason to hurry back, that jumping pogo out of Toronto's snowy airport settled into a slower, lazier groove. Speed is still the enemy of reflection. And Africa's 'keep drifting' mantra has evolved (intelligently designed) into a 'next stop' search. I'm not doing this because I'm addicted to momentum for the sake of it. I'm looking for somewhere to live.

A year On The Road, a year checking out viable alternative lives. Forget Trustafarian divvy hippies and their middle-brow craft stalls, I keep bumping into working-class punters earning usual livings in unusual places – Chelsea Mick computer-programming in Guatemala. Florida Rob spannering in Honduras, Everton John laying bricks in Nicaragua. Others use the jump to make changes – plumbers become actors, barmaids become teachers, teachers become bar owners. All proving that there are bigger, better, broader choices than 'Manchester or London?'

A year On The Road, a year on the bike. The first journey was from Doncaster to Manchester down the tight-as-spoons-in-a-drawer motorway; the last journey was this morning, taking the Canadian to the airport and back to Brooklyn. The girls come and go, the bike remains the same.

Sometimes I want to paint it white and stencil 'PBR Streetgang' across the tank. Sometimes I want to swap it for a black Multistrada or orange Adventure. But most of the time, I just ride it. As long as it's working.

Like all bikes, the Dakar's reliable until it breaks. There's no more malicious god than the God of Counted Chickens and He pecked like an angry cock after my last blurted 'It's ace and never breaks down' blunder. Within a month, the battery had died for the third time, the front wheel bearings had collapsed, the head races had buckled, while everything else carried on rotting like warm roadkill, gnawing at itself like a nervous nail-biter.

Maybe it's my fault – too many jerked-off wheelies slammed down like dominoes, not enough soapy love. Sometimes it disappoints me. Until I remember it's a loan bike, I'm a lucky twat and it's usually a reliable friend.

A year On The Road, a year of friendly faces. Second night of the war, I thought I'd walked into my second fight of the war when I stopped for a drink in a pool hall just outside Camp Lejeune. A platoon of jarhead buzzcuts and Semper Fi tattoos caught the accent and offered a drink to this 'ally'. Sorry, wrong Limey. I think your war's rubbish and your Commander-in-Chief's a murderous liar. If this was a Royal Marine pub I'd have spent the next three days picking bits of broken glass out of my eyes. My biggest fear here was being high-fived to death. 'Whatever, dude. Let's have a beer anyway.' So I drank with them just like I drank with an Israeli lieutenant sitting next to a Hezbollah commander in Guatemala.

Most encounters are less politically charged, just simple friendly. Cops help with directions, shopkeepers are patient with my slow Spanish, everybody waves. Even sailors.

A year On The Road, a year of surprises. Who knew that Niagara Falls

froze? Or that Mexico City was as grand as Rome and cultured as Madrid? I was expecting the Central American Spanish-Indian mestizo mix, but who knew that the Atlantic coast from Belize to Panama and beyond was highly Afro-Caribbean and had been for 330 years, settled by escaped, shipwrecked and freed slaves? Not me.

Nor was I expecting the Irish, English, Scottish, Welsh influence down here. Never knew that Captain John O'Reilly's St Patrick's Battalion fought alongside Pancho Villa in his war with the US. Never knew that Welshman Henry Morgan settled pirate colonies in Honduras. Never knew that he and Francis Drake and a squadron of less infamous but just as ferocious English buccaneers raided and raged across Nicaragua and Costa Rica. And never knew that Drake, the most celebrated of all pirates, was mortally wounded then buried at sea off the Panamanian port of Portobelo, a long way from home but less than a hundred miles away from the doomed Scottish colony of New Edinburgh. Never knew, and it's been a delight finding out.

Best of all, it's been a year On The Road and a year transforming a flatpack monochrome map into a bubbling, laughing, riding, fucking, loving book of waking dreams. A year making crisp, clean travel guides all soiled sweaty and dog-eared damp.

Travel is sensual. That map's been sensualised. By the smell of South Carolina's sulphurous plough mud, of New Orleans' vomit and bleach cocktails, of Mexico City's black sooty smog and of El Salvador's fresh pine cloud forests. By the sight of frozen Niagara Falls, of elephants on Broadway, of the jungle pyramids at Palenque, and of a hundred Pacific sunsets and maybe three Caribbean dawns. By the taste of salsa'd fish tacos in Baja, of dark rum in Managua, of fresh ground coffee beans in

Atenas, and of Cubano cigars in San Salvador. By the sound of sirens on 42nd Street, of the world's worst cover band in Atomic City, of Mexico's best mariachis in crooning Guadalajara, and of Stone Roses wah-wahs and Sean Paul bom-boms in every Caribbean beach bar.

And by the feel of sand and tarmac and gravel beneath thrumming tyres, by the feel of sun and rain and wind in my daft grinning face, by the feel of old cold stone and hot baked beach beneath my toes. And by the feel of spiteful road tearing into this fatbody's too-thin skin.

The latest map to get sensualised, the latest country to be humanised, is Panama. And that word in an atlas now smells like coconut oil on a warm neck, tastes like peppery octopus ceviche served in a roadhouse full of shriekingly happy Down's syndrome kids, sounds like the whistling wind they call the Devil's Breath that tried to blow me and bike into a view, looks like cargo ships sailing through farmer's fields at the Miraflores Locks and now feels like a Canadian girl called Anna.

Aye. In love again. Again. Truth is, the Road is a promiscuous place. Slutty, even. Take hundreds of lost and lonely travellers, pickle them with cheap rum, grinding reggae and leaving-tomorrow anonymity and watch their clothes fall off. Fine if you're a one-night-stander, harder for a headless romantic looking for the One. I'm the fling that refuses to be flung.

It's been a year of wonderful women. All wonderfully refusing to jack and ride away into the sunset with me. Guess that's more of a male fantasy than a female reality. Guess I'm more 'Hobo Layabout on a Scruffy Motorbike' than 'Gypsy Prince on a Shimmering Stallion'. Christ – I'm turning into Jon Bon Jovi.

So. A year On The Road, and I'm as excited and intrigued as I've ever been, still dreaming about what's round the next corner. 'There's no bliss on earth, there's peace and freedom, though,' said a poetic Russian. Trips like this drip and gurgle with the peaceful freedom to dream.

Now this year On The Road's about to be interrupted by a flight. The Panamericana pauses in Panama, dead-ending into the rainforest wall of the Darien Gap, 100 miles of equatorial jungle swamp infested with nothing but mosquitoes and Colombian cartel commandos. Too rich for my blood. So I'll fly bike and body into Bogotá. Risky? Some. But then so is commuting by London bus in these dark days.

Next stop – Cartagena.

THE AMERICAS: PART 3

SOUTH AMERICA

☆ ☆ ☆

**APRIL 2004 – OCTOBER
2005**

Somos todos americanos.
Hugo Chávez

Welcome to Hell. 'Welcome to Colombia, señor,' smiles an aproned waiter. Cue black and white B-movie starlet screaming into her fist. 'Cold beer, señor?' Cut to chubby Pablo Escobar in mirror shades and Miami shirt, slapping a high-heeled, bikini'd behind with a hairy hand that's more rings

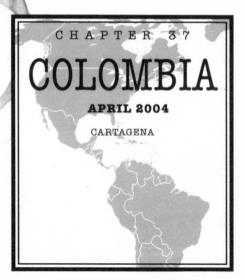

than knuckles. 'Ice cream pancake, señor?' Cut to guerrillas in olive fatigues and red bandanas shooing snivelling backpackers off the bus and into the jungle. 'Or how about a nice relaxing pooh, señor?'

Welcome to Colombia, the Most Dangerous Country in the Americas™, 2200 reported kidnappings in 2003, that's more than the rest of the world combined. The murder rate is eleven times higher than even the States – homicide is the most likely cause of death for men aged between 16 and 25. But sat sipping draught Aguila in coastal, colonial, Caribbean Cartagena's Plaza Bolívar, where the old men play chess in the palm-tree shade and the carriage horses harrumph into nosebags under the cathedral spire, watching nice-but-square Dick and Jane fiddle with their video camera and bicker gently about whether to spend the afternoon visiting the Inquisition Torture museum or boat-tripping round the islands, it's kinda hard to match that grisly map with this groovy territory.

Colombia yes or no is the decision every trans-American traveller has to

make. I always knew it was gonna be a yes. Kinda hard shitting out in front of 100,000 monthly mirrors. And I'm reluctant to write off an entire country and 41,000,000 human beings just because the CIA says so.

My only real decision was ship or fly. I wanted to ship, loved the idea of sailing, loved the idea of, er, working my passage from Colón to Cartagena. But when I rocked up at the shipping office in Panama City, they looked at me like I was puddled. 'Ferry? Not since six years, señor.' Talk about missing the fucking boat.

So I'm flying. We're flying. Dick and Jane, travelling two-up on a GS1150, heading from Alaska to Argentina and on. A married couple from Stoke Newington taking one last Big Trip before they settle down to breed. They're a great team. And it's nice to see that after nearly a year on the road, on the same bike, Dick loves Jane and Jane loves Dick.

We met on the Panama City ring road. I was in a cab, taking the camera to the repair shop, talking friendly rubbish with the cabbie – 'A bike? All the way from England? A BMW? What, like that one?' – when they zipped past, lost. The cabbie chirpily gave chase, we caught them at the lights. Thinking about the amount of variables, possibilities that had to coincide for that meeting to happen, plaited my blood. And kicked my arse. I slipped into their enthusiastic slipstream and finally sorted my Panamanian exit.

No road links Panama with Colombia, joining Central to South America, so everything flies, and the process is normal, simple, easy. Ride out to the cargo terminal, disconnect the battery, drain the tank, and feel that odd mixture of relief and tension as a man in overalls wheels the bike away. And then realise that there's no way back to town. Or wouldn't be if a fella delivering car parts hadn't stopped and offered us all a lift back. Try to imagine white-van man picking up three scruffy Panamanians from a Heathrow cargo depot and running them into central London, just to chat, just because he could. It can't be done.

One last night in Panama City, one last night in Players, the faux London pub with the real friendly welcome. Foamy beer, salty popcorn, rubbish pool and happy nonsense. 'You want to hear some English music?' asks Kathy, the Japanese manageress. Sure. I'm expecting Lulu and the Beatles. I get the Doves and Asian Dub Foundation. 'You want anything else, just download it.' Third world? You're having a laugh.

My bike's gone to Bogotá, theirs to Quito, and we all decide to detour to Cartagena in Colombia for the weekend while the wheels clear customs. I spend the flight trying to spot the line in the jungle that separates these two unlikely neighbours. Panama's so friendly, so relaxed, so peaceful, it doesn't even have a standing army. Which is why the Darien Gap will never be filled. Panama likes the impenetrable buffer.

Cartagena – the original Spanish Main. Founded in the early 16th century as a base for finding El Dorado, it became the Spanish empire's main holding centre for gold stolen from Latin America, and a regular target for Drake, Hawkins, Vernon and other English privateer predators. Now it's a tourist town – Bill Clinton visits, Gabriel García Márquez and, er, Julio Iglesias both have houses here, and the elderly Europeans arrive by cruise ship and pop in for tea.

Without the bike, I'm just another tourist squid in another tourist town. I play the game, wandering the pretty colonial streets, strolling past window boxes and balconied mansions and cloistered monasteries, looking for clues, signs, flashes of La Violencia that haunts this country. And give up, and just like every other tourist squid, I end up in the pavement cafés, chilling out with a beer and a steak, ignoring the constant 'Señor?' interruptions from Polaroid 'Señor?' photographers, pavement 'Señor?' artists, shoe 'Señor?' shiners, tat 'Señor?' vendors. Will you leave me alone, I'm staring at the peaches.

Cor. Blimey. I always thought the biggest crop in Colombia was coke or coffee. It isn't. It's breasts. Round, brown, beautiful breasts, busting out all over, popping out of low-buttoned blouses to say hello. And bums. Juicy apple bums, cheeky as you like, giggling behind too-tight white jeans. The waitress looks likes Angelina Jolie's good-time sister. I can't look her in the big, brown eyes without stuttering. 'Algo más, señor?' Anything else, sir? Christ, yes. Please.

Despite the dirty distractions, I'm uneasy. Somehow, this doesn't feel right. It's like finding Barcelona's Las Ramblas in downtown Baghdad. Somewhere out there, beyond the table brollies and the jars of sangria, beyond the city walls and the military checkpoints, are 30,000 uni-formed guerrillas, countless cartel killers, millions of hungry, angry poor. I can't decide whether this performance is admirable defiance or arrogant disdain.

Not all the poor are outside. Wandering home, I pass a kid asleep on the pavement. A child. Not a stick-naked fool, not a turps-soaked tramp, a child, eight or nine years old, lying on a piece of cardboard, arms and legs tucked into his T-shirt. People tut and step over him. I give him a couple of bucks, but it doesn't make either of us feel any better.

Next day Dick and Jane do the sensible thing and fly on to Ecuador to pick up their bike. And I become very, very aware that I'm alone in Colombia.

Next stop, Bogotá, baby.

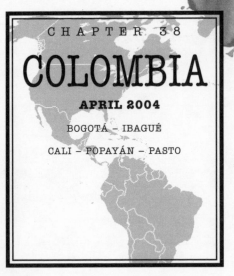

CHAPTER 38

COLOMBIA

APRIL 2004

BOGOTÁ – IBAGUÉ

CALI – POPAYÁN – PASTO

'Ladies and gentlemen, welcome to Bogotá.' Mid-afternoon, mid-week shuttle flight from Caribbean Cartagena to the Colombian capital, and the bilingual announcement's just for my benefit. Bogotá attracts tourists like Baghdad. I spend the flight looking for dangerous faces. All I see are people. And people see me. A cheery fat man says he has a son and grandson in Hampstead, says he left Colombia years ago for Panama, says he loves Margaret Thatcher. And when he hears what I'm planning to do, shakes his jolly, jowly head. 'They will take you.'

Plane becomes taxi in an airport full of soldiers. A hobbled Nissan wheezes out of the car park, past the cargo terminal where, inshallah, my bike's waiting after its flight from Panama City, and into downtown Bogotá.

I'm looking for bodies in the streets, but all I see are steam trains and cycle lanes. The swanky six-lane ring road's separated by a raised and protected bicycle route. 'Five days a year, no cars in the city,' explains the driver. 'It's good for the environment.' Is it dangerous here? A steam train puffs across a level crossing with a cheery Thomas whistle, towing gaily painted wagons full of cheering children. The cabbie shrugs.

We nudge through the early-evening traffic, under new-build tower

blocks padded with falling fog, past normal shoppers going about normal overcast business on normal overcast streets. With army posts at every junction. Three gypsy boys gallop past on donkeys, chased by an armoured car pell-mell through a ped mall. The cabbie doesn't look twice.

Shops, banks, burger bars, then we take a wrong turn, get lost in the cobbled one-way and every corner's ganged up to the angry eyeballs. Rat-faced boys throw me 'when, not if' looks through the grubby glass. A kid on a bicycle bounces off the pavement, onto the bonnet, growling a wild-dog howl. Never trust a boy who barks. The cabbie locks his door with an elbow.

I plot up in a town-centre commercial-traveller hotel. The staff seem delighted to have a guest and fall over each other to fill me with tinto, strong black coffee, and carry my bags to a top-floor room. Which I'm too scared to leave.

I'm scared. Proper scared. Scared of violence, scared of robbery, scared of kidnap. Scared that big boys will steal my smashing new digital camera and groovy pinstriped flares and favourite African bangle. Scared of running out of money, scared of the bike breaking down in the dangerous middle of nowhere. Scared I've made the wrong decision coming here.

Scared, but nosy, and anyway I'm too hungry to hide under the bed. Pull my best gangster outfit out of the dressing-up box and practise 'don't fuck with me' shapes in the mirror, but all I see is eleven-year-old Daniel wearing a pudding-bowl Brian Jones haircut and posh school blazer preparing to run the council estate gauntlet to the bus stop.

Puff up my chest and bounce faux-confident out into the grey, cold dusk. And right into a military operation – soldiers with steel helmets and assault rifles checking papers, chucking paupers into the backs of trucks. It smells like fascism.

Pull my collar up and my hat down, scuttle past, trying to look innocent tourist to the troops but dangerous local to the locals. Downhill, towards the main drag's bright lights, trying to look like I know where I'm going, trying not to look at my city map, and dive into the first bar.

What a difference a beer makes. Outside it's cold realism, inside it's warm magic, smoke and mirrors in a low-ceilinged bar that's wooden like the inside of a barrel, sepia-coloured like nostalgia. Scratchy vinyl tango struts and sobs out of coffin cabinet speakers over the sing-song hubbub of Spanish chatter.

This is the Latin America of dreams, of myth, of fiction, straight out of the pages of Márquez or Borges. The barkeep's doing just that – keeping bar, looking after the bar like a custodian, wiping spills, collecting empties, but most importantly, keeping the antique Argentine tango flowing to a crowd in love – in love with each other, in love with the drink, in love with themselves, but most importantly, in love with the tango.

Sit at the bar with a noisy squad of dissident journalists in seventies suits, scruffy hair looking longer than it is with glasses and moustaches, and watch Colombia vs Peru in a World Cup qualifier. An old man harrumphs. Apparently football was a man's game in his day.

Two soldiers stride in, gun barrels clashing off the door glass. The

spell's briefly broken, until owner Maria, all smiles and tight grey bun, glides over like a nun and offers them tintos. Hard faces crack into grandson smiles, helmets off, guns down. A table of pretty girls in high heels and long scarves giggle. The boys blush.

Back out into the chill cold full of beery warmth. The street's noisy with queuing clubbers, cigarette sellers, more soldiers and a child eating out of a bin. A kid of eight or nine tears apart rubbish bags, finds a lemon husk and sucks hungrily. I give him a couple of bucks and try to talk but he just stashes the bills and keeps scavenging. What else was there for me to do but cry?

Next day's Saturday. Customs is closed for the weekend, nothing to do but wander the streets. Muggy drowsy from the altitude and maybe the beer, I need to eat fast and hit a hot-dog stand. A buck gets me a foot-long sausage smothered in a layer of broken crisps, then a layer of chicken, then more crisps, then strawberry ice cream sauce. I take one bite and bin it. 'Thanks, fatso,' sneers a tramp as he snatches it out.

Hide in an internet café for online reassurance. There's an email from Jerome, an English lad on a KTM. We were planning to meet here, maybe ride together for security. 'Sorry, didn't feel safe, flew on to Ecuador.' Another from Trys, also safely flown to Quito. 'Who shall I contact if you get kidnapped or killed?' And another from a Colombian contact at horizonsunlimited.com, the overlanders' best online resource. He's sent me a route to the Ecuadorean border and the Rules: 'Only travel between 6 a.m. and midday. Park the bike out of sight. Don't go out at night. Be lucky.'

I cheer myself up by reading Foreign Office travel warnings. 'Volatile . . .

violence increasing . . . narcotraffickers, terrorist groups, criminal elements widespread . . . daily clashes between armed groups and military . . . travel by road especially dangerous and should be avoided . . . frequent roadblocks rob and kidnap travellers . . . no guarantee foreigners released unharmed . . . backpackers as likely targets as multinational workers . . .' What the fuck have I done?

The decision to come here was vain, gung-ho, slightly nihilistic. Easy to be tough in a bar in Panama City, easy to shrug 'Kidnap's a great story' under a beer-buzz haze. But now, here, really here, it doesn't feel so smart.

Wander out for a coffee and a think. I hear English voices at a nearby table. Loneliness makes me salesman pushy. Can I join you? 'Well, of course.' 'For sure.' They're expats, not tourists. Jonathan, a minor English aristocrat, been coming here for ten years or more 'looking for the perfect love'. 'I'm not sure it lives in strip clubs,' laughs Joseph, a commercial sea captain and former Belgian Army boxing champion. They both look exactly as they should. And they both express the same concern about the trip. 'On a bike?' Why not? 'Because of La Violencia.'

The Violence. Colombia's been at war with itself for fifty years. On the left, the Marxist FARC and Guevarista ELN, with maybe 30,000 uniformed guerrillas, too strong to be defeated, too war-weary to make the break out of the jungle and into the parliament. On the right, the government and its deniable paramilitarios death squads, the AUC, now backed by the States' neo-colonial Plan Colombia, an aid-for-arms-and-allies operation that pretends to be anti-drugs. In the middle, the cocaine cartels, controlling Colombia's biggest export and an estimated 60 per cent of the GDP. And in the cracks, La Delincuencia, criminals, bandits, kidnappers, thriving on the chaotic instability, the glut of guns and Fernando Vallejo's Law of Medellín: 'Here everything that lives is guilty. The poor produce more poor, and misery more misery. And more misery makes more killings and more killings make more corpses. This is the Law of Medellín which will rule henceforth on Planet Earth. Be warned.'

'They stole my cargo ship,' says Joseph. Er, your what? Ten years ago he was delivering a cargo of fishmeal from Peru to Buenaventura, Colombia. Normal enough run. Until the Port Captain impounded the boat, arrested the crew and, after months of intimidation, finally organised an on-board attack that left Joseph for dead, leaking from a dozen machete wounds. 'Because they could.' The good news? He was found by a dock worker who took him to hospital and eventually became his wife. 'Here she is now.'

Pretty Jenny sits down, smiles and then frowns as Joseph explains my plans. 'They will . . .' Let me guess? Take me. 'Maybe. Unless you follow the Rules.' And a road trip becomes an anti-surveillance exercise. 'If you want to eat, pass the restaurant, turn round and pretend you are travelling the other way. Never tell anyone where you are really headed. Never tell anyone you have a bike. Only stop in major cities. Don't go out at night.' I groan. 'It's not just you. This is what all Colombians do when they travel across their own country.'

Monday morning, dull and early, I check out and cab up to the airport to release the bike. Shouldn't take more than an hour or two. I'll be On

The Road by ten. Nine hours, three offices later and I still haven't even seen the bike. 'Mañana, amigo,' smiles Carlos Espana, a kindly customs officer who found me floundering at the second office and decided to help, driving me from 'no' to 'no' in his own car, translating, encouraging, explaining, even insisting on buying me lunch. Nine hours of help plus friendly, innaresting banter in his second language, just because he could, just because he rides an XR400. Try to imagine a Heathrow customs officer doing the same for a scruffy Colombian biker.

Tuesday morning, dull and early, I check out and cab up to the airport to release the bike. Carlos is waiting for me and he's got a present – my number plate written on a piece of paper, ready to be sellotaped to the back of my jacket. Apparently all Colombian bikers have to do this. 'It might stop you being shot in the back if you miss a checkpoint.' I laugh. He doesn't. Because he isn't joking.

The bike's wheeled out of the bonded warehouse. Normal morning routine overrides specific local fears. Pack up, gas up, fuck off, chasing the landmark crumb trail out of Bogotá and onto the open highway, battling buses and trucks that steal space like a fat man on an aeroplane, getting used to the military posts that litter the landscape and sit at the entrance and exit of every town and village.

On my own again, On The Road again. Everything's going well, and I should be in Cali by early afternoon. 'To make God laugh, tell Him your plans,' say the Mexicans. Heading into another armed village, the bike cuts dead. Nothing. Coast downhill to an army post, smile 'Buenos dias' so they won't shoot me, try to think of something useful to check. Two boy soldiers wander over, chatting happy shit ('You know Meek Jagger?'), gurning for photos, while I unpack the tool kit and scratch my arse. 'Good bike,' nods one and slaps the tank. The lights come back on, it fires up again. We look at each other and laugh.

What to do but keep going? Maybe I can find a mechanic in Cali. 'Please, bike, don't break down' prayers whinge pathetically round my lid. Heading out of another armed village, the bike cuts dead again. Coast uphill to a muddy verge and try to think of something useful to check.

This has happened once before, all the way back in New York State; trying to leave a snowy Albany gas station, turned the key and nada. What did I do then? Had a smoke, kicked it, tried it again? What's the connection?

Slow as Homer, tumblers fall in my daft head. Albany. Bogotá. Albany. Bogotá. Planes? Planes. Cock. I bet I haven't properly reconnected the battery. Cock. I haven't. Cock. That's all it is. Maybe I really will make Cali.

When Pablo Escobar was finally murdered, the Medellín cartel was eclipsed by the Cali cartel as the biggest, baddest coke-dealing network in Colombia and, consequently, the world. So Cali's got a rep for being rough. But in the afternoon sun it looks like any other Latin city. Any other unnavigable Latin city – too many one-way streets, not enough road names. I spend two hours riding in circles, getting nowhere but lost and hungry and frustrated, eventually asking a cab to lead me to a hostel. He does, but won't take any money.

I don't usually do backpacker hostels – too many kids, too many lies, too much noisy nonsense. This gaff doesn't change my mind – a dirty bed in a grotty, stuffy room and a kitchen full of brash Aussie

travellers noisily talking about coke deals over macaroni cheese. I slip out alone.

An indigenous lad slides along the bar. He wants to tell me his story. Go for it. His ancestors ruled the jungle interior when the Spaniards arrived. 'We thought if we fought hard, it would dissuade them. It just made them think we had something worth fighting for.' Turns out they did. That yellow metal that washed up on riverbanks and adorned every peasant hut. Gold. 'We are cursed by our natural resources.' He waves up another round of rum.

He's right. First cursed by gold, now by coke. Different product, same pirates. The victims of cocaine aren't powder-addled twats in west London washing soggy septums down shower drains, not even howling, confused crack babies in East LA. The primary victims of cocaine abuse are the normal people of Colombia. I'll not touch that poison again.

Eight hours later I'm sat sweating on the edge of my dank bed, wired to the stupid, red eyes, chewing on a pipe-blistered lip, listening to Alicia, a cooch dancer from Melbourne, witter on about Legs Eleven in Birmingham. I have to get out of here. 'Can I come with you?' For once I respond with my head not my hips. No, Alicia, you can't.

Guess I really fucked the dog this time. One time when I really need to keep straight, I end up sleepless and shattered from smoking tension. I'm appalled with myself and feel the need to repent – no hiding in a darkened room, no cooch comfort, just get up and get back On The Road.

Cali was hard enough to ride straight. Plait-twisted, rotten as fizzy fish, it's a shrieking, hazy maze. I pay a taxi driver five bucks to lead me to the highway, but he jumps a red and loses me. I stop to ask for directions but people look at me as if I'm a fried foreigner in weird clothes speaking bad Spanish. I end up following a bus.

It's Semana Santa, Easter week, a bigger deal in the Catholic calendar than Christmas, a time for pilgrimages and families. For this one week of the year, the military make a muscular effort to secure the roads. Cali to Popayán is rebel territory – the boy soldiers have become hard men, the sandbags concrete pillboxes, the trucks APCs with armour and mounted machine guns. Helicopters buzz the valleys. Buses and cars race as fast as they can, and the cops don't seem to mind – speeding is irrelevant when the priority is just getting there without getting taken.

Stop for lunch at a busy transport café. Sit down with a buck plate of chicken and rice, avoid the eyes, watch the news. 'No hijackings yet this Holy Week,' runs the headline over library footage of ELN guerrillas in black-and-red bandanas torching buses and blazing away with AKs. That's news?

The road rises, the air cools and the Panamericana hits Popayán, La Ciudad Blanca, the White City, the pilgrims' most popular Easter destination. Pointed-roofed houses straight off the Finchley Road lead past leafy parks into the whitewashed, cobbled colonial streets and celebrants' cathedrals.

'We have a paradise but we live in a Hell,' said, er, Shakira. This is Colombia as it should be, as it would be without the war. Every time I park up, strangers shake my hand, smile, say hello and welcome. Girls giggle and ask me for rides. Boys coo and ask, 'What'll it do?' It takes

me an hour to find a bed, but full hotels take the time to get on the phone and help me hunt. For the first time in a week, I'm properly relaxed.

Maybe too relaxed. I'm spotted by a radio team who ask for an interview. Sure. Broken Spanish, easy questions, stupid answers. I play it for laughs – 'Soy Ricky Martín y bienvenidos a gay Paris' – and the gathering crowd chuckles along politely. 'So tomorrow morning you'll be travelling the road to Pasto on your BMW, alone, si?' And somewhere in Bogotá, I hear Joseph and Jenny chime 'Doh!'

At six o'clock, the town goes to Mass. For the first time in twenty years, I join in. The central cathedral's ram-jammed with hundreds. I genuflect, murmur along the responses, and for the first time in weeks, I'm not a gringo, I'm another Catholic.

Another town, another sepia-tinted tango bar. I chat away with Xavier, a travelling salesman, and get clues about the next stage. 'The most dangerous road in Colombia,' he shrugs. Guerrillas? 'Delincuencia.' Any advice? 'Have another beer.'

Good Friday. The day Jesus died on the Cross. For a superstitious lapsed Catholic with a Messiah complex, this is not a good day to travel 'the most dangerous road in Colombia'. But I'm feeling dagger-proof. The paranoia's made impotent by the road's beauty as it twists and shouts through wet green valleys and hazy peaks, under warm sun and fresh cold air.

No traffic, no macheteros working the fields, no military. Stop for a smoke and a Coke and a look. And realise that this is the first time in Colombia that I've even noticed the impressive Andes views. A shoal of racing bikes whirs past, all thighs and Lycra. A Renault 4 support car pulls over. The driver just wants to check I'm OK. How's the road to Pasto? 'Beautiful.' And he gives me a banana.

Military Suzuki Freewinds swarm past, heading my way. Drab green, pillions riding shotgun, Uzi and Armalite. Never seen a Freewind look sinister before. I tag on the back and we swoop into border town Pasto. And without a bang or a whimper, it's all over. I've survived Colombia. Three weeks across 'the most dangerous country in the Americas' and I didn't see as much as a scared cat, but could never shake the feeling that just out of sight, very bad men were doing very bad things. I got away with it, nothing more. Back in Panama City, a diabolical Dutch brothel keeper warned me off Colombia – 'Dumb luck. Forget planning or precautions: the only thing that keeps you safe down there is dumb luck.'

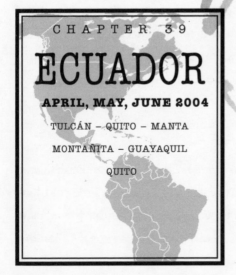

CHAPTER 39

ECUADOR

APRIL, MAY, JUNE 2004

TULCÁN – QUITO – MANTA

MONTAÑITA – GUAYAQUIL

QUITO

'No se puede.' Misty mountain morning at the Colombian–Ecuadorean frontier and we're all getting KB'd. Knocked back. First the old man in the crumpled, once-smart face and suit trying to get to his grand-daughter's christening – ID cards won't do and he's never had a passport. 'No se puede.' Then the indigenous women in the felt hat wearing seven skirts and a gurgling papoose – I filled out her application, but she can't sign her own name. 'No se puede.' And then me – I'm all right, but they won't let the bike in. 'No se puede.' No you can't.

Borders are never dull. Too many weekly variables. Too many corrupt loopholes. Too many uniformed, gun-slinging bureaucrats. The old man sits on his suitcase and shrugs. The indigenous woman practises her signature and sings. I head for customs and grin.

'What's the problem, sir? Why can't I visit your lovely country? 'The customs chief smiles, shakes my hand, sits me down. 'The customs office is closed. Until Monday.' It's Saturday. Arse. Er, which customs office? 'This customs office.' He shuffles and stamps papers, answers the phone, responds officially. I wait till he hangs up and try again. This customs office? 'Yes. Not open today. No one here.' There's an odd silence. We look at each other. 'I'm not really here.' He grins. 'Welcome to Ecuador.'

There's no arguing with that kind of logic. I head over to the Colombian booth. I'll come back on Monday morning. 'No se puede.' Why? 'You can't re-enter Colombia so quickly. Come back on Monday morning.' Cock.

This is a new one. Stranded in no-man's-land in the South American Andes? It's too funny to be annoying. Back to Ecuador, back to the customs officer who isn't there. Can I ride to Tulcán, the first town, and come back on Monday for the paperwork? 'Yes. No. You could, but last week two gringos asked the same and didn't return. There was a lot of trouble. Sorry.' He smiles and gets back to non-existent paperwork.

Can't go back, can't go forwards. There's one bad choice. Spend the weekend in Tulcán and leave the bike here, chained to a lamp post. At the Colombian frontier. 'I take absolutely no responsibility for this bike,' smiles The Man Who Isn't Here. I climb into a taxi as he tries the Dakar out for size.

Tulcán. 'Very little interest to tourists,' says the Lonely Planet. I don't care – I'm just delighted to be out of Colombia, away from La Violencia, away from the feeling of dread that stalked me for three weeks, dread that rattled like a stick along railings, dread that startled like a bottle breaking in a dark alley.

Dread that dissolves instantly upon exposure to, well, several hundred young girls in drum-majorette cheerleaders' outfits trotting through the crowded streets like ponies in miniskirts. Tulcán likes parades like I like, er, tarty-looking teens wearing too much make-up and knee-length red patent boots. Twirl it, chicas. Two hours later I'm barbecuing on the terrace of the best hotel in town, watching a cop

motorbike display team crash through a ring of fire while the drunk chief of police sings a song about an old lady masturbating with a wooden spoon. I think I'm gonna like this country.

Monday morning, foggy and early, and the good news is that the bike's still there. It only takes me ten minutes to readjust every pressed button and tampered switch. Even the rear preload's been changed. I'll be off then? 'No se puede.' What?

The two runaway gringos have really clogged this border up. The geniuses bolted and the customs post took a bollocking. Twats. Now they want deposits, financial guarantees, or a carnet that I don't have. The negotiations take all day – one office to another, into town with an officer on the back, three days' transit bargained up to eight days' transit pleaded up to fifteen days, but then there's a two-hour lunch hour and the boss disappears and the photocopier's broken. Nine hours later, just as it's getting too dark to travel, I get the papers. Three days to cross a border. It's my new world record.

The Andean valley drop and mountain climb to Quito is dizzying in the clear, but just damp in this winter mist. Five blind hours later I'm in the world's second highest capital, and the only one to start with a 'q'.

Quito. High, modern and surprisingly familiar. Trawling round La Mariscal, looking for a hotel, all I see is street after street, block after block, of backpackers' hostels, internet cafés and budget all-day-breakfast restaurants. And in them, round them, between them, the unwelcome return of Jenny and Penny and Chloe and Zoe, gap-year runaways and round-the-world ticketeers, still being awfully authentic and authentically awful, talking too loud about their wonderful host families and all their amazing volunteer work digging latrines for Jesus.

No problem, I'm not here for them, I'm here for real people: Brian, my oldest friend, just escaped from a messy divorce in Vietnam, now heading for a year's teaching in Eritrea, visiting for two great weeks; Manchester Trys, still on his XR, now plotted up painting portraits of self-important expats for a cheeky living; nice-but-square Dick and Jane on the GS (Dick still loves Jane and Jane still loves Dick), and a dozen more motorcycling overlanders, spotted on horizonsunlimited.com, stopping for a pint in the Quito bottleneck.

Headquarters is established in the Turtle's Head, the *Viz*-themed Scottish pub run by the growling ex-dispatch-riding Scot, Albert, the owner of the only 2003 FireBlade in Ecuador. Happy hours become drunken days and woozy weeks lost in beery, bikey nonsense. 'I only remember snatches,' slurs Dick as Jane gets the giggles.

Trys, pillion Bri and I make a break for the beach. An hour out of town I guess I catch a branch in my chain, 'cause I hear it snapping. Two hours out of town, and the rain just won't stop, so we do. We wring out and I glance at the sprocket. It's got fewer teeth than MacGowan's grin. Guess that wasn't a twig. Arse.

Next day I stick Brian on the bus and the bags on Trys and limp back to Quito, hoping the slipping chain doesn't jump off the sprocket and through my leg. By the time we get back to the Turtle's Head, I've got two clutches. 'That'll be you stuck here then,' says Albert.

He's right. There's a BMW dealer in Quito, but despite the liveried logos and shiny new 1200GSs in the showroom, the spares department is empty as a Soviet shop. I play my cheat trump card and call BMW GB's David Taylor for help. He just happens to be visiting Panama City. And they just happen to have a chain and sprocket set in stock. 'I'll Fed-Ex it tomorrow.'

That was two months ago. The parts were sent, snared by Ecuadorean customs and swallowed whole. Two months of emails, phone calls, websites. Two months of 'no se puede'. Two months without the bike, watching the rain fall hard. This town can drag you down.

Say it again, Jack: 'No matter how slick it looks on top, it's a hobo jungle underneath.' Behind the businesses and bars, under the empty, cartel washing-machine skyscrapers, Quito's a nasty den of thuggish muggers and corrupt cops. Every night, Albert warns gringos not to walk home, to spend a buck and catch a cab. Every night they sneer back know-it-all headshakes. Every night they come back with purple eyes and snotty noses. It starts to depress me. I resent taking cabs three blocks. It feels like they've won. Taxis at night, eight locked doors between bed and street – I feel like I'm in prison. 'You should go and see the Manchester guy who's really in prison,' says Albert, right on cue.

El Centro de Rehabilitación is past the old town's whitewashed walls and Indian print shawls, above its sloping streets and steep steps. From the outside it looks like an under-funded museum, with flaky, peeling paint and windows smudged opaque. The security and the queue are the only clue – cops in camos sling carbines from arm to arm while sucking on oranges and whistling at the waiting glamour girls wearing too much pancake and cleavage for any museum.

Half an hour late, they open the gates. Arms stamped, passports checked, bodies patted down. 'Who are you here to see?' A door opens up and, fucking hell, the visits all happen on the wing? The visits all happen on the wing. In the cells. I'm in jail.

The gate clangs behind me. The screw throws the bolt and shoos me inside. I have no idea where I'm going, who I'm looking for, how I find him. I barely dare look up. I kinda see men in cells round a yard. I clearly hear catcalls and jeers. The guards are all on the other side of the gate. Great. A small black fella with a scarred smile bustles up and yabbers in side-of-the-mouth Spanish. 'Who do you want to see?' Alan, el hombre inglés. 'Siga me.'

So I follow him. Down a graffitied, prison-green corridor, past a Gothic workhouse cellar kitchen where grey ghosts are cooking up greyer food, past tumbledown rooms behind rusted shut doors, towards the noise and smell. The noise of door slams, barked threats, running feet. And the smell of men, scared and scarred men, too many men in too small spaces.

In Heaven, every doorway opens up secret wonders, every hallway leads to exotic intrigue, every junction to adventurous choices. Hell looks the same, but every door closes on claustrophobic ambushes, every hall-way drips with lurking menace, every crossroads offers up unzipped predators.

'Is this him?' A white zombie with a recently buckled nose is staring at the air like it's squirming. Alan? Alan? I guess not. 'Is this him?' A pock-marked New York junkie with hair in his eyes is kicking a ball round the yard. 'I'm Scotty. You want the Brit, right? He's in someone else's cell. Hiding from debts.'

More stairs, more stares, more ranchero radio blares. I dunno whether to walk chesty-con tough or goofy-visitor friendly. Someone reaches up and tries to rip out my earring. Goofy it is. Virgil raps on a first-floor door. A spyhole slides open. 'Is this him?'

The cell's twelve by six, two bunks, toilet and shower almost curtained off by a too-small peekaboo sheet. A big guy with Marvin Hagler's shaved head's lying on the top bunk. A little black guy, a very young Spaniard and a sallow white guy with a hooked nose and lead-lidded eyes are slowly nodding out on the bottom bunk. Alan? 'Y'all right, mate? Sit down. Have a smoke.'

Starts awkward, but soon opens up with Manc banter, football chat, Who do you know? Where do you go? and What the fuck are you doing in here? A middle-aged midget prostitute strolls in. We stroll out while she unbuttons 223rd-hand tenderness for five dollars a pop.

Alan's a mule, a medium-time hood from an area that New Labour calls 'a prioritised sink estate' and the rest of Manchester calls 'an abandoned violent shithole' as it hits the central-locking button. Twelve-year-old car thieves, thirteen-year-old mothers, third-generation unemployment. 'If you don't take this call-centre job, we'll cut your benefit.' Kids from Ordsall don't dream of being doctors or lawyers. 'Two hundred thousand pounds. How many times am I gonna get to see that kind of money?'

Bigger boys made and paid the deal. Alan just had to fly over, collect the product, fly it back. 'Twenty-two kilos of pure coke. Two for me as payment. Hidden in mirror frames.' They pulled him as soon as he hit the airport. 'Kid like me stood out like a sore thumb.' No Spanish, no

Cooped up in
Quito while
customs sit
on spares -
April/May/June
2004

'Well?'
Future ex-wife
Grainne looks
unimpressed,
Cats Bar, Quito

Less teeth than a
tramp's smile

'You're very quiet today'
- public art, Quito

'Oh que cuchi rico' -
fresh bacon butties on
the road to Montenita

Mancora Beach — a picture perfect paradise secreted behind a truck-stop

'A shimmering two-lane blackt that cuts up into sandstone mountains then darts down to the roaring Pacific's wind-scooped dunes...', Peruvian Pan American Highwa July and August 2004

Top of the World on the road to Puno

'The world's wild west where deserts and oceans collide with a jagged scream that settles into a soothing spray' – Peruvian Pan Americana

El Camino Sinuoso – possibly the most beautiful road in the world – winds from Nazca to Abancay and Cusco – Peru, September 2004

Monkey mechanics bodge
bleeding brakes

Richard and Jane
celebrate a year on
the road with tequila
smiles, new tattoos
and an electric hat

Magnificent views,
rubbish riding

Plane high on the altiplano

Midget riders surf the Salar de Uyuni salt flats

Dirt track stuck to the canyon wall like spaghetti
on a ceiling - the road to Uyuni

Beautiful, bonkers backwater
Bolivia, baby - October 2004

'The sun burns, the wind chills and the colours glow like a cross-processed paint box' – Peruano altiplano, September 2004

Lago Umayo, Puno

Attention-seeking attempt to get it up on the road to Nazca

Sillustani Funeral Tower, Lago Umayo

'With a packet of sweets...' Buying friends on the
Uros Isles with Dick and Jane

'Buenos Aires nearly killed
me...' BA, Argentina — 2005

Walking the black dog,
La Boca

Monserrat stencil

CAPITALISMO

Sailing off the
edge off the world
— Hotel Ritz, BA

clue, no chance. That was eighteen months ago. The sentence? 'Nine years.' And you'll serve? 'Nine years.'

He chats, I sort of relax, and get a chance to look around. We're on the first-floor balcony of a three-storey blockhouse. The prisoners wear their own clothes but the sickly yellow light turns everyone uniform drab. I'm expecting the ping-pong and pool, the constantly slamming doors, the circular shouts. What surprises is the private enterprise – one guy's selling toiletries, another cigarettes, another burgers, all from their cells. There's even a Coca-Cola-branded fridge. 'He's got an official franchise.'

Not that a can of pop can make this place feel normal. The air tastes sick, thick with feet and arses, sweat and tears, blood and spunk. And it crackles with slovenly violence. 'Seven murders in the last two weeks,' nods Alan.

Saturday I come back again. I've promised to clear Alan's debt. Thirty bucks buys him his life and me a front-row seat in the sickest show in town. Different cell, different floor, same chain-smoking banter with Alan, Danny, a dangerous-looking kid from Ohio with a martial-arts topknot and a tweaker's fidget, and another Manc, Mickey, an old-school villain, with bright blue eyes, neatly trimmed 'tache, and faded green chest-plate tattoo peeking out of a seventies-striped brown shirt.

Mickey's had some drama. Prisoners with money can buy their own cells. 'The best pads have tiles, carpets, boarded-off toilets, everything.' The trick is keeping the buying process secret. Predators hear you're buying, predators know you have money, predators come for the money. They came for Mickey last night. Three balaclava'd macheteros tied his

neck to the bed and threatened to cut off his hands if he didn't give out. He gave out all he had – fifty-seven bucks. They were an hour too late, the $1000 payment had already been made. 'Once I'm sentenced, I'll have 'em.' He pauses and turns away. 'You have not seen the wrath of Mickey Thomas.'

Somehow the mood today's different, calmer, easier. Maybe I'm getting used to it, but the edge is dulled, less shank-sharp. Maybe it's the families – wives and children get to stay over on Saturday nights. Maybe it's the hooch – Nigerian Michel passes round a half-litre bag of something fermented and demented. 'That'll put hairs on your chest,' coughs Alan. Aye, and burn them off again if you dribble.

And maybe I'm dreadfully naive. A posse limps down the corridor. With purpose. With a target. Us. Him. Alan is pulled up by two lean killers in death's-head bandanas, their faces cool as Colombians and cruel as conquistadors. The Spanish is slow, direct and too easy to understand. Another, bigger debt. 'It's been eight months. Business is business. Pay me tomorrow or you will die a painful death.' And added in English, in a whispered grin. 'You will die tomorrow.'

I'm fucking terrified. A Joe Pesci scene has escaped the screen and landed in my lap. I can smell the killers. They can smell me. I try to throw a shape, back Alan up, but my muscles have melted like wax. If they kill him, they'll kill me too. Alan laughs. 'You can't kill me, man. I'm already dead.' The Jackal shows a bandaged machete handle. 'Tomorrow.' And to me. 'Nice to meet you. Thanks for coming to visit us.' One more jackal grin and they lollop off to spoil someone else's day. 'He's just a baby,' bluffs Alan. Danny shakes his head. 'No. He's killed more men than cancer.'

Too rich for my blood. I stutter through another hour and flee. 'Thanks for giving me something to look forward to,' smiles Alan. 'And next time bring a Kentucky.'

The outside world feels rainbow bright and Disney naive. I sit in the park and eat Alan's fried chicken. A crumpled old man kisses a crumpled tiny baby. 'I could eat him!' 'No se puede,' laughs his daughter. A little girl cries over a dirty, dropped candyfloss. 'I want to eat it!' 'No se puede!' scolds her mum. A teenage boy puts his hand up a girlfriend's skirt. 'Let me eat you!' 'No se puede,' giggles the girlfriend.

Man, I just wanna get back on my bike.

Next stop – anywhere but prison.

CHAPTER 40

ECUADOR

JUNE, JULY 2004

QUITO – BAÑOS – QUITO – CANOA

MANTA – MONTECRISTI

GUAYAQUIL – QUITO – RIOBAMBA

HUAQUILLAS – MÁNCORA

Giddy. Giddy as the birthday boy on a trampoline. Giddy like a city dog on a windy beach. Giddy as a grown man about to take a test ride on a dream bike. Giddy.

Two months is too long. Too long to be kicking round cooped-up Quito. Too long to be laid off the busted bike. Too long to wait for a chain and sprocket set to escape customs' corrupt clutches. I've thrown a couple of beach trips between the claustrophobic prison visits and boozy bar crawls, but it's not the same. Only losers take the bus. So when BMW Ecuador, embarrassed by the customs cock-up and keen to redeem, offer me three days on their 1200GS demo, I almost lose a drop of pee. That giddy.

Three days. Free days. Tense becomes tentative becomes tearaway in ten tickled minutes, then, in an afternoon chuckling and charging round town on made-up missions (I'm just off to, er, check that the airport's still there), born-again over-excited by biking's basics. The cars, right, have to queue, but the bikes, right, get to zip between them! Brilliant!

Bikes are brilliant, and this Beemer's an especially brilliant bike, especially out here. Swift enough to create its own race-space ahead of every car-clogged crossroad, nimble enough to be squirted up the inside of every bus like spit through teeth, daft and deft as a drunken courier, chunky enough to swallow a beanpole pillion whole like King Kong scooping up Fay Wray, and with the most astonishing full-stop brakes I've ever used, complete with *Star Trek* swooshing-door sound effects from the sci-fi servos. I fucking love this bike.

Everyone loves this bike. Motorcyclists 'Cor!' then curse their Korean commuters. Car drivers toot. Cops wave. Women swoon and purr 'Que rico!' Not because they love its steroid-shouldered, 'rexic-arsed, robotic-bulldog looks, but because they love its smell. This bike stinks of filthy money. Suddenly I'm rich. Suddenly I'm sexy. 'My Beemer makes all the pretty girls want to dance and take off their underpants.'

So I enjoy a night of bragging rights with the mercenaries and missionaries, copper miners and gold diggers in the Turtle's Head and in the morning head off. Fill up with gas and Marlboro, hit the Panamericana and see how far we can get in a day.

From scruffy southern Quito's jarring scabby judders to the surprisingly smooth sweepers that spiral round majestic, snowy Cotopaxi, whether happy galloping past grunting lines of diesel-farting wagons or squelching about on muddy goat tracks, this Beemer's fast as a Ferrari and classy as a steam-age Pullman carriage. The perfect adventure-touring-viewing platform.

So perfect that I almost forget to stop. Take a moment at the seam between two worlds where the high Andes drop into the spicy Amazon basin, and stare down a valley that's ocean-deep, days long, too vast to photograph, under a sky so high I can see next Wednesday, can spy on incoming seasons. Misty-silver and rain-green spring here, glassy-blue and sunny-yellow summer there. The wind sucks the smoke from my smiling mouth and sends my lid scuttling like a tumbleweed.

Back on the bike, back up the hill, past a gaggle of gringas puffing and pedalling past on mountain bikes rented from some Bureau of Pleasant Trips, sweaty hair stuck to red faces, desperately trying to look like they're having a good time. Twist the throttle, feel that fat twin's lazy chug and chortle away. I love this bike.

It's been the perfect little road trip. I knew I shouldn't have said that out loud. The bike sneezes then yawns then snoozes to a stop, sleep-walking to the kerb on a coasting clutch. Feels like it ran out of petrol, even though the gauge still reads quarter full. The big German liar. Trudge half a mile downhill to a petrol station, then across the road to a baker's to buy a bottle of water to empty and then fill with petrol, and trudge half a mile back uphill, hoping it is just the petrol, and fucking hell I can't find my keys.

There's nothing quite as embarrassing, frustrating, retarding as losing stuff. The flapping, the scrabbling, the searching the same pockets again and again, the blame (You! You've got it!), the childish urge to pray (God, I'm aware you ignore the genocided, the starving, but any chance of intervening for me?), but when something's lost it's lost. And this key's lost.

Cock. From cock of the north to cock in one dumb swoop. After all the holier-than-thou 'this just isn't good enough' guff I've slung at the importer about the missing chain and sprockets, this is gonna be awkward. Humiliating. There's only one option. Lie like a cheap watch. Hello? Diego? Man, you won't believe this, but someone just stole my keys . . .

An hour later, the company pickup arrives. I think I overdo it, throwing

up a ridiculous story about vagabond children and a spirited-yet-hobbled motocross-booted chase. Diego looks as delighted as a man who's had his weekend evening interrupted by a moronic foreigner. I'm heartbroken. My bike's gone. My smell of money's gone. All that's left is the stench of my rotten boots. I stink like a damp dog's dick. Diego coughs and rolls down the window. 'The good news is the Dakar's ready. You can collect it tomorrow.'

Tomorrow. Giddy? Giddy as the birthday boy on a trampoline? Nah. You can't be half giddy. And I'm at least half full of jangling fear. Like a lover, a bike only needs to betray once to be considered forever unfaithful. Four out of the last seventeen months, this git has been out of action. I trust it like Hillary trusts Bill. And its recent dirty week-end with BMW Ecuador has made things even worse.

A BMW dealer service should smoothly reassure like an opium draught. These monkeys have me spooked like a face at a dark window. Despite the shiny showroom floor and flapping liveried flags, the workshop's run by backstreet abortionists. That's not a white lab coat, it's a butcher's apron. First, they fit new sprockets, but not the new chain. Why? They shrug. Er, it's normal to change them at the same time. They look at me like I've got my lad in my hand. 'Mañana.' No, today. Then I catch them oiling a freshly waxed chain on the outside. Er, it's normal to oil a chain from the inside. They look at me like I've just stuck my hand down their sister's pants. Praise the Lord and pass the knitting needle.

A quick test trip round the car park, once I've fixed the newly sloppy clutch, shows that the front brake doesn't, despite a dickhead's too-strong handshake, and the newly slack throttle's got maybe half a turn's play and needs wringing like a wet towel. I hate to think what happened

inside, hidden under the engine casings. Smile and say thanks and get out of their harm's way.

Southern Quito sprawls like a fat man on a couch. Round the cobbled old town, through clogged, coughing tunnels, past the city jail where Manchester Alan's still recovering in the hospital wing, and the bike shudders, dragging its arse like a dog that's been hit by a car, and stops dead in the outside lane. Trucks and buses parp past and rasp round. Two lads from the Indian market help me bounce the bitch to the safe side. Nothing to do but smoke, shrug and murmur 'I wonder what the fuck's wrong with the back brake?' as a Gatorade splash sizzles into sweet steam.

For appearance's sake, I dig out the tool kit. Trying to prise apart the lock-jawed pads, I snap a screwdriver, which makes me burn my hand, which makes me bang and scorch my head on the pipe. The market claps like they're watching Punch and Judy. All I need now is a rake to stand on. Painful, but works a treat. What to do but wobble off?

There's an urban myth that medical students play a game, an anaesthetist's relay, where they jab each other with ketamine and see who can run the farthest before the sleepy drugs kick in and the muscles collapse. That's how this trip feels. Not if, but when. I'll see just how far south I get before the bike nods off.

Ahead lies a couple of days of Andean altiplano plateau, a couple of days of tropical lowlands and the Peruvian border. Sounds ideal. But the same details that turn a journey into an adventure twist into ordeals on an iffy bike. And the recent affair with the 1200GS has made the Dakar feel sloppier, skankier, shoddier than ever. From mouse's ear to wizard's sleeve. From saline twins to spaniel's ears. It's gonna be an odd few days.

Three days. Tense days. Every time I hear a bird chirp, I pull in the clutch. Every time I smell a wagon's brakes, I check my calipers. I see nothing but problems, feel nothing but tension, look forward to nothing but seized joints and gravel rash. Proper paranoia's set in. Ecuador is conspiring against me. Road signs point to dead ends. Petrol stations refuse my money. Clouds whisper my deeply sensitive personal details across a sniggering sky. This is getting out of hand.

Enough. Stop. Relax with a cigarette. And notice that someone's been blowing oily smoke rings up my fork leg. Either that or the seals have been culled and burst. Throw a cheeky wheelie just to make sure. Super-duper. That'll be my nineteenth nervous breakdown.

The frontier arrives just in time to stop me getting all Eeyore. The border change is gradual, organic, but noticeable. For a start there're road signs. Proper road signs that point me in the right direction at junctions. Then the sun comes out. And the Panamericana returns to its true home, the Pacific coast, and the ocean sparkles on my right as a desert appears on my left, happy trails slithering away from the tarmac into the sandstone mountains and shifting dunes. I can't resist. The bike's jaded, but I'm not: proper happy off-road with the freedom to mess about, play about, kick up dust, ride anywhere I want. Until the back locks up again and I call it a day in Máncora.

Máncora. From a passing bus, it's just another one-street non-event,

non-stop. Get off the bike, and behind the breeze-block shops, a beautiful white sand beach, some rustic bamboo hotels, some fish restaurants, some surfers. It feels like a secret. I like it here – can I stay?

While I relax in a picture-perfect paradise, the Dakar deteriorates daily. A squeak becomes a rattle becomes a knock. It's not a bike, it's a game of KerPlunk, and any moment now marbles and straws will clatter out of its bottom.

'Sounds like yer bearings are bollocksed, lad.' His name's Ian, he's a 61-year-old farmer from West Yorkshire and he's travelling the world on an Africa Twin. 'I told the wife I were going for four months. That were in '99. She's not best pleased. Shall we have a look at that hub?'

I've been riding this luck too long. And what once felt pleasingly punk-rock now grates as dumb. Big trips mean taking more responsibility, not less. Rather than bitching about bad services and depending on the kindness of strangers, I should be grown up enough, organised enough, knowledgeable enough, to fix my own problems. Until I sort that, I'm still half stuck at home.

So. Giddy. Giddy as a windy dog on a trampoline. Giddy like a beach on its birthday. This road, the Panamericana, stretches more than 3000 miles from northern Peru to southern Chile. Farther than Glasgow to Lagos, Nigeria. I feel like I'm staring down a well.

These are the days that must happen to you? Abso-fucken-lutely, baby.

'Have you run away, too, lad? Good, innit?' Perfect Peruano afternoon on Máncora beach and Africa Twin Ian's throwing yarns at anyone who'll listen – me, you, the jowly growler trotting past with his lead in his mouth. Ian pats El Perro with talk-to-the-animals farmer's hands. 'That's how I used to feel, like a scrap-yard dog, chained to an oily puddle. Never go back, lad. Pump it. Hold it.'

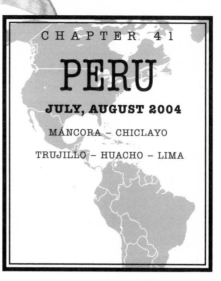

CHAPTER 41

PERU

JULY, AUGUST 2004

MÁNCORA – CHICLAYO
TRUJILLO – HUACHO – LIMA

Bleeding brakes. I've got a sticky rear end. The workshop's a tree-shaded yard off a cool blue-tiled alleyway, outside Cucho's Welding Shop. Cucho dabs at a wheel rim with a flame, his señora gently scolds a spark that hisses into the washing line and I get the giggles about bleed nipples. 'You slacken off that bleed nipple while I nail my willy to this doorframe.' Yes, mistress.

'Pump it. Hold it.' Mechanically, I'm as awkward as a left hand trying to scratch a left elbow, but Ian speaks fluent spanners. And perfect non-sense. He never shuts up. Despite not having a single word of Spanish. 'Yes I do – obrigado.' That's Portuguese. 'Oh, bollocks.'

Ian spent a year riding a 30,000-mile coastal lap of Australia, fixing tractors and shearing sheep, then skipped across to Argentina to gaucho. 'Milking, mostly. Two thousand cows in t'morning, two thousand cows at night. That's an awful lot of tits. Right, lad, we're done.'

That's good and bad. Now I've no excuse to stay. Máncora's proper perfect – a pretty, working fishing village on a beautiful beach with a long left break that attracts the Peruvian surf crowd. All ten of them. Quiet enough to feel like a secret, isolated enough to deter most backpackers, so laid back it took me two days to realise I'd lost my shoes, so honest my shoes were exactly where I'd left them. My two weeks here have been a happy, healthy holiday, strolling the sandy shores, jumping two-footed into panting games of beach football, then collapsing into the sand to watch pelicans dive for wet fish, and whistle at the bouncing bikini-girl surfers.

It's my birthday. Thirty-three. One more year and I'll have finally beaten Jesus at something. Sip pisco sours by the Panamericana with Ian, kite surfer Jacques and Colombian Danny and watch the wheels go round. Big-rigs funnel speed into sound through scattergun stuttering Jake Brakes. Impatient tourist coaches squeeze into gaps that aren't. Passenger squids peer out of tinted letterboxes then disappear behind fiddly curtains. Stare far enough up the night's light-streaked darkness and you can see Ecuador, Panama, Santa Monica Boulevard, even. 'Want to dance?' winks a Colombiana cutie. Love to. 'Have you got a grand-mother, love?' chuckles Ian.

One last walk home to the sleeping hotel down the night-time beach, cool sand massaging my feet. Hubble-bubbled hairy hippy chicks, high on spiky cactus juice, huddle round a driftwood fire. 'Hey, mister man. What beats green?' Dunno – red? 'Ooooh. Look, sand.' Hop into a rock-a-bye-baby hammock and smoke a weed as the star-sparkled sea whispers a lullabyed 'shhhuuuuussssshhhh'.

Next morning, Ian heads north on his overloaded Africa Twin, looking for a rainforest road that he knows doesn't actually exist. 'I do enjoy life, me.' I'm heading south towards Lima, 1200 km down the coastal desert. Should take two long days.

Make that three. It takes time to get back into the groove and find the road's rhythm. The bike's struggling on 84-octane low-go juice, straining like forced laughter on every mountain climb. And even though there's only one route south, I somehow manage to get lost. Call it a night in Chiclayo, a town that says, 'Rather than sit inside and watch TV, let's stroll the cathedral square tonight and smile at strangers.'

'What charm the world acquires when it is wound up and moving like a merry-go-round,' said a poetic Russian. He must have ridden the Peruvian Panamericana. I've spent years searching for this best of all possible roads. Sometimes you find what you're looking for. A shimmering two-lane blacktop that cuts up into buff sandstone mountains, then darts down to wind-scooped dunes by the roaring Pacific. Bridges leap across paper-dry creeks full of dust and lizards, then green stripes of linear oases worked by busy farmers. Best of all, this happy shit goes on for days.

The traffic's light enough to let me relax, regular enough to reassure that I'm not hopelessly isolated. Rusty orange Dodge Challengers, thirsty V8s ripped out and replaced with organ-donor diesels, turn family trips to the relatives into *Vanishing Point* death rides. Quartz-hauling road trains with too many axles for the hairpins judder up slopes in low-low, slowing me down long enough to read the 'Randy from the Andes says Tigers Pay, Dogs Steal' slogans slapped below cargo doors barbed theft-proof with thorn trees, then air-honk 'hola' as I slide by.

Fast boys find their drama on the dark side of 150, hanging off like bats at upside-down lean angles, fighting to stay on the black and out of the green. This is my drama: steady sixties, fast enough to feel alive, fast enough to feel the breeze, slow enough to see, slow enough to feel, slow enough to whoop and point and grin and well up at the engaging, raw beauty of this open-space place.

This is the world's Wild West, the edgy West End where deserts, mountains and oceans collide with a jagged scream that settles into a soothing spray; where skies are so high, it's disorientating; deliriously, delightfully dizzying. This desert's defined not by its cities or towns but by the empty spaces in between, by the dramatic pauses between the noisy people.

I'm in love. In love with this road and the way it makes me feel. Bubbling, warm, soulful, real love that sings inside like Otis. Slip-slide down a dirt track and up a cathedral dune 'cause I want to look down from the gods. When the bike topples sideways in soft scrunch, I don't bother picking it up, but keep going on foot. Collapse outside a cave and look. Two buzzards watch me from the wooden arms of a giant, paganised cross. Stick my hands and face in the sand because I want to smell the land, fuck the rocks, make love to the desert, eat shamanic berries that taste like burning and fly with the eagles. I settle for a hot shower and a cold beer instead.

Three days later I hit Lima. Off the bike, this sophisticated city of eight million seems too quiet. I miss the deafening wind rush, the anonymous momentum, the stimulation that stretches thoughts like gum as riding alerts interrupt every internal conversation. The Road works.

Next stop – back to the desert.

Gloomy as an old Andes Indian, Lima lurks under a shivering blanket of wet Pacific mist. Chic Peruanos pull hats down and collars up and huddle double-handed round steaming espressos in coffee shops that smell of cigars and shared secrets. If only I knew the right cipher, I'm sure that beauty in the Audrey

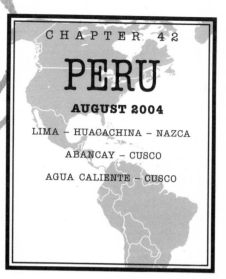

CHAPTER 42

PERU

AUGUST 2004

LIMA – HUACACHINA – NAZCA

ABANCAY – CUSCO

AGUA CALIENTE – CUSCO

Hepburn scarf and shades would hand over the East Berlin dossier.

Welcome to Peru, home of potatoes and Paddington Bear, llamas and lost Inca empires and some very weird weather. Two days north, Máncora's surfers are playing in the sun. Half a day south, sandboarders are sweating up and down desert dunes. But Lima's stuck in a wrong-way-round winter. Which is why I'm hitting the road.

Back in its touring fat suit, the Dakar stutters through the traffic's kaleidoscopic crush of swarming taxis, swerving buses and dozy tourist pedestrians with all the confidence of a posh girl wrestling a double bass through a rush-hour tube. Excuse me, sorry, pardon me. Past Parque Kennedy's Gothic cathedral, past the McDonald's with more armed guards than happy eaters, past the Honda garage where Beto resealed my forks, and out onto the Panamericana.

The city fades like footprints on a beach as the highway heads south into the coastal desert. Truck traffic clogs and bunches round 'eight wheels pay, two wheels don't' tollbooths, leaving as far as the eye can see both kinds of free for me and the bike.

Steady sixties, happily singing past grifo gas stops marked by flaming oil drums, past coach-driver lunch stops marked by Inca Kola hoardings, past puncture-repair shacks marked by tyres speared like missionaries' heads. Rust-bucket Dodge Coronets and Ford Galaxies bounce along parallel dirt tracks. It feels post-apocalyptic. And it kinda is. Six hundred years ago, the indigenous Incas had their perfectly serviceable civilisation torched and tortured into nothing but slaves' memories by cruel conquistadors and vicious Vatican vandals who make the Taliban look like Happy Clappers. 'Mother Earth, witness how my enemies shed our blood,' said last Inca rebel Túpac Amaru just before a Christian slit his throat in the name of love.

The only thing better than falling asleep in an oasis is waking up in one. I overnight in Huacachina, an arched arcade of quiet hotels and open-air restaurants round a wet mirror protected by loping palm trees and towering dunes. When I'm woken by the morning sun, all I can see through the window are two giant stripes of colour, sky blue and sand orange. Morning, glory.

This coastal desert is thousands of miles long but only tens of miles deep. I cut inland at one of the wider parts, 100 sandy kilometres from Nazca. Miles-long straights sear across shimmering plains whispering 'Blackbird or Busa', but bus-sized clusters of tragic crosses warn of hidden dips, snatching crosswinds, deadly overtakes and distractingly low planes full of 'ooh, a giant monkey picture' tourists day-tripping over the famous desert drawings.

I'm not here for the lines; I'm here to meet Dick and Jane on their GS1150. Parked up, we make an odd team. My rag-and-bone dustcart versus their Touratech-catalogued Tonka. 'Once you get used to the weight, she's a great ride,' says Dick as Jane gets the giggles.

Happy with the company, concerned about the compromises, we're all prickling with 'Who's faster? Who's smoother? Will he mind if we stop to pee? Will they mind if I stop to smoke?' nonsense. Irrelevant meta-clutter that becomes just that as soon as we stop worrying and start riding.

The sign reads El Camino Sinuoso, the winding road, but it could read 'The Most Beautiful Road in the World'. Ten minutes out of town and we already know this is gonna be very special. Smoky ochre hills concertina like folds on a bulldog's neck, and as we climb into the Andes there are snowy peaks above, sandy desert behind and below, the road falling away like coiled rope.

Magnificent views, rubbish riding. The Dakar's under-steering and 'umm?' vague. Stop for a smoke and kick the tyres. They're proper hot. 'When did you last check the pressures?' asks Dick. Umm? He whips out a digital gauge: 18 and 23. He whips out a compressor. And the bike's transformed from squelching in wet wellies to strutting in slutty heels. Air pressure, you say? Who knew?

The road levels out as it hits the altiplano plateau. We plane-high, bitch: 4500 metres high, 14,000 feet up, where the sun burns, wind chills, and the colours glow like a cross-processed paintbox. Everything that lives this high is woolly and fringed – the long-lashed llamas that have us cooing vowels, the kissing donkeys, the clever farm dogs, even the stonewalled thatched cottages. Indigenous kids in woven ponchos and goblin hats stare from the roadsides, cheeks stained salty with last night's tears, top lips crusty with this morning's snot. They don't look very well.

We stop at the bluest lake I've ever seen. Miami-pink flamingoes strut out of place among the llamas. 'That's rich,' they squawk. The air's thin and I'm not. Gentle strolling leaves me wobbly woozy. Marlboro Lights hit like crack. So it's not all bad.

Up, down. Scoured yellows and cloudy whites become wet greens and woody browns in valleys of Alpine triangles, pointed pines and sloping roofs. Then the road dips from Austria to Mars, into a valley that's as pink as a cat's mouth, as pink as lipstick kisses. Pink dust settles in pink mounds, pink water bubbles round pink stepping stones in a giggly pink river. Pink landslides tear, er, soft pink gashes in pink cliffs. Pink rocks painted with moss and shadows melt into angels' faces and giant frogs as easily as stoned clouds. It's like riding through a smile. 'That's not how you described it earlier,' laughs Jane.

Swooshing round easy open bends, bike rolling as smooth as a pool ball on felt, black visor down, belly in, showboating past farm workers walking home for their tea with that end-of-the-day last rush of energy, chasing a too-soon afternoon moon, and I just can't stop laughing. This is a physical happiness that flows from nose to toes, that lifts like dancing to great music, that hums like sub bass somewhere behind my balls and somewhere above my eyes. I feel good.

And then the sun sets. I'm scared of the dark. South American roads that are dodgy during the day become dog shit at night. Too many too-dim donkeys and too-bright wagons. Too many potholes, not enough street lights. 'Stick close to my rear,' orders Dick as Jane gets the giggles and he turns up the HID spots.

If it was a book, I'd speed-read this bit. But it's a bike, so I have to ride every word, every 'I can't see' sentence. Even ghosting Dick's smooth lines and Jane's stickered box, I hate it. A long hour later we arrive in Scottish-sounding Abancay. Plot up in a transit hotel where no one's ever unpacked, eat dinner in a transit restaurant no one's ever visited twice, laughing at things that aren't funny. 'You're rubbing off on us,' scolds Dick as Jane gets the giggles.

It's a hundred miles from Abancay to Cusco. The buses take six hours. It takes six minutes to see why as we wallop over another pass and this time see the coiled-rope road spilling away in front of us. If only I had brakes, it would be perfect.

There's fluid seeping from the master cylinder. I ignore it for an hour or so, hoping it will go away, but it gets worse. There's more fluid on the disc that's too hot to touch. Not that that stops me. Cock. Dick pulls up, looking worried. Problem? 'Something wrong with my helmet,' he shouts as Jane gets the giggles.

Dick fiddles with helmet cam, intercom and MP3 player connectors while I look pathetic. Eventually he gets the hint and takes off my caliper. 'Whatever you do, don't pull that lever?' This one? Cock. 'Now we need something hard and long to prise this apart,' he groans as Jane gets the giggles.

Monkey mechanics can't fix leaking brake seals at a roadside, but I'm not living in this lay-by for the rest of my life, even if the views are great. Nothing to do but keep on, head full of disaster rehearsals. If the brakes fail, will crashing through the box and hitting the kill-switch dump enough speed? If the brakes lock, will I have the balls to jump off the back before the bike slow-mo cartwheels off a sky-high cliff? These are not happy thoughts.

I'm distracted by a waterfall that has hidden a hundred yards of hairpin under icy cold bubbles and glistening gravel. The brakes hiss as I chug across. It's so damn refreshing, I ride it twice. Dick's not so keen. 'I don't want Jane getting all wet,' he says as she gets the giggles.

Half an hour outside Cusco, I hear a clunk and a drag. The back light and number plate are hanging by a wiry thread. Gaffering it up, I watch a fiesta in the field below – indigenous women in felt hats and too many skirts playing football with teenagers in Real Madrid shirts, a guitar, pan pipe and squeeze box band crooning drunken country ranchero tunes, an MC chattering in Quechua, the language of the Incas, over a whiny PA. The MC spots me, switches to Spanish and asks me to come on down. How could I say no?

They're celebrating a tap – the first time they've had running potable water in the village. I'm expecting some interest, but I'm overwhelmed by the no-angle hospitality. The bike's surrounded by 'Who? What? Where? Why?' questions, handshakes and hugs and I'm showered with shots of chicha.

Halfway through my second cup of cold sick, my host reminds me how this moonshine is made – the raw maize needs an enzyme to break it down before it will ferment. An enzyme found in human spit. Old women chew the grain for hours then spit it into barrels. A gurning gummy granny offers me a refill. How could I say no?

Dick and Jane follow me down, English hesitancy drowned in grubby kids' kisses. Three lads produce a table and chairs and we're sitting targets. Kids on knees, hanging off arms, climbing over heads. 'Will you dance with me?' a pigtailed girl whispers in my ear. Why would I say no?

Exhausted by the hokey-cokey, dizzy from ring-a-ring o' roses, half-cut on granny phlegm, we hit Cusco just as the setting sun's backlit the red roofs like dashboard light. An hour later we're plotted up in the Norton Rats pub, admiring owner Jeff's '74 Commando. Two hours later we're in a back room with a pint, a pie and pipe of Peruvian pollen, chuckling along to *Easy Rider*. 'I never wanted to be anyone else.' Stumbling back across the grand plaza, we pass a line of backpackers squabbling onto a night bus. Why travel at night? 'Because there's nothing to see between here and Lima.'

The world and his second wife pass through Cusco on the way to Machu Picchu, South America's iconic archaeological sight. No private traffic allowed beyond the Sacred Valley, so I'm on the train with the cag-in-a-bag two-weekers and too-much-too-young gap-year round-the-worlders. 'My prep school's older than this place,' squeaks one little darling.

Ignore that wretch, believe the hype – Machu Picchu is the most dramatically beautiful sight I've ever seen. A citadel carved into a mountain top, surrounded by misty peaks and dizzying drops, snowy caps and jungle witchery, all buzzing with what explorer Hiram

Bingham called 'the fascination of finding . . . the rugged masonry of a bygone race; and of trying to understand the bewildering romance of the ancient builders who . . . sought refuge in a region . . . designed by nature as a sanctuary for the oppressed, a place where they might . . . give expression to their passion for walls of enduring beauty.'

Mesmeric and ingenious. Quarried terraces allow the steep slopes to be farmed and grazed. Clever Incas. Fresh water was channelled from springs to bathhouses. Clean Incas. Best of all, the Spaniards never found it. No one knows what it was called, when or why it was built, when or why it was abandoned. Mysterious Incas.

Back at Norton's, all we can talk about is that road. Not only but also – desert, plateau, valleys, and a reason to ride. 'The best ride I've ever had,' says Dick and Jane gets the giggles. Why so? 'Hard to explain. You really had to be there.'

He's absolutely right. These are the days that must happen to you.

'You coming or what, Dan?' Gah. Sunday morning in Cusco, and last night's Cuban rum's turning today's breakfast run into a lunchtime slouch. Dick and Jane have been knocking every half-hour since Christ knows. I suppose I'd better get up.

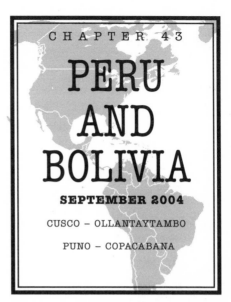

CHAPTER 43

PERU AND BOLIVIA

SEPTEMBER 2004

CUSCO – OLLANTAYTAMBO

PUNO – COPACABANA

'Afternoon.' They're pink and scrubbed, curled and fluffed, nice but square in matching riding gear. I'm still half-cut, night-sweat damp, chuckling about that Japanese girl blurting, unprompted, 'I can't kiss you because of this cold sore, but you can have a go on my boobs if you like.' Sleazy like Sunday morning.

The gang's all here. Dick and Jane on their banana-yellow VW camper van GS1150, Nutty Jerome from Richmond on his matt-black KTM Adventure with Akropovic horse-scarer, and expat Jeff, our leader, owner of the Norton Rats pub and a very shiny '74 Commando.

A proper bloke on a proper bloke's bike, with a proper bloke's tank badge, kick-start and pretty, ponytailed pillion. We're all proper jealous, this old Brit iron making our Teutonic plastic look as desirable as disposable razors. And damn, does he know it. The old boy double keen to prove that his old girl's still got it, he charges away, bouncing up steep-as-spires cobbled alleyways, down 'it's not a road, it's a storm drain' short cuts, and out into the Sacred Valley. It ain't what you ride, it's the way that you ride it, fatty.

The Sacred Valley, a line of forts, temples and farms through the Incas' spiritual homeland, becomes the Scared Valley as I fail to keep up, then give up and accept fourth place. These kinds of 'mine's bigger' comparisons only matter if you care. And I don't. 'Being able to ride fast is no more impressive than being able to throw a ball a long way,' reckons *Bike* contributor and old friend Gary Inman, and I'm so slow I have to agree.

We stop for coffee and shim adjustments under towering Ollan-taytambo, last in a series of forts whose impregnability seemed to rely upon their utter unpronounceability. 'Ollantaytambo? Sacsayhuamán? Oh sod it, let's invade Chile instead.' This was the only place where the Incas defeated the Spaniards in open battle – a guerrilla-tactic inspiration to the young Norton-riding Guevara. 'Picture?' ask Tokyo tourists on a JAL-sponsored 'Che Trail'.

Comfortable Cusco's an easy place to lose a week. Once the puma-shaped head of the Inca empire, now it's Peru's tourist capital, its whitewashed walls and grand plazas lost under pizza parlours and faux Irish pubs, travel agencies and cybercafés just as its sun temples and golden courtyards were buried under Catholic churches and Spanish palaces. Two-weekers from Warrington in khaki shorts and long socks dodge gangs of street kids selling snide cigarettes and cute finger pup-pets. Coaxing girls flap menus at tour groups in matching hats, waving them towards tables of English posh kids, girls neighing unembarrassed loud about 'mummy and daddy', boys slouching unconvincingly in mockney: 'Just the seven pints for me last night then.'

The best place to watch this circus, out of reach of Dragoman Overland trucks and Israelis on hired dirt bikes with exhausts as obnoxious as their manners, is the upstairs balcony at the Norton Rats, which nestles between the cathedral and the Jesuit church, as inappropriate as Angels in the Vatican. I stay still for days while the square fills and empties like stop-motion photography. A religious procession for Blessed Saint Martín blurs into a crowd of thousands watching local heroes Cienciano beat mighty Boca Juniors on a big screen blurs into a protest about insensitive tourism.

And behind me, in the bar, more overland bikes – the Creepy Californian on his KLR who makes the girls shiver with his 'Eeww, bad touch', and Too Tall Tom, a Canadian on another GS riding Alaska to Argentina in annual monthly chunks. 'This year it's Lima to Buenos Aires.' He's a nice guy, so I don't mention that it seems like running a marathon in twenty-six separate stages.

Then the bawdy, back-slapping Brazilians on muddy DR800s breeze in, bringing bad news from the Bolivian border. The Peruanos have tightened up and are impounding overstayed bikes. Which means we've gotta leave. Which means I have to fix my bleeding brakes. Again. Now the seals seem rotten, weeping then sobbing from the master cylinder and caliper. Maybe it's the altitude, maybe the monkeys in Quito spat in the lines. Whatever, the brakes don't work.

Back in Lima, Antonio's the man to know, working out of his yard beyond the railway tracks, past the giant Condor statue. While he finishes off a CR500, I amuse myself buying a can of Fanny and a bag of Ace from the local shop. The grocer really couldn't understand why I was laughing so hard I almost choked.

Peru is blessed with good mechanics. Chirpy Tatu resealed my forks in a workshop rammed with high-maintenance crossers, WRs, KXs, even a Husaberg, while bantering about whether or not his mate Beso is gay. 'Beso, do you like girls?' 'No.' 'Do you like boys?' 'Yes.' 'So you are gay?' 'No, but boys, er,' he makes a ring with thumb and finger, 'are tighter.' No smutty nonsense from Antonio, just a steady fluid flush. 'Agua.' There's water in the lines. 'Ay, que sucio.' And rusty dirt too. Run half a litre of blue DOT through and hope that will do. We've gotta break for the border.

Two dashed days later we roll up at the Lake Titicaca frontier. Now I'm square and the kids are rock-and-roll rebels. My papers are in order and I'm waved through. Theirs aren't and they're not. Five hours of excuses and tears, bribes and fears changes nothing. The little man in the big boots stamps impounding orders and their home-from-home is locked up in the customs compound. I'm shooed into Bolivia and they're put on a bus back to Cusco and the British Embassy.

These aren't the days that must happen to you.

'Love isn't always on time, cha cha cha cha.' Breathtakingly high, drop-dead gorgeous afternoon on the Peruano–Boliviano frontier, and my first impression of Bolivia is crooned by the customs coronel, another little man in big boots soft-rocking out to the radio and asking increasingly odd questions.

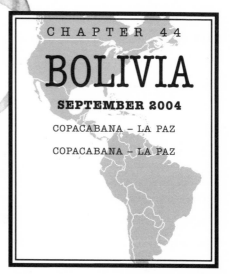

'How much is a day in Miami? Why are you so fat? Which is your favourite Spice Girl? I like Scary, La Negrita.' And I've got a couple of questions of my own. Like why is he wearing a T-shirt that reads 'Fucking Situation', and why has he given the bike ninety days, but me only thirty? He stretches out on his camp bed. 'Welcome to Bolivia, gordo.'

Welcome to beautiful, bonkers, backwater Bolivia, baby, Latin America's craziest cousin, landlocked away in this high Andes attic. Home to the bowler hat for her and the coca leaf for him. Death spot for Che Guevara's last romantic adventure and Butch and Sundance's last great train robbery. And resentful harbour for that worldwide joke, the Boliviano navy, marooned in Lake Titicaca (titter) like goldfish in a bag.

Lake Titicaca (arf) – 100 miles long, sky-high, the puddled remains of an ancient inland sea. The Peruano side's industrial and touristy. Backpackers brave polluted Puno port's open sewers and strangle muggings to day-trip out to the Islas de Uros, floating islands built from hollow reeds, spongy wet weave woven into springy floors, pigtailed houses and cat-faced canoes by isolationist Indians escaping imperialist Incas. The men still fish for freshwater trout, but now the women survive selling cheerful tat and surly pictures of their snotty kids to camera-clicking tourists.

Bolivia's three hours away, via the town of Ilave, now nationally notorious after its citizens beat their mayor to death then hanged his mashed-beet body off a bridge, via a border post that's now overlander infamous after they impounded Dick and Jane's GS, and into lakeside Copacabana. And no, it isn't the hottest spot north of Havana.

Five bucks buys me a room in quirky terracotta La Leyenda, a room with an Incan sun god's view of the lake's soft-lapping, wet-slapping shores, smudged-mountain horizons, and sky-blue beauty. Beauty that moves and grooves and soothes everyone who sees it. Beauty that mesmerises anyone who stares into its shimmering mirror. Beauty so profound that it squashes the need for ugly small talk. This gaff's so relaxed, even the hippies can't annoy me. They don't play the didgeridon't and I don't criticise their decision to style themselves like Jesus just for the tourist blow jobs. Perfect.

Lazy days, chirpy nights in English Tom's bar, Nemo's, with Brendan, an ex-ICF hooligan turned London club promoter, and Leslie, a script editor for *Emmerdale* who actually got to say 'And then they lezzed up'. And Tony, a dole snooper from St Albans. Who inevitably gets bounced off a couple of walls. And if this isn't nice, what is?

No one's ever called El Alto 'nice'. El Alto's a slum suburb that sprawled so far it became a city. As attractive as that first sight of your naked father bending over a bath, as flattering as your first view of your mother (and your mother's first view of you), El Alto is La Paz's furry flaps and chicken-skin sacks, its dangerous streets littered with dead dogs and smashed breeze blocks.

Plastic bags flap like dying fish in the dusty gusts. Bomber-jacketed XT bike cops blow hard on ignored whistles. Pedestrians lurch in front of over-filled minibuses and overloaded cement trucks, staring at angry swerves and cursing horns with eyes like cows on the way to the abattoir. Then the six-lane highway funnels into a black market and tumbles out the other side into downtown La Paz.

La Paz. It ain't pretty, but it's authentically South American, a million miles away from Lima's Miami-lite Miraflores. Little brown folk hustle and bustle up and down too-steep streets, swapping money and kisses, flowers and colds, snide Marlboro and pirated Harry Potter DVDs. Rich girls in boob tubes and miniskirts swish past indigenous dustwomen in dust masks. Mohawked punks sneer at giggling teens queuing for *Alien vs Predator*. Sharp men in sharp suits get their shoes shined by boiler-suited and balaclava'd boot boys.

A new city means playing the new-city routine, riding in clumsy circles for a couple of confused hours, forcing the map to fit the territory, hunting for a hotel that takes bikes, a cashpoint that takes Co-op cards, a café that brews proper coffee and serves breakfast till mid-afternoon. And, obviously, a decent bar.

I don't just need a bar because I'm a wet-brained wanker. I also need to

meet Bolivianos. Backstreet La Luna is perfect. Down the steps, knock three times on the cracked orange glass and trip into this beery cellar. Five minutes later I'm flirting with frothy Marta the manageress, chewing coca leaves with 'Andsome 'Arry the jungle guide and clinking chilly suds with Out and Proud André, laughing at a gang of Stoke builders cracking onto a table full of plain-clothes Irish nuns. The guide book calls La Luna 'Bohemian', which means that a man who looks like the bass player out of Spinal Tap tries to sell me coke every time I duck into the toilets.

Three weeks later, I'm still there. I was gonna leave sooner, but frankly I just couldn't be arsed. I'd run out of keen steam. This wasn't an existential crisis, just a break. It happens. Some people take this as a cue to bail home, but I'm used to this two-wheeled-travel mental cycle, and know that quitting would be a premature evacuation. The trick is just to stop. And sidestep the guilt that resting breeds. Guilt that gets kinda noisy when I realise that I've spent the length of the average British annual holiday doing nothing but plucking hairs from my balls and learning to play 'Comandante Che Guevara' on the guitar in a bed crunchy with crisp-butty crumbs.

Until one morning I wake up at seven, three days sober, and an unavoidable voice is asking, 'What now?' Pack the bags, pay the bill, and ride off to the dynamite shops of Potosí.

Next stop – the Potosí mines.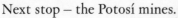

'Eight million died in these mines during three hundred years of slavery.' Nearly three miles up the Bolivian Andes and I'm breaking my teeth trying to crunch obscene numbers. A dozen Euro day-trippers, decked out in fluoro rubber pants and gas-lit helmets, suddenly stop sniggering at each other's

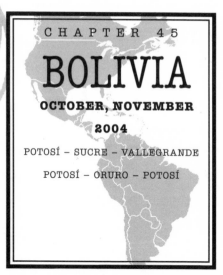

CHAPTER 45

BOLIVIA

OCTOBER, NOVEMBER

2004

POTOSÍ – SUCRE – VALLEGRANDE

POTOSÍ – ORURO – POTOSÍ

'Santa's Big Fat Helpers' garms and try to think of an appropriate response to this underground genocide. Jahira, the only female indigenous guide in town, responds for us. 'Bolivia is a donkey burdened by silver.'

Welcome to the mine tour in Potosí, the highest city in the world blessed and cursed with the richest silver mine in history. It starts out as a hoot, diving into the dressing-down box and emerging smothered with obligatory health-and-safety gear, then trotting up to the market to buy gifts for the miners. Er, are you sure we're allowed to buy this stuff? 'Of course.' OK then, I'll have two sticks of dynamite plus blasting caps, fuses and nitrate boosters, half a kilo of coca leaves and a bottle of 96 per cent proof 'Bolivian whiskey'. 'Certainly, señor.' And suddenly the duty-free Lacoste store in Panama City is my second favourite shop.

'They say you could build a bridge from here to Madrid with all the silver the Spaniards stole.' This healthy seam was discovered by the

Incas then ripped into a tattered gash by conquistador-cruel concentration camps of Quechua and Aymara Indians and imported West Africans. The slaves worked six-month shifts: six months below ground – 'Never surfacing, working and living underground' – and six months above ground, working the toxic processing plants. 'They preferred to work underground. The processing used mercury. The death rate was higher here, above ground.' She points at the grey rows of sheds, still belching with bubbling vats, still shuddering with sleeve-snagging, elbow-snapping grinders. 'Now they use cyanide instead of mercury. Let's go down.'

Going straight to hell, boy. Which is why we must pay our respects to a devil, Tío Jorge, Uncle George, Quechuan God of the Underworld. His after-life-size effigy squats on a throne in a dark cave shrine, hands, horns and hard-on decorated with curled-dry coca leaf confetti, stained with over-proof rotgut. 'For luck. Every miner pays respect here every day. We must too.'

It's a serious ceremony and nobody's sneering. Sitting in this deep hole, listening to the walls creak and the tunnels rumble, I'll take any extra luck I can get. Flutter coca onto Tío's lap, push a pile into my own mouth. Splash whiskey onto Jorge's rubber boots, then scald my own lips. And get the giggles wondering exactly how I've ended up worshipping Satan in a medieval mineshaft, high on coke, drunk on moonshine and loaded up with TNT. Dynamite in my pocket, baby. 'You seem very happy. You can lead.' Arse.

Up here, down here, the air's suffocating and thin, now cold and dank as fishes' kisses, now hot and stuffy as a mouthful of sand. Words are strangled at birth, dropping from my mouth like dead birds. Crouched ceilings and jagged walls drip with noxious oxides and 'Don't touch that!' residue. My leaking wellies squelch like Aunt Fanny's farts as we stumble, trudge, crawl deeper into this labyrinthine anthill.

Hand-pushed bogie wagons thud out of the darkness, scudding along the rails in a spray of sweat and muscle strain. I was so exhausted playing working class for the day that I'd forgotten that people still worked this unlit, unventilated dungeon. We stop in a cave to swap gifts for answers with two workers, deep-chested Quechuas, cheeks bulging with wadded coca golfballs. What do you earn down here? 'Three dollars on a good day, nothing on a bad day.' How dangerous is it? 'The tunnels kill you now, the lung diseases kill you later.' How does it feel to be a tourist attraction? They chuckle. 'It's fine. We appreciate the gifts.' Makes sense — back when I earned a living leaning on a scaffold, I'd have been fucking delighted to meet foreign tourists bearing gifts of booze, fags and narcs. 'And we appreciate the help.' Help? Er, why have you given me a shovel?

Tough, topless teenagers wrestle a handcart out of the pitch and dump two tons of rocky rubble at our boots. The cave fills with shovel-shriek and red-eyed dust, as the rubble's shovelled into baskets and hand-winched to the surface. Five minutes in and I can't see or breathe. The real men haven't broken a sweat.

Three hours in this handmade hell is more than enough and we run back into the light, puffed and pummelled, humbled and horrified. 'Who wants to blow something up?' And now it's a hoot again. Small boys and big bangs. Strolling back from the bomb hole, body still quivering like a bass bin from the high-explosive hardcore, we pass a line of old dears hand-picking through slag heaps. What's this about? 'They are miners'

widows. The company lets them sort through the rubbish for silver, tin and zinc.'

It's a *Naked Lunch* moment. The 'moment when everyone sees what is on the end of every fork'. Behind the pretty packaging, the fluttering FTSE figures, the ironic adverts, sit the world's poor. Panamanian children picking supermarket bananas for a dollar a day, Colombian Coca-Cola workers tortured to death for organising trade unions, this Bolivian widow feeding her family by picking through industrial waste. It's arse over tit, sugaring arseholes while slashing udders, punishing the real producers and rewarding the phoney marketeers. Paying motorcycle journalists more cubed than miners. Everyone knows this, but it's still a shock when the poor pop out of the shadows and shake your hand. Once upon a time, inequalities like these made men like Che Guevara pick up AKs and head for the hills. Now they just make boys like me jump on motorbikes and head for the spot where a CIA death squad turned a revolutionary into a T-shirt.

'My name is Che Guevara and I have failed.' Che's last romantic adventure died with him in the jungles of south-eastern Bolivia on 9 October 1967. 'It is better like this, I should never have been captured alive.' After six months wreaking havoc with a miner-led guerrilla group, Che was tracked, wounded and captured in Vallegrande by a mixed bag of US Green Berets and Bolivian Rangers commanded by Félix Rodríguez, a fascist Cuban CIA operative. 'I know what you have come for and I am ready.' After a day of pointless interrogation and celebratory torture, Rodríguez ordered Bolivian Sergeant Jaime Terán to execute the wounded prisoner. 'Know this, you are killing a man.'

Rodríguez and the smiling executioners posed for gloating pictures over the corpse. The hands were cut off, pickled in formaldehyde and sent to Argentina for fingerprint confirmation. The body was buried in secret under an airstrip. Rodríguez kept on killing commies for mommy, in Vietnam and Laos, in El Salvador and Nicaragua, in Washington and Guantánamo. He now lives in Dade County, Miami, where he actively campaigned for Dubyah's re-election. Rodríguez still wears Che's Rolex.

On 13 July 1997, Che's exhumed remains were returned to Havana, Cuba. All that's left in Vallegrande is a plaque and a bust, a strange tang of history and a great reason to ride. Which is why so many overlanders end up in nearby Sucre.

Sucre — with its whitewashed walls, red roofs and blue skies, it smells like summer holidays. With its grand colonial churches, palm-tree shady plazas and wealthy middle class, it feels nothing like the clichéd 'bowler hats and donkeys' view of Bolivia. Fifteen dollars buys a quiet wooden room off a cool stone courtyard. Headquarters is set up in the Dutch Joyride Café. Plot up at the bar with owner Dirty Gertie, tuck into Belgian beers, Argentine steaks and Manchester music and watch the bikes roll in.

All the nicknames are here — Nice-but-Square Dick and Jane on their GS1150, Amish Kids Renee and Amy on F650s, Lonely Bob and his Peruana Pillion on another Dakar, Oz and Curly Kylie on a Dominator and KLR250, Typhoid Tony on his KLR650, plus me — Surly Dan, aka the Terrible Cunt.

Most of us have met before, on horizonsunlimited.com, in Quito, Lima or La Paz, but it's the first time we've come together as an English-speaking group. It's nice to be among friends. Nice to relax with other

travellers and swap routes and rants, horror stories and dreamy plans. Nice to break the bar's drinking record, race quads round sleeping streets, dance on tables to the Smiths, and learn how to say 'fanny like a donkey's yawn' in Spanish. Made extra nice by the knowledge that in a week or so this comfortable company will split as we head our separate ways.

Everyone's going to or from Che's memorial, from or to the Salar de Uyuni salt flats. I change plans. Because I can. Delay Che, back-flip south to the salt with Dick and Jane. Which means serious dirt. Which means serious flapping. 'Cause Dick and I are scared of the dirt. We blame everything else – the bikes are too heavy, the tyres too road, the pillions too precious – but the truth is we're just shit and slow. Dirt's as different from tarmac as two wheels are from four. Dirt means more concentration, more physical commitment, more painful risk. Dirt needs practice. And I've only ridden seven serious dirt days since leaving London, plus maybe another week's worth of playful trail riding. Fitting Tonka-toy MT21 tyres should make me feel fitter, but on tarmac they skate like football studs on a changing-room floor. By the time we get back to Potosí and the trail head, I'm seriously worried.

Potosí to Uyuni is less than 200 miles. The Amish Kids rode it in a steady seven hours. Dirty Gertie raced it in four hours on his WR400. Somehow, it takes us nine hours. Nine ball-banging, teeth-grinding, front-sliding, head-aching hours. We need someone to kick us in the arse, show us that faster is easier, smoother, safer, but we just slow each other down. We even pretend we like travelling this slowly ''Cause you can look around'. But all I see is the patch of the ground just beyond my wobbly front wheel.

There's always a reward. Every dirt road, no matter how tough, eventually leads to at least one glorious run, always produces that Dakar Rally helicopter shot of a small bike kicking up dust in a big landscape. Today it's a dramatic single track stuck to the steep canyon wall like spaghetti to a ceiling. But I'm still glad when we finally bounce through the tin-roofed whistle-stop where Butch and Sundance robbed their last train and into outpost Uyuni.

The Wild Boys from the Hole-in-the-Wall Gang and the Train Robbers' Syndicate would recognise Uyuni. Its sandy streets still full of nothing but wheel-biting mongrels, Spanish kids, Indian markets. Its dead-end narrow-gauge railway still shunting ghost trains to a real graveyard where locomotives rot and rust picturesquely under the desert sun. There's even a mission church with a high-noon bell, ready to be rung by bullets as the Pinkerton shootist stuntman-tumbles from its Spanish steeple. 'We're just popping to the internet. Meet in the pizza parlour?' spurts Dick. Spoilsport.

You get what you need. Next morning, lined up for petrol behind the 4x4 tours, we meet the Good German. Mid-forties, On The Road perma-tanned, riding a fifteen-year-old R80GS. From the early-nineties Arai and Dainese and the wide-open smile, I'm guessing that he hasn't been home in years. He's headed north, beyond the salt, towards La Paz. I've heard that road is a sandy pig. He chuckles. 'I've been riding too long to worry about things like that. Come, ride with me.' And he's onto the dirt, up on the pegs, second, third, fourth, fifty miles an hour, relaxed, fast, smooth. I only keep up for five, ten minutes before running out of puff, but it's enough to prove his point. If his outdated, hard-luggaged pig can cope, then so can my Dakar. I'm almost disappointed when the rough stuff stops and we hit the Salar. Almost.

The Salar de Uyuni is the largest salt pan in the world. Thirteen thousand square kilometres of nothing but bright-bright, white-white salt surrounded by purple-shadowed volcanoes. Thirteen thousand square kilometres of shimmering, dazzling, tangy salt. No people, no animals, no plants, no nothing. Just salt. Geometrically perfect salt that rises from the earth in a never-ending hexagonal lace. It looks like a giant snowflake has fallen up out of the ground. It looks like God's oddest jigsaw puzzle. It looks like nothing I've ever seen before. It's absolutely astonishing.

Something this astonishing, this desolate, this quiet, needs to be ridden alone. Dick and Jane follow a jeep track, I cut off into the glaring white nothing. Damn, this feels free. No directions, no restrictions, nothing to hit, nothing to miss. Just hours of crisp, salty silence. It feels celestial. It's the closest I'll get to heaven. And the closest I'll ever get to riding across a sea.

The Salar used to be part of an inland sea that covered Lake Titicaca (arf) and, wait for it, Lake Poopó. The islands are still there, dark and vague, dotted with tough cacti and marooned chinchillas. Pick a shape that could be ten or a hundred miles away and tack towards it, carving swooshing figures of eight, seeing how long I can ride with my eyes shut. Damn this feels free.

An island looms, the surface changes, the salty hexagons now standing upright like clamshells until the bike crunches through them like teeth through prawn crackers. In the distance, a dumb bell rings. Last night, a German guide warned about the mud round these islands. 'Get too close and it's "Ciao" your bike.' Ever get that sinking feeling? Er, why have we stopped?

I guess it's called 'mud' but it looks, feels and, ugh, smells like a coughed-up cocktail of filthy axle grease, snotty clay and congealed dysentery. Wet underground, it soon sets solid in this sharp sun. And my knobbly MT21s lost underneath a 250-section shitty slick. The back wheel still spins, but we're stuck as tight as an exercise bike. Oh, bollocks.

Fun facts jostle round my brain. I am properly stuck FACT in a salty desert wilderness in the Bolivian Andes FACT where I haven't seen another soul for over an hour FACT with no means of communication beyond snivelling prayer FACT with nothing in my pockets but half a pack of biscuits and an extra pack of smokes FACT. I'm fucked. Facted.

A Marlboro-jacketed bouncer keeps Panic behind the velvet rope. Maybe a tour group will veer off course and spot me. Maybe I can find a hut on the island and survive the night. And maybe I'll die out here, frozen solid, mouth choked with shitty mud, lips blistered from drinking petrol. Just as I'm about to choke down my first drop of pee, the yellow submarine appears in the hazy distance. Never thought I'd be so pleased to see a Dick.

Uyuni back to Potosí – same route, but an entirely different journey. The Good German's long gone, but I've pickled a slice of his confidence. Double the throttle means half the pain, less stress, more laughs. An extra 20 mph makes the bike float over corrugations and sand traps, not battle through them. Best of all, I've found time to look up and around. Ancient mountains have burst through an even older desert and thrust it two miles high. Martian reds, lunar silvers, earthy creams rise and fall

under a *Simpsons* sky. Fluffy clouds, close enough to catch, blot out the sun and polka-dot the bright afternoon with cold splashes of dark midnight. It's uniquely, beautifully Bolivian.

Six hours later I hit the tarmac in Potosí. Sit by the roadside, smile, smoke, pat the bike, wait for the kids to catch up. Miners roll by, whistling and singing, racing barrowloads of beers and girls. I guess today was a good day. Tonight I'll say goodbye to the kids. They're heading west to Chile and the Pacific, to catch some sun. And I'm heading back east, to Sucre and Che, to catch some typhoid.

Next stop – hospital. For quite a long time.

'Get up, ya lazy bastard Pom!' It felt like the hangover that had finally killed me – room spinning like a seasick merry-go-round, eyeballs aching like pinched plums, stomach cramping like a knees-to-chest period, aching body sweating like stinking rotten meat. Heart banging like that Aussie at the door. 'Had a couple of beers last night?' I try to

CHAPTER 46

BOLIVIA, CHILE, ARGENTINA

NOVEMBER, DECEMBER 2004, JANUARY 2005

SUCRE – ORURO – ARICA

IQUIQUE – ANTOFAGASTA

LA SERENA – LOS VILOS

PAPUDO – SANTIAGO – MENDOZA

say 'No, I came straight home', but it just comes out as 'Ummf'. 'I bet ya did. We'll see ya down the road, eh?' No Oz, don't leave, man, I'm proper sick and really could do with some help. 'Ummf.' 'Cheers, Dan.' Arse.

This is typhoid. A filthy Bolivian brain-boiler that's born in sewage-infected pipes and borne by wet sneezes, rubbed eyes, puddle splashes. I recognise the symptoms 'cause I just spent a week hospital-visiting Typhoid Tony from Stoke. Same nose-to-toes aches, same inability to walk or talk. Difference is, I'm on my own. I was supposed to ride out this morning with Oz, so I said my goodbyes last night. Everyone in Sucre thinks I've gone. I could call the front desk for help, but I don't know the Spanish for 'ummf'. Besides, they're not talking to me since the deeply Catholic manager's deeply Catholic daughter caught me rooting through her father's drawers (easy) at three in the morning, looking for the key to the beer fridge, deeply drunk and, er, deeply naked. Guess I lost the towel somewhere in the courtyard.

So it's two long, lonely days before the Boss forces entry and retches 'Ay, Dios'. There's sick on the towels, shit on the tiles and the shower's flooded, clogged up with sticky sheets. I'm sprawled on the floor 'cause it's cooler and cleaner. That's the second time this week the hotel staff have seen me naked. It's starting to look deliberate. 'Vamos al hospital. And please, put some clothes on, señor?'

'Welcome to the second best hospital in Bolivia,' trumpets a tatty banner. The bald doctor tells me it's altitude sickness. The hairy doctor tells me it's meningitis. I tell the fat doctor it's typhoid and a blood test backs me up. Painkillers in my arse, a tap plumbed into my hand for mainlined antibiotics and a constipating glucose drip, and a bed in the infectious-diseases ward, slotted between malaria and dysentery. Morning, Sweaty, how is it, Shitty?

Glaring, blaring days and grotty, potty nights, trying not to hear the old boy shitting his soul into a washing-up bowl, trying not to see the lad getting undercover hand relief from his curly girlie. Life reduced to sleep and not-sleep. Sometimes I get up, pad about in my dead midget's bleach-stained pyjamas, take the snagging drip stand for a walk, reeling like a drunken sailor with the staggers. Sit in the garden and smoke with Jesús, a sweet twenty-something melted monstrous by the worse kerosene burns I've ever seen. We hide in the shade 'cause the sun makes him sneeze and weep. His bandaged hands can't light a light or smoke a smoke. So I do it for him. People stare. 'Look at the burned boy smoke,' laughs Jesús.

Two weeks of this claustrophobic bedlam and I'm ready to throw myself out of a barred window. Two weeks is too long to suck hard on this death, disease and detergent. Two weeks of no-insurance medical bills have mounted up and I've missed this month's work deadline, which means I don't get paid. Worst of all, the drip's fish-hooked into my wanking hand. 'Oh my God, Danny, there you are!' Hallelujah. Anna's arrived.

Anna, the Canadian cutie I hooked up with in Panama, Ecuador and Brooklyn (Where do motorcycle travellers go on holiday? Coney Island, baby), just bussed in from Peru. She appears at the end of the bed, haloed hazy in the window light like a soft-focus, soft-porn angel, all baby blue eyes and pouty princess mouth, Farrah Fawcett locks a-slow-mo-blow in the cool breeze. 'Gosh, that fan's powerful. Let's get you out of here.'

A week later I'm back in my boots and ready to get back on the bike. We're heading west to Chile, racing expiring visas to the border. We. A long time since I took a pillion further than the shops. Anna's never been pillion further than the shops. She's all excited, dressing up like Penelope Pitstop and packing picnics. I'm not so sure. A small bike's the perfect place to make a great couple grate.

The rain starts ten minutes out of Sucre and doesn't stop for the next ten hours. The route across the altiplano highlands, so beautiful in the sunny dry, feels isolated, desolate and fairly fucking dangerous in this freezing wet, the road lost under muddy landslides, the Andean views drowned in foggy storm clouds that we ride through, not under. And I start to feel like one of those idiots who gets rescued from Ben Nevis wearing sandals and shorts. 'But the weather turned' is right up there with 'But the bend tightened up'. Sometimes I don't take this shit seriously enough. I've got someone's daughter on the back.

By lunchtime the sandwiches are soggy, the rain's hardened into heavy hail and we're dangerously cold. Stop for a snivel and a soaked smoke and nearly fall sideways off the bike, knees buckling with spastic shakes. Anna's still smiling, though she's shivering like a shitting dog. 'Isn't that a Peter Kay joke?' Er, yes, it is.

And then we hit a roadblock. Bolivia has a fierce tradition of civil disobedience. Problem with the government? Roll out the boulder and balaclava barricades, make the bastards stop, look and listen. The hooded spokesman's poor and hard, cold and wet, friendly but firm. 'No pasarán.' He points at the queue of buses with his stick of dynamite. 'Everyone must wait.' How long? He shrugs. This could go on for weeks, and my visa's only good for half a day. Usually I'm happy to show solidarity, rub up against the revolution and pull Che faces. Today I'm ready to scab like a Nottingham miner. What would happen if I just burst through? I don't have to. Anna flashes the baby blues, the hard man winks and waves us on. Revolting peasants prefer blondes, too.

What feels like several days later, we splosh into Oruro, a pretty name for a low-rise crossroads slum. My fingers and toes are pruned before I get into the steaming shower. Everything's soaked, so we hide in bed with a Chinese takeaway. That was the worst day's riding of the entire trip. 'Thank God you said that out loud,' says Anna. 'I thought that was normal. I was just about to go home.'

Bad days fade, good days stain. Next morning the sun's out, the

breakfast patio's warm, the salty butter and home-made jam just melt into the oven-hot bread. Even the bike looks perkier, locked up in a derelict pharmacy, surrounded by prescription litter and sleeping alley cats. While I'm loading the bags, a Quechua granny cycles up. 'Your wife is very beautiful.' Yes, she is. 'You should appreciate her.' Yes, I should. 'Because one day she will look like me!' We all laugh and Gran rides off, wrong way down a one-way. I'll miss this country.

One last happy waltz with the Bolivian wilds, under this domed cathedral sky, feeling the sharp high-altitude sun burn away yesterday's dampness, letting the fresh highway wind blow away yesterday's stress, and I've beaten the visa's clock. Which is good and bad. Because for the first time this trip, I'm not especially excited about the next border crossing.

Welcome to Chile, the South American country with the big ol' but. 'It's nice but . . .' No one ever falls in love with Chile. No one ever falls in love in Chile. Travellers want to settle in Peru, get married in Colombia, build bars in Brazil or apartments in Argentina, but Chile? It's a qualified success. 'It's beautiful but . . .'

Ruta 11 drops from the 5000 metre-high border post to the Pacific coast, from ski runs to surf bums, in just over a hundred miles, nosing and diving, whooping and hollering round mirrored lakes full of fluffy clouds and angry volcanoes, through flamingo flocks and wild llama herds, and as the Andes fold into the Atacama Desert, through sandstone canyons spiked with candelabra cacti. I've never seen black and white Friesians grazing rich green grass under yellow dunes overshadowed by snow-capped Andes peaks before. It is very beautiful. But something's not quite right.

First, the border crossing was just too damn easy. Polite professionals in coordinated uniforms helpfully guided me through the immigration process, asking logical questions and entering the answers into a working computer. No daft 'I heart Disco' hand-me-downs, no 'Favourite Spice Girl?' non-sequiturs, no 'Not if the day starts with a "t"' bureaucracy, no '$50 white boy tax' corruption. It's shockingly normal. And after nearly two years in Latin America, normal feels very fucking odd.

Then there's the roads. Two hours in, and I've still not met a car on the wrong side. Drivers actually wait until they can see it's safe before overtaking. They've got odd orange lights on their corners that blink when they're turning and rear red lights that flash when they're stopping. Which is a damn good idea, 'cause they stop at the oddest places – traffic lights, 'Give Way' signs, even pedestrian crossings. Even when there are no cops watching. It's really freaking me out. Normal is the new odd.

If I'd just flown in from the UK, it would all be pleasingly exotic, but I haven't, so it isn't, and I can't fake it. If I'd just shipped in from New Zealand, it would seem fantastically cheap, but I haven't, so it isn't, and I can't afford it. The bare essentials – petrol and food, booze and fags, motels and Lacoste shirts – are three times the price of Bolivia or Peru. And not half as interesting.

Normal traffic clogs up normal towns – Arica's all McDonald's and malls, condos and casinos, and though Iquique's prettier, with its colonial streets of pointed, painted wooden roofs and iron balconies, it's strangely subdued, like Old Orleans or the Mild West. I just can't find any mayhem.

Last Christmas I was drinking in Nicaragua with on-the-run revolutionaries. This year I have a nice dinner with the hotel owner and a retired couple from Quebec. Last New Year I was stoned in the Costa Rican mountains with an ex-AMA racer spinning *On Any Sunday* yarns. This time I'm watching family fireworks with backpackers from Leeds. Ooh. Aah. The evening's only saved when an old boy sets up a telescope, selling the stars for a peso a peep. All together now. 'How much to see the rings around your Uranus?' Oh, come on.

Poet Pablo Neruda described Chile as 'a long petal of sea, wine and snow'. Up here, there's only sea, wind and sand. From the northern border to central Santiago sits 1000 miles of coastal desert, desert so pure it's never seen rain. I guess from the 'Wake Up!' rumble strips that some drivers find these shimmering straights kinda dull, but I love listening to the roaring gales tear across these empty places, love watching the subtle-soft ochre and terracotta colour changes, love smelling the ocean crashing off these endless shores. And I love finding the quirky corners that the express buses miss – the nowhere, no-reason sculptures, the abandoned mining ghost towns, the forgotten cemeteries spilling sun-scorched spines into the trespassing sea. Favourite roads usually last for minutes, maybe hours, but this happy shit goes on for days.

Next stop's Santiago. Spend a weekend with the Saturday shoppers and Sunday strollers, up and down streets selling nothing but hot dogs and ice creams, round a mall full of nothing but hairdressers that stinks of menthol fags and ammonia, and find cultural refuge in the Allende Museum.

Salvador Allende was elected president of Chile in 1970. After decades of colonial piracy, the Chilean people yelled '¡Ya basta!' and voted in

Allende's radical coalition of socialists, communists and Christian Democrats. As promised, Allende started the process of nationalising the lucrative mining industry, reasoning that Chile's natural resources should belong to Chileans, not foreign multinationals. Unemployment dropped, inflation stabilised, wages rose by 50 per cent. The US reacted with typical good grace. 'We shall do all in our power to condemn Chileans to utmost poverty,' cooed the US ambassador as he declared sanctions. 'Make the economy scream!' squealed President Dick Nixon as he cut off World Bank loans.

By 1973, economic pressure had become open political destabilisation. 'I don't see why we should stand by and watch a country go communist due to the irresponsibility of its own people,' purred Henry Kissinger as he masterminded a military coup. On 11 September 1973, General Pinochet stole power from the elected government. Allende died defending his democratic revolution with an assault rifle. 'They have the might, and they can enslave us, but they cannot halt the world's social progress with crime and guns.' Kissinger proved him wrong by winning that year's Nobel Peace Prize. Pinochet closed Congress, abolished all political parties and the US returned to business.

This is fascism. Steel-helmeted, jackbooted, goose-stepping fascism. 'The following names must report to the National Stadium for re-education' fascism. Unknown thousands of Chileans were killed, kidnapped, tortured or just 'disappeared' while the General enjoyed the military and financial support of every US President bar Carter. Pinochet finally stepped down in 1988.

I've gotta get out of this place. It's time to head east, cut across the mountains into Argentina. The Panamericana continues south out of

Santiago for another thousand miles or so, but the thrill is gone. The joy of this unique road comes from standing at the top, in LA or Mexico City, and staring down this well towards Guatemala and Peru. All that's left now is more Chile. The see-saw's tipped, this ladder's become a snake.

For me, Chile will always be South America's supermodel sister – very beautiful but too long, too skinny and too expensive to ride, and despite the groovy exterior, unpleasantly right-wing underneath. I'm glad I saw it for myself, glad I punctured the dumb prejudice that South America's nothing but bowler-hatted peasants riding donkeys through *Flight of the Condor* postcards, glad I learned that for millions of Chileans 'South America' means glitzy holiday resorts, corny malls, modern lives. But I'm even more glad to be leaving.

The border's reassuringly chaotic. The Chileans have lost the exit stamp, the Argies have found a kilo of coke in some chump's trunk, so everyone's just waved through. First thing I see is a 'Las Malvinas Son Argentina' billboard. Second thing I see is Aconcagua, the southern hemisphere's highest peak. Third thing I see is a mixed-bag bike gang, ZX10s riding with XR650s. We chase round painted mountains, through coloured creeks, down into Mendoza, a quiet town full of noisy people. Miguel on the DR800 leads me to a hotel and on to the Irish Pub, where I get my bum pinched by a trannie, my pocket picked by a grifter, and a gun pulled on me by a one-eyed, one-armed midget who's upset 'cause I winked at him. These are the days that must happen to you.

Next stop – Buenos Aires, baby.

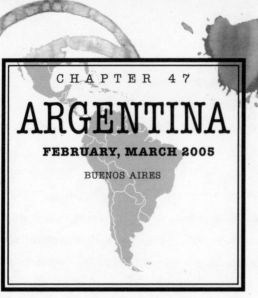

CHAPTER 47

ARGENTINA

FEBRUARY, MARCH 2005

BUENOS AIRES

In the beginning Buenos Aires was all good.

I say that, but I don't really mean it. Sitting here, writing this, knowing that, knowing that it all went so shit-shaped in the end, I feel as phoney as canned laughter. Like I'm talking with a corpse's mouth. Like I'm forging a fresh first love letter to a bitter, hateful ex. But Buenos Aires deserves a decent write-up. So forgive me while I fake it. You're the biggest, baby, you're the best.

In the beginning, Buenos Aires was all good. It's two days from mountain-shadowed Mendoza to the wild, Atlantic-spray shores, two days from the vineyards wet with Andes melt, across the flat green Pampa, to the glamorous River Plate capital. Which means I've got just two days left of this two-year road trip.

Two days on after three weeks off. Three lazy weeks in white-walled, white-trash Mendoza's shady parks and cobbled streets, munching squid salads and fat fillets in so-good-yet-so-cheap all-you-can-eat tenedor libres, happy to just hang out and be, be with pillion girlfriend Anna and Norton Rats Jeff. Jeff's travelling to Ushuaia from his bar in Peru, wants me to ride with him. I'd love to, but I just don't trust the bike. 'Are you fucking kidding me?' He laughs, looks at my 2002 BMW, then at his 1974 Norton Commando, then at me. And laughs some more. 'I'm sorry, man. Let me buy you a pint.'

One last night in the imaginatively named Irish Pub, learning snappy slang from the tattooed boys in the sloppy shorts and tight vests, then practising the new words on the saucy girls in the ass-wrapped denim and nipply shirts, while Jeff tries to start the pre-war Royal Enfield that's nailed to the wall. A gang of British soldiers, pretending to be a rugby team but training on Aconcagua, knock my cap in the gutter when I tell them where they can stick their war. 'I think it's maybe time to leave, Danny.' I think you may be right, darlin'.

It's good to be back on the bike. The stuttering start-line cross-town traffic gives way to lazy grooving along the two-day highway. Some riders reckon this flat-line dash is boring and stick their bikes on the train. Not me. I love the amplified quiet of these wide open places, love the big sun, the windy-skied serenity of these faraway spaces. Heaven in a breadbasket, relaxing into the easiest of easy riding, past the wineries set up by Jesuit missionaries looking to repeat everyone's favourite 'water into wine' miracle, through sneezy seas of snoozing sunflowers and across the Pampa's wet green bovine paradise. Mootopia.

'Lunch?' Anna throws a smile over my shoulder. Yep. Here. Nowhere. Sometimes it's good to cosy up inside the buzz of other people's noise and strangers' smells. And sometimes it's better to be almost alone. Enjoy the silence, share the sandwiches and split the iPod. Outside an abandoned dairy we find a rusted bus stop, scored with scratched graffiti that stops suddenly in October 1993. Here. Scooch on the shaded bench with a hand on my knee, with mustard beef in my mouth, with Jeff Buckley in one ear. Hallelujah.

'After the first ten, women are all the same,' said a man who probably lives alone. Some days, some times, I feel the same about roads. Some times, some days, everywhere reminds me of somewhere else. Minding my own business, trying to concentrate on the riding, and suddenly an unknown catalyst sets me off into road-tripping flashbacks – a smell of green, a taste of cooking fires, a chunk of chapped lip, a judder of Jake Brakes, and I'm off, gone, lost, brain blinded, hijacked by a pirate broadcast, flooded with uninvited cut scenes, and I can't wake up, can't put the lid back on the box till the dream's been identified. Spastic flailing back and forth through time, from Goa to Guatemala to the A47 from Peterborough to Leicester, then Anna squeezes my leg or a dog lurches into the road and I'm back, with no idea how I rode the last two miles or ten minutes or fuck knows how long.

'Are we there yet?' Dunno – we've no particular place to go. Ride till five and plot up in a one-night-stand town whose name I'll never remember. The restaurant's closed, so stock up in the petrol station on hot dogs, Pringles and chocolate milk. Collapse on the crumby bed and fall asleep watching dubbed *Buffy* and dream those flashing highway-sign dreams.

Final day. A jumpy dirt-road diversion is the last thing I need but the last thing I get. I'm worried about the bike. Ride the same bike for long enough, and it becomes part of your body, an organic link. Over the last year, the Beemer's deteriorated from cocky third leg into a rotten hump. I feel like I'm dancing with a dead Siamese twin. Seals bleeding, gaskets oozing, gearbox limping, this piece of roadkill's heading for its final death rattle. So it's a sweet relief to finally find the end of the road.

Pan-American Highway, Kilometre Zero. This is my chequered flag.

Two years of my life smeared across its bends and beaches, bars and boobs like flies on a visor. Where else could I celebrate but on a petrol station forecourt? Choke down a trucker's triple espresso and a microwaved milanesa sandwich steak and smoke while patting the bike, waiting for someone to ask me 'Where have you come from?' And when they do, all I can do is laugh so hard I nearly come. Whupped 'em again, Josey.

Where? Toronto, man, fucking Canada. I've ridden this bike from Toronto to Buenos Aires, with no GPS, no maps, no internet packing lists. No camping gear, no spares, no puncture repair. One contact lens, no insurance, no licence. I've cheeked, mooched and slunk across 26,000 miles and fifteen countries. I've cheated and I've won. And right now, that's the funniest joke I've ever heard. 'What are you laughing at?' says Anna, trying to join in. No wife, no horse, no moustache. She and the pumpster look at each other and shrug. I don't care – I've come a long way to get these giggles, and I'm gonna savour every chesty chortle. Who says nothing feels as nice as tits?

Victory lane's a flyover expressway. Capital city, busy and shitty, fast and nasty, just the way I like it, baby. Desert-highway dreaming and mountain-climbing dramas are good, but for me, nothing beats six lanes of early-evening anarchistic traffic playing race-around-the-ring-road. Cops swoop alongside, looking like Mussolini's outriders with jackboots and Moto Guzzis, and throw me 'No problem' nods and 'Join in' grins that say we're riding, not ticketing. So we ride, fly over the suburbs' stained-cement slums, fly over the 'this could be anywhere' industrial estates and truck parks, fly over the international airport and mainline straight into the sticky sweet heart of Buenos Aires.

ARGENTINA   333

What's new? Everything. I'm a junkie for this uncut novelty, ripped to the tits on this blurred speedball cocktail of 'Where are we?' white-washed walls, 'Who is he?' national hero statues and 'How do you say "Pacheco de Melo"?' street signs, goofy gandering at a million people I've never met reflected in plate glass and shiny steel. First impressions blast.

Park up outside a hotel because it's next to the Communist Party Headquarters and the Ham Museum and opposite the Bar Pelvis. Anna sorts the room, I watch the bike. Them's the rules. Lid off, fag on, stretch my back, scratch my arse, rub my eyes and smile a 'Made it' smile.

Hot in this city's upside-down February summer. Stilettoed secretaries tut at late buses and fan themselves with 69 sorpresas sexuales of the semi-famous in *Hola!* magazine. Wide post-room boys spit and jabber into mobiles, eyes willing the secretaries into undoing just one more blouse button. Chuckling strong-armed labourers slap round, brown bellies and help clucking umbrella-shaded wives into the wooden backs of old Ford trucks. And in the hotel lobby, a sweating director bawls out a soapy lead for fluffing another line while the lanky cameraman yawns and laps up his overtime. 'We're in. You can park underneath.' Perfect. I don't know it yet, but I'll never ride the bike out of town again.

Hotels are all right for the odd anonymous nights, but after 137 of them since Toronto, I've had enough of the days. Time for another apart-ment. Time for a front door and a fridge, for home-made cheese on toast, and cold milk cornflakes, time for that morning pot of proper coffee without having to get dressed and go downstairs first.

In Honduras, behind the general store on the beach, I found an air-conditioned breeze-block bolthole that smelled of stale water and someone else's wife. In Quito, behind half a dozen slamming gates and snarling dogs, Trys found a sweaty studio slum that stank of fried chicken and spilled rum. And in Buenos Aires, behind a chirpy uniformed doorman and an entry phone, Anna found 'Oh my god, the loveliest apartment you've ever seen.' And it smells of? 'Well, fresh flowers and clean linen, I guess.' Perfect.

Five hundred dollars a month divided by two equals this fancy-pants top-floor flat with two balconies, cable TV, and a lift full of tucked and nipped smeared old dears in pink Chanel suits. Unpack the bags, spend a few happy hours with a beer, trawling through two-years-on-the-road junk, while Anna orders up T-bones and mash from the chop shop next door and starts planning dinner parties. Sweet home, Buenos Aires.

Sometimes you find what you're looking for. Old, bold, beautiful, brash Buenos Aires, with its swirling tango soundtrack, with its scratched-vinyl melancholy-theme sound of long shots and lost hopes, of punch-drunk fighters dragging themselves off the ropes for that one-in-a-million knockout right-hander, of sunken-ship sea shanties for stranded sailors, feels like Calvino's mythical city.

The tango – its erotic, dramatic, aggressive roots writhe under the bordellos, where it started life as a man-on-man stylised knife fight, something to kill time while too many cowboys waited for too few hookers. In the tour-bus dinner shows, too many sequined matinees can reduce it to tourist-titillating stood-up fucking. But when it's real, when the eyes connect, when the foreheads press together, straining but as still as a wheel hub as the sweaty spoked arms clutch and the legs

stamp and snap and slide, it's an entire love affair condensed into its most dramatic three minutes, from pursuit to lusty consummation to inevitable, unavoidable exhausted end. 'Toward it heaves the shuddering, longing ache of contact.' Wipe away the sweat, look around the room for a suitable partner-collaborator-victim and do it again, do it again. 'Next.'

We find the reeling deal in the Café Resistencia, a cool, dark cavern with wine-barrel tables and wax-stained tablecloths, where a sexy sticky couple dressed in greasy black writhe and shimmy to the rancid sound of the accordion and a middle-aged journeyman singer crooning the white man's blues, 'Por una Cabeza', the lament of a dock worker who gambled all and lost all on a sure-fire racetrack winner that lost by una cabeza, by a head. 'In any other country in the world, a man with a cabeza like that would be a plumber,' says Anna. I like women – they're more unpredictable company than men. I respond predictably. Guess what I'm gonna say now? 'Umm, shall we go for a drink? Sure, Danny.'

'Don't trust a man who says he never feels the need to get drunk – he's either a fool or he's not paying attention.' There's always a bar. Sometimes there's a great bar. In Venice Beach, LA, it was the Townhouse, where the forlorn Angels, limping Crips and busted flushes sit at a bar so long, deep and dark it can suck the sunlight out of a Californian July. In Roatán, Honduras, it was the Twisted Toucan, a coconut-roofed, wooden-floored beach shack where the saucy-as-salsa-dancing-on-the-bar staff threw cold beers and salty margaritas at the half-dressed, fully relaxed never-gonna-grow-ups getting twisted tight and louche loose. And now, in Buenos Aires, there will always be the Gibraltar.

It didn't start well. Cosy-looking, understated British-style pub, found by accident on a cobbled back street in boho slum-chic San Telmo. 'You're not gonna like this,' says Anna, pointing at a sign over the door: 'This is not an Irish bar.' 'Kin cheek. Why not add 'no blacks and no dogs', you fucking bigots? 'Fok's sake, calm down, chief,' says a prop forward dressed for golf in an equally mongrel half-Irish, half-Porteño accent. 'It's not a fockin' Irish bar – I'm not fockin' Irish, this isn't fockin' Dublin, and I'm fockin' sick of all these phoney plastic paddy pubs in town.' Fair enough. 'So. Pint of porter for yourself? And how about a Beef and Guinness pie with spuds and cabbage? What's so fockin' fonny?'

His name's Alex, spent seven years running pubs in London with his wife Natalie, mostly round Paddington. Fun? He shrugs. 'Always full of fockin' football hooligans. Bristol coming to London or Millwall travelling away. Though the rugby fans were worse. Why do they shit in pint pots?' Dunno. How did Millwall feel about an Argie landlord? 'They didn't care. Only time I thought we'd have problems was up in Newcastle. Having a drink with the missus and suddenly the pub fills with Newcastle fans, drunk and noisy, you know? We're surrounded, and I've said to the missus, "Just try to keep quiet." Didn't work. This big tattooed bastard comes up and goes, "Where yous from?" And I said, "You're not gonna like it." And he says, "Why? Yous not from fookin' Sunderland, are you?"'

Gary Inman turns up on a Mazda junket. The marketing department are paying the bill, so he's staying in BA's most expensive boutique hotel, the super-snooty Faena Universe, with its rococo rooms filled

with all the toys that idiots enjoy – phone in the toilet, revolving telly, remote-controlled curtains. And an Experience Manager. Gary laughs. 'She'll get you anything. Watch. Excuse me, we'd like to see a football game.' 'Certainly, sir. Three tickets for the River Plate–Quilmes game will be in your room . . . now.' Blimey, that is good. 'Try it.' OK – I want monkey sweat and an electric hat. 'Ah, *The Simpsons*. Viva Ned Flanders. A classic.' Dayum.

We head downstairs into the over-designed bar that smells of air-conditioned money and has the dead air of a bank vault. The kind of place where you always put your drink back right in the centre of the coaster. The snapper tries to fake it, orders champagne and foie gras, but it's just sandwich spread and fizzy wine in an empty bar designed by ponces for bastards. 'We should have stayed in your Irish bar,' says Gary. It's not an Irish bar. 'Eh?'

Couple of great days later, Gary leaves for the airport in a limo. I try to sneak another afternoon round the infinite pool, hoping that Shakira will pop in, but I don't belong here. A zombie in a braided crombie throws a shadow over my sunbed. 'Room number, sir?' The Experience Manager appears in a puff of cologne. 'Taxi, sir?' An old man in gold Speedoes sneers and stares. You ain't rich, dog, you just got money. 'Taxi, sir!' Oh, I see, it wasn't a question. No thanks. I've got the bike. She follows me out with a mop.

Dusk along the banks of the River Plate (from the banks of the River Irwell), across the slippery tram-tracked bridge, into the dusk on San Telmo's cobbled streets. Sepia music and light spill from café windows onto tiled pavements. As I'm hitting the cashpoint, a boy with no arms wanders up. 'Can you help me use my card?' Sure. 'It's in my back pocket.' Er, OK. 'This is the PIN.' No problem. Drink? 'Sure – but I'll need a straw.'

Warm orange light and dark wood inside the Gibraltar. Bottle of red wine and fish 'n' chips. 'I hate the smell of vinegar,' pouts perky Milena, the braless barmaid. 'It reminds me of Christ's wounds.' 'Who the fuck are you? Mary Magdalene?' His name's Bruno, he's German, and he's a Muppet Operator. 'Usually Rowlf, the dog. And once, only once, Kermit. Such a privilege. Salud.'

Salud. Cheers. Slan. 'What's so funny?' says the boy with no arms. This. Them. You. Buenos Aires. The Road. All of it. This world that can only be seen from the dusty seat of a long-range motorcycle. A world that the experience managers and the business suits and presidential suites can never see so can never spoil.

'Oh God, oh God, I'm so fantastic, watch me now! I'm a sexual spastic.' Javier the bar manager stops waggling his knob ring at the backpackers and sticks Frank Zappa on the jukebox. An English girl throws her drink in my face 'cause I won't sleep with her. I walk home at dawn with my new mate. Completely Legless and Mostly Armless.

These are the days that must happen to you. All of you.

Huh. I almost convinced myself there. Almost. But sitting here, writing this, knowing that, knowing that this time I really fucked the pooch, I feel as phoney as canned laughter. Like I'm speaking with a corpse in my mouth. Like I'm forcing out a wank over a bitter, unfaithful ex. So forgive me. 'Cause I'm faking it.

CHAPTER 48

ARGENTINA

APRIL TO DECEMBER 2005

BUENOS AIRES – PANAMA CITY

BOCAS DEL TORO – ATENAS

Buenos Aires nearly killed me.

I say that, but sitting here, writing this, knowing that, knowing that I obviously survived in the end, I feel like I'm putting on the poor mouth. Self-harming for attention. Whining like Gwyneth Paltrow's multimillionaire husband. But the good people who pay my wages deserve an explanation. So forgive me while I fake it, climb back onto the balcony wall and self-indulgently splutter, 'Nobody said it would be this hard . . .'

In the beginning, Buenos Aires was all good. After two years On The Road, the cultured, cluttered, clued-up capital of the deep, deep south was the perfect pissed-up pit stop. Truth is, I needed a rest. Long-range, long-haul, long-time-from-home travel is liberating, stimulating and astonishing, but tiring too. Behind the fizzy spectacles, the friendly strangers and the laugh-out-loud lunacy is a background hum of stress. Border stress, breakdown stress, 'Bloody hell, that was close!' stress. Every time a child, a dog, a lorryload of llamas swerves into harm's way and misses by 'Sheesh!' inches, the stress volume gets cranked up another notch. And the whisper becomes a nag becomes a 'this one goes to 11' shriek. A shriek that sweet home Buenos Aires shushes and soothes away with a randy cuddle and a brandy-stained kiss.

Rest and explore. First, a penthouse month strolling haut bourgeois

Recoleta's tiled pavements, dodging the professional dog-shitters dragging their furry tangles of leads and cocked legs to the pedigree pooch parks, and the meretricious rich girls begging their sugar grandaddies to pawn one more swastika-stamped purse of golden Reichsmarks at the boob-'n'-lip-mongers. Then a bohemian month in slum-chic cobbled San Telmo, its paint-peeling mansions filled with squatters' kids and clothes lines, its pavement cafés frothing with the smell of wine and tango. And then, a third and what should have been final month in the faded 'cigarette holders and monogrammed luggage' glamour of the Buenos Aires Ritz.

The Ritz, a once-grand, now-shabby, still-charming old queen of a hotel with double-height ceilings, a creaking cage lift and dusty slatted shutters that open onto the colonial snobbery and neo-neon of the downtown microcentro. Best of all, it has a balcony – my own royal box overlooking the opera of the Widest Road in the World.

Avenida 9 de Julio is nineteen lanes of marvellous, motorised mayhem. I spend hours just watching the tides of traffic, racing dispatch riders between the lights like Poohsticks on a river, wincing at emergency vehicles stranded on stagnant central reservations, and saluting the waves of demonstrators.

Every Friday they march, from the Plaza de Mayo, where the headscarfed mothers and grandmothers of the disappeared still dance alone, to the parliamentary Congreso, via my fourth-floor front door. Twinset-and-pearls Perónistas with Evita hairdos link arms with Malvinas veterans in combat fatigues and Indians in hard hats and pigtails while the hooded hardcore with the balaclavas and baseball bats block traffic, bang terrace drums, brandish Che banners and bait riot cops. That's entertainment.

Email from the family. 'Why aren't you coming home, Dan?' Because I've spent the last months living in the Buenos Aires Ritz. Because my girlfriends have my telephone number but my bosses don't. Because I can get a rare steak, a real coffee and a cold beer at four in the morning in the always-hissing café below. Because the bars never close.

Because I'm three days' ride from the Bolivian Andes, four days south of saucy Rio, five days north of the Ushuaian End of the World, and a million miles from any Gatso. Because licences and lids, shirts and shoes, speed limits and sobriety are optional extras for Argentine riders.

Because down here, Numero 10 Diego Maradona is more important than Benedict XVI. Because down here 'tango' means a stylised, sensual knife-fight-in-a-brothel dance, not sugary crap in a can. Because down here 'revolutionary' means the angry poor invading the presidential palace, not a really small phone that's also a camera. Because down here 'visa' means three free months in a new country, not a lifetime of dreary debt.

Because I can no longer smell the difference between Blair and Howard, or between a 2003 and 2005 Gixer Thou. Because in England I'm a bitter, useless shit-heel, and down here I'm kinda happy. Because I've got tickets to see Boca Juniors and the White Stripes next weekend. Because 'I function better with the sun in my eyes'. Because I'm scared of the Welsh. Because I am home.

Life is good. New World all around, best girl Anna by my side, insides overflowing with two years of bubbling memories, and if this isn't nice, what is? But this idyllic idleness can't last for ever. 'Ask yourself whether you are happy, and you cease to be so,' said a wise old misery-guts. Somewhere, Beckett's headwaiter is murmuring an unavoidable 'And to follow?' Eventually I'll have to get back On The Road. And that means sorting out the bike.

Bouncing off Buenos Aires and trampolining into Brazil and beyond doesn't just need refreshed enthusiasm, it also needs confidence in the bike. The bollocksed bike. While I've rested, the bike's rusted, abandoned and ignored in the basement of a downtown multi-storey. It takes Anna weeks of gentle nudging and sexual blackmail just to make me look at it.

I've been dreading this back-to-school day. Mad Roland, the expat German motorcycle mechanic who likes to dress as a pirate, comes along to shine his eccentric expert spotlight on my shame. We drag the dusty Dakar from its cleaning-cupboard cell and bump it down an up-ramp. In this underground echo box, it sounds like a horse smithing its own shoes.

I smoke, Mad Roland examines my dog-eaten homework. He's appalled. 'I have never seen one so bad.' And genuinely upset. 'These are great bikes, if you look after them, but . . .' He shakes his head like he's found bad bruises on a good kid. Just spit it out, Kraut. 'OK, OK. Gearbox, main bearings, rear shock, oil pump, water pump, radiator – all ruined. Brakes, front and back, from cylinder to disc, also ruined. And then . . .' He shrugs and waves his toy cutlass at the bent bars, dinged rims, cracked plastics, pitted forks, rusted-through pipes and oil-smudged engine cases. 'For sure, we can fix it, but I think it would be cheaper to buy a new bike, yes?'

Yes. It's not the labour, it's the parts, amigo. Mad Roland will get the bike seaworthy for shipmates' rates, but Argentina's 100 per cent import tariffs make the parts prohibitively pricey, and I'm stony broke. Need to work and write to get the bike fixed, need a fixed bike to work and write. Arse. I'm trapped. I feel like a cat stuck up a tree. Without my bike, I'm a blind man who's lost his dog. I decide to go and get drunk. It's February. When I finally sober up, it's somehow September.

'There must have been a moment, at the beginning, where we could have said "No". But somehow we missed it.' I missed it. Anna didn't. After three weary, wine-stained weeks, she calls time, intervenes, suggests we escape to Brazil. I should say, 'Yes, darlin', help me get out of here.' But I don't. Instead, I call her 'boring'. And six months' worth of pent-up resentment splashes out of her sulky mouth. It's not a comfortable sight. Anna's too nice to do angry. It doesn't fit her. A little girl wearing her daddy's work boots is kicking me to death.

'Boring? Boring? You're the one who wants to go to the same pub every night just to get drunk with the same people. You're the one who spends all day in bed, too hung-over to move, groaning and whining till I get you food and cigarettes. How dare you call me freakin' boring?' Freakin'? It's after 9 p.m. You're allowed to swear. 'Fuck you, Danny. Fuck you. Not that I ever do any more. You haven't been near me in weeks.'

I walk onto the balcony and smoke. She sobs and packs. Last time she did this, I locked the door, hid the keys and asked her to sleep on it. This time, I help. Pull a pretty black dress off a hanger. How come I've never seen this before? 'I bought it for our Valentine's dinner. It was supposed to be a surprise.' Eh? We didn't have a Valentine's dinner. Oh. I see. She shakes her head and turns away.

Next morning Anna catches the ferry to Uruguay. It takes me a year to realise that she's never coming back.

Online AA questionnaire. Has alcohol abuse affected a) your health, b) your relationships or c) your work? Check, check and check, mate. When I get wet, the words dry up, my always flaky output reduced to smudged notes and stolen quotes on damp cocktail napkins: 'There's nothing finer than Latin satin in Chinese silk and noisy heels,' and 'If all the statues in the world came to life and went to war with the monkeys, who'd win?' and 'I am the cat who walks alone and to me all supermarkets are alike.' Even I can't get away with submitting that kind of drivel (oh, shush now), so instead I email an honest surrender to the office. Tell them that I've lost my bottle and found a glass. Tell them that I've forgotten how to write and travel. Tell them that I'm a useless phoney. An exasperated editor throws it at the readers' letters page with a snide aside. Shamed by the glare of 100,000 mirrors, I slink back to the bar.

A lucky life reduced to slinking, drinking and stinking thinking. Slinking past the hotel lobby, avoiding the manager and her charge sheet of unpaid bills. Slinking past the internet cafés, avoiding the inboxes full of 'Sender: John Westlake, Subject: We really need words' and 'Sender: Mike Walsh, Subject: Where are you now, my blue eyed son?' missives. And slinking through the city's streets, shrinking from

the bright lights into the alley shade. 'Mira,' laughs my cigarette man, 'el Hombre Invisible.' I fade into anonymous, ghostly invisibility. With no place in society, no role in the wheel, there's no reason for anyone to notice me, no criteria for anyone to judge me, and no cause for anyone to ever say 'No' to me.

The normal friends fall away, bullied, boored and bored, until all that's left is the junkie drunk rump. We're just the boys who can't say 'No' – Peruano mafiosi, Dutch dealers, English ex-cons, Argentine runaways, African stowaways. Different routes, same destination, we're all déclassé, lumpen elements who've fallen through the net, all pursuing our own self-righteous suicide missions. No, I'm Raskolnikov. You can be Scarface.

So we create a nocturnal hobo jungle of casual criminality, loveless violence and petty sex. Even nihilists need a schedule, and ours seldom changes. Meet up at midnight in the Gibraltar, where the hood element can sling pills and powders to the backpackers and where I've still somehow got credit, then swagger round to slum-'n'-bass speakeasy Guevara's for the dance and the five o'clock fight, before finishing up in the espresso-hiss and toaster-clunk old-world elegance of the Café Británico. Dignified waiters in bleached aprons serve coffee and croissants to the respectable ready-for-workers, and frosty beers and colder smiles to our crew of growling idiots crouched in the corner round a table full of empties, listening through our arseholes, scratching at our eyeballs and chewing off our bleeding lips.

'Wine is a mocker, strong drink is raging.' I wake up in a cubicle, pants round my ankles, clammy face stuck to the cold tiles. Someone's rapping at the door. An elderly waiter lifts my chin, touches my cheek and says softly, 'Ay, los esqualidos.' The squalid ones. The door swings shut and I piss away the last drops of my soul.

¡Ya basta! Enough. This isn't fun any more. I hide in my hotel for three weeks, escape the scene, kick the habits, get fat on hot dogs and banana milk. But even though I'm kinda clean, my insides still feel rotten. Everything's turned to rust and lard. I feel guilty and pathetic that I've blown this best of all possible chances, tarnished this best of all possible worlds. Buenos Aires should have become a beautiful base of operations, the perfect launch pad for the next ten years' two-wheeled rally raids into the southern wilds. Instead it became just another popshop. I may as well be on Chapel Street, Salford, staring at the rain through the Black Lion's cracked windows.

'Never trust a man who says he never gets depressed – he's either a fool or he isn't paying attention.' But this is too much. This is the counsel of despair. I gambled everything precious – love, time and trust – on one Big Idea. That running away on the motorcycle would make me a better person. That running away on the motorcycle would make me a different person. That running away on the motorcycle would cure the bad chemicals and faulty wiring that have always hobbled me. But two years down this road, five years away from England, I'm as bad as ever. I feel like a first-class fucking failure. And I feel betrayed. Like an old greyhound who's just realised that the rabbit wasn't real.

I try to walk up some magic but the city's been soiled. Buenos Aires is still beautiful, but I don't see the spires and skies when I'm staring at the porn in the hedges and the dog shit in the gutters, at the shoeless kids begging in their doorways and the handcuffed drunks bleeding onto their pavements. A tramp peers out from under his cardboard duvet and

shrugs, 'We lost.' An old gypsy woman lurches out of an alley with a dead child under her arm and laughs, 'Is this yours?' I have drunk and seen the spider.

Ya fucking basta. Enough. I can't take this any more. Back in Nicaragua, an Irish friend asked me what I was running from. It took me two years to work out the answer. The one thing I can never leave behind. Me. I'm the problem. And right now, I can think of only one solution. Who else can you blame when you break your own heart?

Back at the Ritz, Next Door Norberto's washing his socks in the sink and whistling 'Ave Maria'. 'Whisky, Daniel?' Nah, man. I'm running late. Kill the conversation with a locked door and a loud TV. Kim Basinger's talking to Al Pacino.

'Do you think we'll ever know why your brother killed himself?'

'I guess some people just get tired.'

Huh.

The maid's been in. Bed made, clothes folded, books stacked, papers tidied. I glance down. A printout of Hunter S. Thompson's suicide note glances back. '*No More Games . . . No More Walking. No More Fun.*' I get the message. The only thing we're missing is Joy Division 'Atmosphere' muzak in the elevator.

I walk onto the balcony and smoke. Sully God's view on my vulture's perch. Then crouch on the ledge, a pot-bellied gargoyle leering out of Chapel Perilous. What the hell happened, man? I guess I just had to

know. I had to know what happens if you just keep going. And now I do know. You sail off the edge. There is no bottom step.

'Dan – what are you doing? Get down from there, please.' Jesus, woman, don't sneak up like that. You nearly made me jump.

'God is never further than the door,' say the Irish. Today God looks like Olivia, a local girl who tried to save me from the booze and the blues with big brown boobs and hot breathy kisses, with arty smarts and pop-star friends, with walks in the park and trips to the seaside. I never really knew why. 'No one's seen you in weeks. We were worried. Why don't you come inside and lie down?'

I come inside and lie down. Olivia gets her wriggle on, but I don't want to play. The best part of my heart's gone to Rio in a rucksack, wrapped up in a little black dress that she never got the chance to wear. And besides, beautiful Olivia's too hairy for my blood. It would be like fucking a spider. So I pretend to be asleep. And she pretends to believe me.

We're woken with a start and a terrible stop. It's late. Two too-fast skids plus two too-loud bangs equals one dreadful scream. I walk onto the balcony and smoke. Two cars have collided hard and fast. A Peugeot's on its roof in Lane 13. A Renault's buried in a lamp post under my window. They're both crumpled like paper. The screaming man climbs out of a broken window, staggers round through the headlights' glare and horn's blare and forces open the driver's door. The driver falls sideways, very heavy and very dead. 'That's just where you would have landed,' says Olivia, cheerily.

The cops arrive. The screaming passenger takes a packet of cigarettes

from the dead man's pocket then places a denim jacket shroud over his dead head. The nightshift from the cafés stare but won't get too close. Even after the dead man's been moved to an ambulance, no one gets too close to the spot where he lay. Emergency workers must see these death spots all over the city. Emergency workers must have their own secret maps of the secret city of the dead. Olivia shudders. I throw out an arm and pull her close. Damn, her back's hairy.

The next day I buy a plane ticket. Buenos Aires and the bike have become burdens, so I bin them both. Suicide's for shithouses. Real men run away. That night I fly to Panama.

'Guess what is my favourite English song.' Midnight in the Unplugged Bar in uptown Panama City. The tattooed rockers round the pool table sing along to 'Ramble On', the smoky smugglers circle the table of uncomfortable gringos I've just ID'd as US Coast Guard, and the drunken sailor wants to talk chirpy rubbish. 'Guess! Guess!' Er, 'Hey Jude'? 'Ha, no! "Ballroom Blitz" by the Sweet. It reminds me of Bristol. And bristols, yes? Another beer?' No thanks, man. That'll do me for now.

Out into the bright noisy night, holding hands with Heather, the pretty redhead stewardess I met in the pub where John le Carré wrote *The Tailor of Panama*. We kiss on the corner and wait for a cab. 'Coming back to mine?' No, thanks. That'll do me for now.

Next day I catch the puddle jumper to the Bocas del Toro islands. Bare feet flap on salty decks, Caribbean waves slap painted wooden fishing boat flanks, and the warm tide laps at peachy, beachy bottoms. I get a job in a mate's rum bar and a room on stilts over the bay. Lying in bed, listening to the sea gurgle beneath the floorboards, I feel a weird easy warmth wrapping round my head. When I realise what it is, I laugh out loud. Shit the bed. I'm happy.

'Who the hell is that? The poster boy for "Gay Nazis for Peace"?' Sunny December morning outside Atenas, Costa Rica, and I'm chuckling into a spiced rice and runny eggs campesino breakfast with the Good Gringo, wondering why there's a signed photo of The Hoff sharing the double-espresso 'Wake up!' view that tickles our noses. The café veranda collapses into a volcano valley that funnels vision past the comical peaks, across the coffee plantations and distant-down to the crashing Pacific surf. A view we've spent the last week riding in, running in a dozen KTM 640 brand-spankers, ocean back and mountain forth, up and down this particularly pretty stretch of the Pan-American Highway. 'Enough of this bullshit, man. Let's ride.'

It's that easy. Riding my bike – this is all I really want to do. Because it's the only fucking thing in the world that makes me feel awake, properly awake, and alive, really alive. Even when I am tearing up and down what's known locally as 'The Mountain of Death'.

We hit a red. Farmers, families and timber-toting truckers all backed up by a hard-working road gang. Zip to the front, coast to a stop alongside an old yellow school bus full of brand new souls. We wave hands and tongues. I cut the engine and smoke.

I'm better now. The Buenos Aires Blues have faded away. A couple of

months in Central America, and most importantly, a couple of months back on a bike, have given me some perspective. Some understanding. It wasn't just about the darkness and the drink, it was deeper than that. It was more about unfair comparisons and unrealistic expectations. I compared every day with those first giddy escaping-from-home months and, when they didn't always match up, I felt like a failure. I expected the Road to act as a cure-all paregoric, as Dr Quack's Miracle Snake Oil, and when it didn't, I felt that it had failed. But the Road didn't fail me – I failed the Road. The Road works.

'Adelante, hombre.' The lad with the flag and the walkie-talkie waves me on. The kids with the bowl cuts and satchels wave bye-bye. Flip-flop slap it into first, ping the clutch and fishtail through the fresh gravel towards the Pacific. Plot up on the hot black sand with a smoothie, a smoke and *The Place of Dead Roads*. A surfer wanders up, wondering what's written on my arm. And for the hundred-thousandth time I wink wise Whitman's words.

'These are the days that must happen to you.'

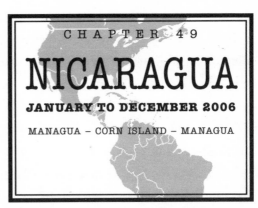

'So you're going back to work, Danny Boy?' Dusty dusk in the Shannon Bar, Managua, and the wanted and the unwanted are supping suds and sundowners. The dart-throwing boys from the bank clunk frosty cans of Guinness, the birthday girls from the Peace Corps shoot wincing tequila shots, and I share a bottle of dark rum and light chat with Irish Miguel. 'You ready for that?' Er, yeah, I guess.

For most British riders, the happy process of jacking it all in to ride off on the bike has become fairly familiar. Even the lowest-mileage gravel-drive cowboy knows the escape drill. First, find inspiration in Ted Simon slash *Bike* magazine slash a mate of a mate just back from Mali. Then spend six-months or so obsessing over 'Americas or Africa? KTM or Beemer? Hard bags or soft?' choices while honing your 'Ewan and Charley – admirable adventurers or camera-mugging rich kids?' arguments on horizonsunlimited.com and UKGSer.com. And eventually, finally, a year later than you'd hoped, make it all real by telling the boss to take this job and shove it.

But I don't live in Britain. I live in Oddworld. Also known as recently-revolutionary-again Nicaragua. Which means I'm sitting in Central America, planning a return to LA or London to buy a bike so that I can get back On The Road. Which means relaxing in Managua or on a Corn Island beach, courting magazine editors, trying to rustle up enough

commissions to pay my boozy way. Getting back on my bike means going back to work. And right now, after a lazy, hazy year of bare-minimum part-time writing and beer-and-burger-money bartending, that's as scary as the Sahara.

'Watch your glass, Danny. Jaysus, did you see that?' Muggy midnight in the Shannon. The boys from the bank have lost their ties and found the Rockanola's Guns N' Roses. The Peace Corps girls are lapping Baileys and dancing on the bar. And, Jesus, I did see that, two kids on a TDR have just robbed that Iranian girl at gunpoint. The Persian Princess shrugs and orders another round of car bombs. So Irish Miguel and I shrug and order another bottle of rum. 'Didn't you just ride from LA to BA?'

Yep. March 2003 I skidded out onto the Toronto snow on an F650 Dakar, heading south on a six-month jaunt to Panama. Two years later, I hit Buenos Aires. Three years later, I'm still down there, out here. A month back in Manchester showed me I can never go home. 'England? That's a dead end. I never believed in it anyway.'

But this isn't about negatives. I love Latin America for what it is, not what it isn't. I love Central America, love its Pacific black-sand shores and Caribbean mangrove swamps, love its secret-pirate-lair islands and crumbling colonial cities, love its unique jumble of cultures cluttered beneath a backdrop of crinkly volcanoes, sulphurous lakes and tropical sweat. And love its contrast with South America's clean lines and snowy peaks, winking llamas and bowler-hatted mothers, spicy jungles and endless skies. Central America's a saucy salsa-dancing good-time girl with a brother in Miami. South America's a snooty supermodel with legs from here to Chile and her head lost in the Bolivian clouds. Er, I'm getting carried away, aren't I? Told you I was in love.

In love with a road? I used to dream of women – now it's all about that road. The Road. The Pan-American Highway, the Panamericana, the nearly-network of nearly 32,000 miles of interstate, two-lane blacktop and dirt track that nearly runs from the Alaskan Arctic Circle to the Argentine Tierra del Fuego tip, via fifteen countries, via everywhere you've ever dreamed of and never heard of on this side of the Atlantic – Hollywood and Huehuetenango, Rio de Janeiro and Riobamba, Acapulco and Atenas, all joined by this best of all possible roads.

There are sexier, noisier, quieter rides, but no matter how sexy, quiet, noisy, they are just rides, and this is a journey. More than the road-movie truck stops and tollbooths, more than the Amazon, Andes, Atacama Desert *National Geographic* encyclopedia backdrops, this high-way is a spine, a nervous system that links the history and culture of a thriving, swirling, changing continent, connects a dreamscape of cow-boy and conquistador archetypes, links Francis Drake to El Dorado, Che Guevara to Pancho Villa, General Pinochet to Secretary Kissinger, Kurt Cobain to Carlos Menem, Túpac Amaru to Biggie Smalls, the Cali cartel to the Californian credit-card choppers . . .

This ain't working. How the hell can I describe three years' travel across a continent in a paragraph? I can't. And even if I could, it still wouldn't be right. The difference between reading and riding is as vivid as the experience gap that lies between 'sex is a pleasurable encounter that provokes euphoria' and getting your Cialis-addled brains fucked out by a stripper from Suriname with pierced nipples and the kung-fu grip. And I think I've just talked myself out of a job.

Let the route speak for itself. Starting in chilly Alaska, the Panam runs down into the west of Canada, becomes the Pacific Coast Highway in

the States, passes through Big Sur and LA en route to San Diego, where it cuts east across the desert and south into Mexico. And south into Guatemala, El Salvador, Honduras, Nicaragua, Costa Rica and Panama, until it dead-ends in the jungle of the Darien Gap, re-emerging across the border in Medellín, Colombia, cuts west through Bogotá, to Ecuador, where it opens its legs and shows its class as it begins the long drop south, plummeting through Peru and into Chile. Done? Nope. In Santiago it switches east, across the Andes, past Aconcagua, across the vast Pampa, all the way into Buenos Aires.

Despite the Kilometre Zero signposts, it doesn't really stop there. Like all weary travellers, the Highway takes a well-deserved BA break, enjoys a step of tango and couple of dozen bottles of cheap red wine in the Gibraltar pub, and eventually gets its shit together, jumps on the ferry across the River Plate to Uruguay and it's off again, racing through Rio de Janeiro, up, up, up to Caracas, Venezuela, back west to Medellín, Colombia, and Finnegan begin again. This is the journey that never, ever ends.

Too good to be true. No, really. The Panamericana doesn't actually exist. This is no Panama Canal. No pith-helmeted project manager ever threw a 'one hand on cocked knee, the other shielding eyes from the Alaskan sun' catalogue shape and hollered 'Buenos Aires or bust, boys!' This International Highway is nothing more than a scribbled sequence of local roads that inevitably, obviously, meet at borders. This is no feat of engineering. This is a metaphysical marvel of genius, praxis and poetry.

The genius came in 1923, when the Conference of the Americas decided to name the barely-there route from Nuevo Laredo on the Tex-Mex border to Santiago, Chile, as 'The Pan-American Highway'. A show of soft hands, a container full of signposts, an updated map and suddenly the continent was united. Genius. But until it's used to cross borders, it's just a theory. The road stays still, it's the travellers that move, and the actions of these travellers, commercial or recreational, on two wheels or ten, on donkeys or bicycles, that make this highway truly international. Praxis. And the poetry? Maybe that's in these travellers, when they stare down into their futures, back into their pasts and almost, sort of, realise their role, kinda understand that until it's travelled, this road is no more than ink on a map, notes on a score, words on a page, that need to be felt, whistled, read into life. 'I didn't realise you wrote such bloody awful poetry.'

Three years down here and I'm still a fumbling beginner, excited as a chicken about another trip. Repeating myself? Give over. All I did was draw one narrow line. Anything on either side of that was missed. And my breakdown in Buenos Aires meant I never saw any of the south-east – which means I've still got Venezuela, the Guyanas and Brazil to explore. Which means I've gotta get back on a bike.

Motorcycle travel doesn't really make a lot of sense. Expensive and exposed, often filthy and frustrating, there's no obvious reason to pick two wheels over four. More comfort, more room, more security, and no one ever fell off a Jeep, right? Maybe on paper. But we don't ride on paper. We ride in Mexico. 'In a car, you're watching a movie – on a bike, you're starring in it,' as some cowboy poet slurred. A starring role that's maybe produced by the rider's unique opportunity to be two things at once – sat still while swooping swift, heavily armoured but completely exposed, dagger-proof and always vulnerable, fully concen-trated and miles away. And I've gone again, haven't I?

I'm not as dippy as I sound. More than most, I know that fishtailing away into the sunset creates just as many problems as it escapes. Once upon a time I hoped that riding away on a bike would cure my ills. It couldn't and it never will. This is riding, not rapture. It's still real life. But real life beats still life. An argument with the boss, a stolen wallet, a broken heart, all fade quicker on a foreign beach than in a familiar bed. And a week On The Road always beats a year in the office. Even though I now live on a beach. Damn, this is getting confusing.

'I said, "What are you running from this time?"' Closing time in the Shannon. The boys from the bank are powdering their noses and shouting about strippers. The girls from the Peace Corps are holding each other's hair back and crying in the toilets. And Irish Miguel's feeling smug about his million-peso question. What am I running from this time? Easy. Same as always. The one thing I can never leave behind.

'Put the two of us in a sack, I don't know which one would crawl out first. Right, sweetie?' Lazy maybe Monday morning in the Hotel Paraíso and neither Ooh La La nor I are in any hurry to get out from under the mosquito net. She, because it's her once-a-week day off, and me, because, well, I'm scooched up with a 20-year-old Caribbean beauty queen called Ooh La La. What the hell is she doing here? Christ knows.

But this ain't the time to get over-analytical. This is the time for a little slap 'n' tickle. So pass me a handful of cordobas — I wanna spend a happy hour bouncing coins off that ripe-apple arse of yours. Right, sweetie? 'Right, sweetie.'

Welcome to Big Corn, a Central Park-sized tropical island fifty miles off Nicaragua's wild Atlantic coast. A British pirate lair turned refuge for escaped and freed Jamaican slaves turned semi-autonomous backwater bolthole in one of Central America's poorest corners, it is now half undiscovered potential paradise and half ramshackle rum slum on a littered beach that the US State Department have only just taken off the 'Don't Go' list. One day it could be another Cancún. Right now it feels like a secret. And for the past two months, a thatched cabina on Brig Bay has been where I've called home.

'Morning, lovebirds.' Morning, Mike. The Paraíso manager is a disconcertingly pretty Dutch whizz-kid who recently swapped his Audis and Monte Carlo weekends for this new off-the-grid life. He's hovering round our eggs and coffee table, hopping with enthusiastic impatience. Last night, he threw me by asking if I wanted to run his beach bar. 'I'd only been here three days when I decided to sell the IT business and buy this hotel.' He smiles his deal-closing smile. 'Why not take the bike and have a think?' I thought you'd never ask. 'About the bar?' Nah, geez. About the bike.

The bike — a drum-braked, twin-shocker junkyard knocker, a Honda XL185 of indeterminate age. Like all old peasants, no one's too sure exactly when it was born. And no one really cares. This a barely working bike, an errand-limping bike, a hobbled donkey bike that's slumped beyond the standard snotter, rotter or grotter. I know teenage Irish tinkers who'd turn their gluey noses up at this old knacker. But right now, it's perfect. I'm not trying to shave a tenth off a lap of Laguna. I'm just popping out for a ride. 'You gonna take me home, sweetie?' Sure, sweetie.

I jump on. The seat falls off and the rusted-through tank stains my shorts. Mike talks me through its idiosyncrasies. 'No key, no brakes and there's a problem with the clutch.' It slips? 'It slipped off.' Oh, I see. Guess I should have spotted the missing lever. 'You sure you've ridden a bike before, sweetie?' Yes, sweetie.

Rotter or not, I'm delighted to be back on a bike. Any bike. Three months is too long to be out of the saddle. Even a saddle that needs holding down with duct tape. Rock it into neutral, clatter the spiny kick-start, give it some gas, crunch it into first and, woah, hold on, sweetie, lurch and go.

Out past Irma the cheeky monkey, out past Hildi, Mike's beautiful Hungarian wife, and out onto the beach and its deep truck-and-taxi-worn ruts. Ruts that would be a nightmare on any overloaded over-lander, but on this light, bright piece of shite are a laugh-out-loud joy. Even when the pack of sandy strays stop tearing chunks out of a turtle shell to snap at heels and wheels. Even when a pack of drunks stop playing Conquistadors and Indians in the reggae palace to wave machetes and whistle catcalls. Even when we pull into Brig Bay.

Brig Bay's the closest this island has to a small town, but it takes more than a cop shop, a customs post and sprawl of run-down homes sand-wiched between the swamp and the commercial port to give this place any kind of charm. The bars are aggressive, the cafés unappetising, the shops Baghdad empty. The sour-milk stench of a stagnant too-shallow gene pool clings to the big-eared boys with their feet on backwards. It's not my favourite place for a stroll.

But we're not strolling, we're rolling. Walking's too, er, pedestrian, cars

always feel like reruns, but there's something special about the rhythm of riding, something special about the tempo of two wheels, that takes the flattest notes and mixes them into the freshest tunes, grabs the grungiest images and edits them into the grooviest road movies, turns grotty Brig Bay into a lively montage of flashing colours, smoky smells and grinning faces. Maybe it does have some charm — just as long as we don't stop. Always easy on a bike with no brakes.

Past the internet café that's rarely online, past the radio station playing its curious Creole mix of roots reggae and corny Christian country, and back onto the only-road ring road. The traffic's light but sometimes heavy. A supersized 4x4 swishes by in a smeared blur of blacked-out windows and buzzing bad bwoy bass. 'White lobster fishermen, right sweetie?'

Right, sweetie. 'White lobster' is the local euphemism for cocaine. These islands are an important staging post for the go-fasts speeding north from Colombia. With the coconut groves wiped out by hurricanes, with the lobsters fished out by greedy foreign giants, who can really blame a poor boy for taking an easy dollar? Once a pirate, always a pirate. And while the USA remains the world's biggest consumer of this screeching tension, it's hard to be too judgemental.

It's also dangerous to be too judgemental. Couple of years ago, the Managua authorities decided to disrupt the smuggling. The response was brutal. Stone-cold cartel killers walked into the police station and cut the throats of five top cops. So now it's don't ask, don't tell, and tax what you can. People round here don't dream of winning the lottery. They dream of finding a wash-up. Even the most respectable families have a bale or two of beach-combed coke buried in the yard for a rainy

day. Takes a strong man to burn hundreds of thousands of dollars in a country where teachers make less than $100 a month. So much of that gear washes up on these beaches that the Colombians have issued a 'lost and found' number. 1-800-I'VE GOT YOUR STASH. Call and they'll buy it back. Though I'm guessing that could be a fairly tense midnight rendezvous.

'Right here, sweetie.' We stop by a sign for Sally Peachy. Sally Peachy? Was your barrio named after a stripper? 'You're looking to get a hot slap. Call me at eight.' Which eight? 'Big eight. Bye, sweetie.' Bye, sweetie.

Sally Peachy becomes North End and the island changes. Brig Bay's mostly Mesquito Indian and mainland Spanish. North End is mainly black. The people here call themselves Islanders and speak Creole, a sometimes sing-song, sometimes sludgy English patois. It's nicer round here. Fresher, cooler and if not richer then more comfortable, more established. The centuries-old Anglican, Baptist, Pentecostal churches all boast new roofs and towering spires. The houses are well-crafted wood, not crumbling cement, with proud fences and watered lawns. The dogs are on leads, the baseball team have uniforms and the grannies rule these roosts. Fat-thighed old dears sit on high porches with their legs too far apart, daring passers-by to take a peek at the one thing they never want to see. Sometimes I love being short-sighted.

Despite the disturbing distractions, there's still no better place to do some serious thinking than the saddle of a motorcycle. And right now, I have me a big decision. After a weird year of failed plots, lost plans and too much drunken inactivity, I've suddenly been hit with two world-class choices. Ride LA to BA for a couple of motorcycle magazines or fulfil another lifelong dream and finally open that barefoot bar in the tropics.

I need a sign. 'Queen Hill.' That'll do. I wander off-road, heading up the rocky track towards the muddy ghetto. Another potential nightmare on a two-up touring rig that's a sweet dream on this little shitter. Even when a wide-assed woman hitches up her skirt and hitches a bike hike. I say 'Yes' only because I can't think of a polite way to say, 'Don't be ridiculous, love, you're far too large.' This is motocross on doughnuts. But the bike doesn't complain. So neither do I. 'What you doing up here, anyway, son?' Me? I'm going to see the Pyramid.

Behind the children's park, behind the tangled scribble of noisy kids playing overlapping baseball, football and catapult wars on the same scrappy space, a group of Spanish artists from souloftheworld.com are building a pyramid. And as usual, chief sculptor Rafael, the prophet lookalike with the luminous white clothes, white beard and white pony-tail, is struggling to explain why.

Imagine an enormous cube inside the world, a cube sized so that just the tips of its eight (count 'em) points peek through the earth's surface. Still with me? Rafael reckons that there's only one possible way to position this hypothetical cube so that all eight points emerge on land. And his latest, greatest and maybe last project is sculpting pyramids on all these far-flung sites. Why? 'It's all about Platonic forms and . . .' He's interrupted. 'I'll tell you what it is.' Oh, hello again, fat pillion. Go on then. 'It's a drug-detection device. Right, son?' Wrong, ma.

I run Rafa back down the hill. 'I hear you have an important choice to make.' Weird news travels fast. 'If you decide to ride, let me know. I

need someone to scout our next location in southern Chile. It's called El Porvenir.' He smiles his messianic smile. 'Which means "The Future".'

Back at the beach bar, Big Archie's comforting little Anna Banana 'cause her favourite duckling's just been kidnapped by a crab. Little Archie's slapping Littler Archie with a wet fish. Ooh La La's sitting on the bar talking rings 'n' tings with her impossibly pretty posse. Pop a cold Victoria and wander down to the seashore, where the red-and-blacks are a-flapping in the wind, and watch teens clamber over a shipwreck climbing frame. I love this easy island, where even the sun sets slow. Ly. But it never really was a tough decision. I'm still not ready to give up the Road.

Mike bounces over with his new baby in his arms. 'This isn't such a bad place to live, you know.' I know, but . . . 'But you're leaving anyway. I understand. Maybe next year?' Maybe next year. Ooh La La dances over, a kinky slinky in a denim miniskirt and painted-on eyebrows. She squeezes my hand and gives me an amber-eyed wink that makes my nuts crinkle. 'I'll miss you for a week. Right, sweetie?' Right, sweetie.

Next day I catch the puddle jumper back to the dust, the diesel and the dead dogs in mainland Managua. 'Somos todos americanos,' said Venezuelan President Hugo Chávez, 'We are all Americans.' He's right – despite the linguistic hijacking, 'American' doesn't just mean 'from the US', it includes anyone and everyone from Alaska to Argentina, and the Panamericana proves it every day. Not only, but also.

'Somos todos Panamericanos.' Long live this Pan-American dream.

Appendix One

THE BIKE

Cut to the chase. Reduce a favourite bike to one hardboiled sum-it-up scene. Say hello to my leetle friend. Blue and yeller TDR250 stroker powerband smoking an uptight RC45 in Stoke town traffic on our first ever mission. You talking to me? Two-up, pegs-down big black XJR round the outside of a kindergarten-koloured upright knee-downer on a Peterborough roundabout – scratch that: two-up on a black and yeller XJR SP, heads full of Friday feelings, picking the front up way higher than expected out-dragging an 840 Beemer into a Waterloo sunset. You torquing to me?

And roll XT VT. A rusty makeshift bridge over a muddy red Mozambique river, just a single stained steel girder barely wider than the knobblies. No barriers, just topple and splash. Shouldn't be a problem. But midway across, I stall it. Tightrope wanker.

'Nobody move a muscle, I've got a plan,' whispers Michael Caine above the 'Can you swim?' taunts of the water and the 'Can't you fly?' laughter of the birds. There's not enough room to put my boots down. I'm just hanging there, wobbly legs dangling, somehow balancing. An old man pops up – he throws me a look like a horse peering over a fence.

Hold my breath with a stomach full of empty. Reach ever soooo slowly for the starter. Nudge it. It fires. Eeeeease off the clutch. Tiniest tickle of throttle. And off. But still on. Me and the old man wink at each other. What's the point? That an overloaded, overlanded XT has the perfect poise and built-in balance of a ballerina. Even when ridden by a chimp.

We've come a long way, baby. 16,000 miles, eighteen (or is it nineteen?) countries in twelve dusty, sandy, swampy, sweaty months. How do you design a bike to do all that? How do you design a bike that's tough enough to carry 50 kilos of luggage over a continent of pounding corrugations, but light enough to be picked up with a bent back? How do you design a bike to be equally competent hustling through spice markets and camel-trotting round dunes? How do you design a bike to be so damn jack-of-all-trades versatile? Answer – by avoiding absolutes, by ignoring ultimates. By compromising.

Compromise has become a dirty word in modern motorcycling. 110 brake, 155 mph VFR? Old man's bike, innit? Flat slide carbs on an R1? Soo last century. You not got the balls for a Gixer Thou? Er, no, I haven't.

As mainstream biking atrophies from an anything-goes way of life ('Wanna know whether someone's a biker?' asked Hell's Angels Prez Sonny Barger. 'Ask them whether their bike is the first or last thing they'd sell in hard times.') to a sunny-Sunday-afternoon leezure pursuit, so the bikes become less like two-wheeled tools and more like playtime PlayStations. That only whistle one tune – Horizontal Bungee 2001.

Anything that isn't totally dedicated to head-down, bum-up cardiac arrests is considered second-rate. To the point where Blades and ZX9s become all-rounders, because there's room for a U-lock under the beer-mat pillion perch. All-rounders, my arse. Damn good sports bikes, obviously, but as versatile as a crack pipe. Even with bungee hooks. Three-up, laden down with crab claws and Tusker lager, heading for a full-moon beach party down a route that's half potholes and half sand. That's useful. The XT is a horny-handed handyman in a world of manicured marketing managers.

So. Mission accomplished, time for the interrogation. Strap the XT to the dentist's chair, bang it full of Pentothal and subject it to the rigours of a Bike Test interrogation. Is it safe? Engine, chassis, value, finish, wow factor.

Engine and gearbox. Er, yep, one of each. The gearbox is anonymous like all good gearboxes, only noticed when I regularly try to change into ghost sixth because yet again we've run out of puff. That's not the box, it's the engine. Which is slow. Very slow. A 33 bhp air-cooled single is never gonna make neck hair stand on end. I'd go as far as saying that it's dangerously slow in Europe, not enough zap to get out of the way, not enough pull to sit out of the slow lane. And it lacks that feeling of 'Gwan!' oblivion that a bike should deliver when wrenched through the box. Get rid of the lid, drink a couple of beers and it's slightly more entertaining, but it's still more old-man-running-for-a-bus than Ryan-Giggs-running-down-the-wing. But it never let me down. Dead slow, but never dead. And dead easy to fix. Apparently.

Chassis. Shazee? Does that mean the frame and suspension? The frame's all right, still sort of straight, and it's still full of oil. Maybe too much oil, judging by the leak round that nut on the engine cover. Oil that's got so hot it's melted the grease on the headrace bearings, so the front now flops like a chicken with a broken neck. The shocks have always been soft, but that's OK 'cause I'm no hard man. Soft is perfect for learning. My first desert racer.

The rear's flopped softer. It now sags like a big dawg's jowls. But it still all works.

Value. Invaluable. This bike got me safely across Africa. How much is that worth? Ask my ma. And it's the only way to travel. I've been driven across Lesotho in a Land Cruiser – overenthusiasm meant I'd dashed out of base camp without filling up. So I had enough petrol to get up and get down but not run around. No problem. Jump aboard with my Swiss mates. But it wasn't the same. The feeling of enclosure. The twee dashboard teddies and dried flowers hanging from the rear-view mirrors. The Europop soundtrack. And the feeling that I was now an extra in someone else's movie. Also featuring Dan Walsh.

And I've been across South Africa in a coach. Same mine-scarred landscape, same elephants' feet escarpments, same enormous skies. But it wasn't the same – sitting next to a born-again Geordie po-facedly arguing that the best way to combat Aids was to preach 'no sex before marriage'. Not my choice of pillion. Scheduled lunch stops at soulless service stations, tatty-tached driver barking, 'Twenty-five minutes and no longer!' That's not what I call an adventure. That's not what I call travel. Two wheels really are better.

Finish. Yep, it's finished. In fact, it's rotting like Senegalese roadkill. I tried to take the wheel out to shrink it for an airfreight crate and the bolts melted. Now, either I've been eating spinach or they've corroded. It's the salt's fault.

I'm sorry, I tried. Left with such good intentions – keep it clean, leaks and problems will be easier to spot etc. But eleven months of coastal raids, beach pistes and salt flats has left the XT kinda moth-eaten. Funnily enough, people in rural villages seemed to object when I asked to use three days' worth of well-drawn water to wipe off my toy. So it suffered.

But this isn't a concourse gleamer. The rougher it looks, the better the reaction. In Mozambique I parked up next to a Belgian couple on over-accessorised Beemers, his and hers 1150 and F650 GSs. He threw the XT a mournful look. 'It just looks so much more adventurous than mine,' he spluttered. Damn right.

What's gone wrong? Not a lot – and so it shouldn't. After all, this was a brand-new bike, lovingly prepared by a Yamaha UK workshop who knew that the bike would be receiving magazine attention. But but but. Bikes do go wrong. Especially when taken apart by this clumsy chump and put back together by well-meaning but underqualified bicycle repairmen.

The wiring's suffered the mostest. Damn electrickery gets me every time. Once a week the starter motor turns prima donna and refuses to stop starting: 'Why should I shut up? I'm very important.' Whining on and on. Turn the key, it still won't quit. Hit the kill switch, nope, nada. Like all attention-seekers, the trick is to ignore it and eventually, eventually, it sulks away. Then reappears elsewhere like a cartoon bump. Touch the brakes and the engine cuts. Eh? Throw an indicator and the same shit happens. Again, I just utilise ostrich mechanics – bury the bike in sand and forget it. Stop, have a smoke and hope it goes away. Works for me.

Wow factor. Depends where you live. Up the Zambezi valley or downtown Bamako, it caused a lot of wow. And now that it's back and suitably travel-worn, it even turns cynical London heads. Shell station on the A14, a couple of kids in a Merc stopped to ask me where I'd been. Er, Africa for a year. Wow.

What's the score? Gotta be perfect, 100 out of 100. Why? Because it did what it said it would. I needed a bike that would get me across Africa with minimum fuss. The XT got me across Africa with minimum fuss. The XT is the best bike for crossing Africa because it's the only bike I've crossed Africa on. Does that make sense? Sure, next time I'd prefer stiffer springs and a louder woof, of course I still lust after KTM Adventures and Yamaha WR426s, but for now, I'm happy to raise a glass and salute the XT600. King Off the Road.

Appendix Two

Why are you so Holier Than Thou and simultaneously ignorant of American policy and George Bush?
I'm just another monkey staring at the sky, trying to work out what the hell is going on. Wasn't 'Holier Than Thou and Ignorant of Foreign Policy' a Bush election promise?

Do you think anyone could manage a journey like that?
Absolutely. It's just going on holiday on your bike – for a really long time. There are no experts out here. All you need is horizonsunlimited.com, an overdraft and an imagination.

What do you think of Ewan McGregor and Charley Boorman's trip. Do you think that they missed out on something by not doing it solo?
Fair play to them, I'm sure they had a hoot, but it looked more like a very expensive, over-nannied enduro ride or a stage-managed World of BMW

promo than an unpredictable, unscripted road trip. I think they missed the point by taking the superstar safety net with them. But it's their ride.

How much does your average day cost? Is journalism the only financial support he has had?
In Latin America, a never-average day on the road costs about $50 for petrol, street food, a couple of beers and a soggy bed. A US day costs about $100. And yep, my writing pays my way, boosted by the falling dollar. Cheers, George.

If we could send you a food parcel, what would be in it?
A pint of Dublin Guinness, a Manchester meat'n'potato pie dripping with HP sauce and a crumbly block of strong Cheshire cheese. Wrapped up in an HPN Beemer, please.

What drives him forward?
Dread. Alcoholic dread.

When do you know it's time to move on to the next destination?
See above. I behave so badly I have to keep moving. It took all of two days for me to get barred from my first Buenos Aires pub. Three months seems to be the ideal time for any country – long enough to get beyond the obvious, short enough to keep things pleasingly fresh.

Why do you glorify drug taking? Are you trying to be the second Jack Kerouac?
I always wanted to be the second John Cooper Clarke. Glorify? I enjoy a weekend toot and a bedtime spliff. Hardly controversial these days, copper.

How much is a gramme of coke in Colombia and Bolivia?
Between $8 and $10 for a vague sized baggie, depending on who you know and whether it's cut gak or pure Scarface. The flophouses of La Paz and the beaches of Colombia are haunted by skull-faced white zombie travellers who just can't get off that rollercoaster.

How do you get away with having so little obvious mechanical knowledge? Did you ever consider taking a Haynes manual and a bag of spanners with you?
I don't understand how women or computers work either, but it doesn't stop me enjoying them. A Haynes manual's like the instructions for spanners, right? Lefty loosy, righty tighty? Abroad's surprisingly well-stocked with good mechanics, and the bike can always be slung on a truck.

How can you manage to knacker your bikes so quickly and comprehensively? How come you spend so much time on a bike and never feel the need to look after it or clean it?

I am a bad mother. I lock my bikes in the cupboard under the stairs and make them eat spider sandwiches. The Dakar's had five services in two years, three from BMW dealers. Compared to my forty-a-day, beer-for-breakfast, beaten-up body, the bike's a pampered poodle.

Knowing what he knows now, what bike would he pick?
The Dakar's a great bike buggered by bad bearings. I don't regret choosing it, I do regret believing the 'Ready for Adventure' blurb and not propping it properly.

Do you subscribe to the Nick Sanders rule of touring i.e. Pair of undies and a toothbrush only? What is the 'essential' stuff you take in your bag, and what are the luxuries?
Everyone (apart from Nick) over-packs then spends the first few weeks junking clutter. Somewhere in the Sahara, a shepherd is using my towering Touratech tankbag as a guestroom. Whatever makes you happier, comfier, more confident, becomes essential. For some people, it's tools and gadgets. For Nutty Jerome, it was a push bike bungeed to his KTM. I've got one pannier full of terrace-dandy clothes, another full of smart-arse books, so I guess they're my essentials. Luxuries? A pretty pillion is always nice.

What's your secret for punching above your weight with women?
I have no idea, but it's good, innit? Maybe it's the attraction of a temporary distraction – they know I always leave. Maybe it's that family heirloom I inherited from my dad. Maybe it's the over-the-counter Cialis. 36 hours, baby.

Which country had the best women?
I reckon that Senegal is the best looking country on the planet – the women look like Naomi Campbell, the men look like Terence Trent D'Arby. In South America, Colombian girls are hot in a lap-dancing, Angelina Jolie kinda way, and the Argentines are super-stylish.

How does Dan avoid getting sexual diseases from all the Peruvian hookers?
Paid company's never been my bag. I prefer keen amateurs. But off-duty working girls are always funny, bawdy, clued-up company and make the best city guides.

Does he miss his old Africa Twin?
Is this another hooker question? I never had an old African twin. But I did meet some young Costa Rican sisters?

Dan, was it worth it, are you now more complete and happy with yourself?
Is this from an ex? Yes, I am much happier, thank you. Darling.

Are you ever coming home? What do you miss most about our little island?
Not if I can help it. I miss family, friends and the football, but not enough to drag me back and besides, my best friends visit, the family are selling up and running for the sun and Brazillian football's hardly shabby.

Dan, a while ago you said 'You weren't trying to live on the road, you where looking for somewhere to live'. What's come closest to what you're looking for and why?
The place I want to settle is always somewhere I've not yet seen. It was Buenos Aires, but now I'm here it's Rio. When I get to Rio, it'll be Havana. And so on.

What was Dan's favourite place from all of his travels? What place would he rather forget? If he was going to start again what would he change?
Roatan, a Caribbean island off the coast of Honduras had the perfect blend of bends, beaches, bars and boobs, but the whole trip's been (and continues to be), the best two years of my life. I wouldn't change a thing. As the Butthole Surfers said, 'It's better to regret something you have done than regret something you haven't done'.

What was the worst example of globalisation on the region that you experienced?
Chile seems the keenest to spread its cheeks for multinationals, hide its Indians in remote reservations and turn its towns into ped-malled Miami-lites.

Do you ever think you'll take life seriously, or is this your reality of one day at a time?
This is as grown up as I get.

How did you manage with being on your own, were you ever afraid of an injury to you that could have been fatal?
Not until now I wasn't.

How do you get away with it? Lucky bastard.
I have no idea. Really. I'm as appalled and surprised as you are.

People treat me differently when I have my bike gear on in England e.g., I get all the train seat to myself. What is the attitude of people to you as a biker? does it vary from region to region?
From Timbukto to Timperley, riding a bike gets you a respect and credibility that car drivers can only lie about.

What's the worst disease you picked up?
Typhoid. It feels like your blood's been transfused with sewage.

What's your most favourite bike ever that you have ridden and owned?
Owned favourites? The Gilera Nordwest 600, dispatched to death then sold to fund an India trip. The TDR250, stolen from outside Old Trafford by two helmetless urchins last seen being chased by a cop van across a housing estate. And the XT600 – took me across Africa, then sold to Melancholy George to pay my rent. He rode it to Kazakstan and sold it to a cigarette smuggler.

When are you planning on coming back and will you still be writing for *Bike* when you do?
Ask the boss. For the last eight years, the phrase 'Walsh, you're fired!' has tickled every *Bike* editor's face, like a sneeze that just won't come out. Basically cause I'm an unreliable arsehole. *Bike*'s the only motorcycle magazine I read, and the only one I want to write for.

Where did he learn to write, making you feel like you are there with him? Who influenced your entertaining writing style?

It's difficult answering this without sounding like a pompous prick. To me, my writing reads like clumsy cover-versions of real writers. Everyone wants to be Hunter S. Thompson. Everyone apart from the actual Hunter S. Thompson, who was so tired of being Hunter S. Thompson that he blew his brains out while chatting with his wife on the phone.

Would he consider leading a bunch of amateurs on a world trip?
Absolutely. But would a bunch of amateurs actually follow me? I tried to lead a gang of *Bike* readers to the Bol in 98 or 99. It was like herding cats. 15 became 3 when we all caught different ferries, 3 became 1 when I lost 2 on the autoroute, 1 became 0 when the sole survivor was hit by a Merc. If anyone fancies a laid-back guided romp from Mexico to Panama or Lima to Rio, email mundogonzo@gmail.com and we'll see what happens.

Will he be gathering his writings together in a book?
It's been suggested, but I'm not convinced anyone would read it. I never said I was hot stuff.

You are paid to travel the world and seek out beautiful locations, Why is it that your face always looks as though you dog has died?
That's very funny. Blame the art queens, they choose the pictures. Or blame The Smiths. I'm sorry, I'll get all boy band and smile more.

Appendix Three

Thank you, thank you, thank you. I couldn't have done it without you.

Africa

The Bike
Dan Harris and everyone at (or used to be at) Yamaha UK for supplying a perfectly-prepped XT600 and selling it to me for mates' rates.

The Kit
Arai for the lid, Furygan for the jacket, Alpine Stars for the boots, Gialli for the pants. I crashed, they broke my fall and nothing else. Pants and boots survived both Africa and the Americas.

The People
Lou for our amor fou, Al Munira Hotel in Tangier for the Beat Generation inspiration, Kentucky Ken for the grins, Caritas Hannes in Bissau for the bed and the education, Dutch Mike and Angela for the cold Cokes (http://www.deprobeurzen.nl/crossingafrica.html), Josh Pritchard for the drunken sanity, Werner for the routes, Melancholy George for buying my XT, and Diani Hughie and Magdalena for taking me in after I was locked up.

The Supporters
I sniveled for sponsorship, hoping to attract big-budgeted marketing departments – instead I found big-hearted Bike readers. So enormous gratitude to – Barry Beamish, Sean Beamish, Andy Cushing, Ian Elsey,Miles Finch, Richard Fincher, Phil and Gill Flup, Dave Holmes, Naeem Hussain, Dave Lochhead, Nick McGivern, Alice Meacham, Sean Merrick, Patrick Norrie, Richard Pickford, Jim Pippit, Steve Read, Audrey Rodkiss, Speed Couriers ov Manchester, Liisa Steele, Mark Stoddart and Grace Todhunter. And anyone else I've inadvertently forgotten.

The Americas

The Bike
David Taylor, Kylie Maebus and everyone else involved at BMW Motorad GB for supplying a suitably-scrappy F650 Dakar. Sorry it never came home. Really. And to Mitch Boehm at Motorcyclist Magazine for organising a service and tyres at Marty's BMW in Torrance, CA.

The Transport
Mike Mandell at Motorcycle Express very kindly supplied airfreight from
Heathrow to Toronto and three months' insurance. Top-notch service,
thoroughly recommended, definitely the smoothest, swankiest way to cross
the Atlantic with a moto.
http://www.motorcycleexpress.com/

The Kit
Thunderchild for the Roof lid, Furygan for the jacket, but, mostly, the ever-
inventive kit-monger Andy Goldfine at Aerostich who supplied unburstable
Ortlieb panniers, plus the courier bag and deerskin ropers that bounced across
Africa and the Americas, and are still used daily. One of the good guys, and the
catalogue cheers up any toilet trip.
http://www.aerostich.com/catalog/US/index.html

The People
Trys for the company, the friendship and the pics, Cotel Kerry for the bed,
Grainne for the love (it might have been the city, but something touched my
heart), Chelsea Mick and Julio for the La Salla late-nights, Scarlet for the
twins, Irish Miguel in Managua for too much to list (venceremos, companero),
Chip for fucking everything (no greater gifts a man can give than a place to
sleep and a bike to ride. Sorry, I fucked up, brother), Sweet Anna Banana for
what turned into years of love, Stefan and Olga at El Pecado in Bocas for the
tastiest treats and daftest laughs in Panama, and Dick and Jane for their square
but nice twist on company, friendship and even more pics.
http://www.eastofthesun.co.uk/

And breathe. Aaaaand Albert at the Turtle's Head, Quito, for beer and
parking, Alan in the jail for reminding me why I don't smuggle drugs, Ian
Coates for senior inspiration, Jeff at Nortons Rats for shits and classic bike
giggles, Gert and crew at The Joyride in Sucre for playing The Smiths, Ehlke
for the tequila, Clara for the compassion, and all the Buenos Aires Gibraltar
crew – too many to name, but it was a hoot, no, Gav?

The Riders
Trys (again), Chip (again), Dick and Jane (again), Renee and Amy, Oz and
Jess, Lonely Bob and Angie, Jeff (again), Typhoid Tony, Javier and Sandra
from Dakarmotos (www.dakarmotos.com) and anyone else I turned a wheel
with.

General

The Catalyst
Gary Inman – you were right, brother. Next time?
http://www.sideburnmag.blogspot.com/

The Website
www.horizonsunlimited.com
Without Grant, Susan, and the hundreds of keen amateurs who keep this
amazing site ticking, I'd never have made it out of my street. Essential for pre-
trip planning, mid-trip crises and life-long friendships. So vital that it's
entered overlanders' vocabulary. How do you know that? Thread on the Hubb.
Where did you meet them? Thread on the Hubb.

Plus an honorary mention to advrider.com for its inspirational ride reports.

Bike Magazine
Richard Fincher and Rupert Paul for giving me a job, Hugo Wilson, Mick
Phillips, Tim Thompson and John Westlake for not sacking me when they
probably should have done. Jeff Porter and Simon Weir for suffering dudlines.
All the design queens who made me look good. And Jenny, for years of
invoices and maternal concern. Ta.

The Rest
One Eight, great mate. Brian. Our Dom. All the old comrades in both Red
Armies. And all the Sisters of Mercy it would be classless to name.

The Walshes
Mike, Margaret, Charlotte for a lifetime of love, support and happy drunken
singsongs.

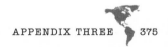